Woodrow Wilson Center
Current Studies on Latin America

Published with the Latin American Program
of the Woodrow Wilson International Center for Scholars
Joseph S. Tulchin, Director

Peru in Crisis: Dictatorship or Democracy?

edited by
Joseph S. Tulchin
Gary Bland

LYNNE RIENNER PUBLISHERS
BOULDER
LONDON

Published in the United States of America in 1994 by
Lynne Rienner Publishers, Inc.
1800 30th Street, Boulder, Colorado 80301

and in the United Kingdom by
Lynne Rienner Publishers, Inc.
3 Henrietta Street, Covent Garden, London WC2E 8LU

Library of Congress Cataloging-in-Publication Data
Peru in Crisis: Dictatorship or Democracy? / edited by Joseph S. Tulchin and Gary Bland.
(Woodrow Wilson Center current studies on Latin America)
Includes bibliographical references and index.
ISBN 1-55587-543-2 (alk. paper)
1. Peru—Politics and government—1980– —Congresses. 2. Democracy—Peru—Congresses. 3. Peru—Economic conditions—1980– —Congresses. 4. Insurgency—Peru—Congresses. 5. Civil-military relations—Peru—Congresses. I. Tulchin, Joseph S., 1939– . II. Bland, Gary. III. Series.
F3448.2.P4726 1994
320.985—dc20 94-14646
CIP

British Cataloguing in Publication Data
A Cataloguing in Publication record for this book is available from the British Library.

Printed and bound in the United States of America

∞ The paper used in this publication meets the requirements of the American National Standard for Permanence of Paper for Printed Library Materials Z39.48-1984.

Contents

Preface

The term *autogolpe,* or self-coup, now appears to be a permanent part of the lexicon of Latin American affairs and US–Latin American relations, following the decision by democratically elected President Alberto Fujimori to close down the institutions of representative government in Peru on 5 April 1992. As if the drug issue, a growing and vicious insurgency, and a depressed economy were not enough, on that day Peru was faced with yet another crisis, this one with major repercussions for countries of the region that had grown confident that democratic government was around for good.

The issues raised by the crisis of Peruvian democracy and the international community's response to it are many and varied and they cannot be separated from developments of Peru's past and the history of US–Latin American relations. Believing the time was right for examining the country's political and economic system within the context created by the *autogolpe,* the Latin American Program convened a major conference, "Peru: Democracy in Crisis and the International Community," at the Woodrow Wilson Center on 1 and 2 June 1993. The chapters of this volume are the revised papers commissioned for the meeting, coupled with edited transcripts of the remarks made by the commentators.

In addressing the issues, we particularly wanted to allow Peruvians themselves to express their views on the challenges facing their country and on the appropriate response of the international community. We sought to provide some of Peru's leading scholars and analysts with an opportunity to exchange their views on three key issues: the prospects for democracy, civil-military relations, and the state of the economy. Therefore, while some of the commentary is provided by North Americans, the six main chapters of this book are the original work of Peruvian experts. For the introduction we turned to Carol Graham, a visiting fellow at the World Bank, who provides an excellent analysis of the events and issues covered in this volume. We are particularly pleased that such an excellent group of Peruvians, as well as Peruvianists from Washington, DC, and other parts of the hemisphere, were able to join the program in what proved to be a most informative event.

These chapters have been substantially revised since the conference with use of the comments and discussion provided at the meeting. We hope the volume will contribute to the ongoing scholarly and policy debate on the democratic crisis within Peru and throughout the international community.

Of course, the production of this, the final product, required the excellent work of the program's staff. Gary Bland, senior program associate and coeditor of the volume, organized the conference, served as a moderator, and prepared the manuscript. The program's two associates, Bernice Romero and Allison Garland, were tremendously helpful in ensuring a successful conference. Lucy Hetrick, program assistant, also was most helpful in organizing the meeting.

Joseph S. Tulchin

1

Introduction: Democracy in Crisis and the International Response

Carol Graham

Few countries in the world have experienced economic deterioration as extreme as Peru's in the past decade. Fewer still have experienced as dramatic a change of their political spectrum under peaceful—if not fully democratic—auspices. And throughout this same period, Peruvian society has faced a challenge from one of the most brutal and violent insurrectionary movements to operate in the hemisphere, *Sendero Luminoso,* or Shining Path.

Although the extreme nature of Peru's crisis requires an exceptional response on the part of the international community, the unconventional and nondemocratic approach that President Alberto Fujimori has taken to resolving the crisis—in particular his April 1992 closing down of representative institutions—makes the nature of that response problematic. Pressuring Fujimori to return to democratic norms by withdrawing economic support for Peru, for example, could lead to an economic collapse that would ultimately play into the hands of Shining Path. In contrast, the lack of an international response sanctions the president's authoritarian tactics. Adding to the complexity of the situation is the president's high level of domestic political support, which to some extent was institutionalized through the constituent assembly elections of November 1992 and a referendum on constitutional reform in October 1993.

On 1 and 2 June 1993, the Latin American Program of the Woodrow Wilson International Center for Scholars convened a major conference on the crisis in Peruvian democracy and the international response to it. The papers presented, which in revised form are the basis for this book, as well as the commentary and discussion

---

Carol Graham is a visiting fellow at the World Bank.

at the conference, reflected the dilemmas that the Peruvian situation poses for the international community. No one "solution" emerged from the event, and it was widely accepted that President Fujimori's position was unlikely to be challenged in the near term. Yet, there was substantial optimism about the viability of democracy at the grassroots level and about the gradual strengthening of the formal democratic opposition to the Fujimori government. There clearly was agreement that the formal political institutional framework, such as the party system, is in a process of major transformation. There was some disagreement about the future strength and nature of Shining Path, although most observers agreed that Abimael Guzmán's capture signified an end to the movement as it existed prior to September 1992 and to its ability to challenge the Peruvian state. In addition, there was disagreement on the viability and sustainability of the Fujimori government's economic reform program, although the basic sentiment was, again, one of cautious optimism.

The Peruvian Crisis: A Paradox for the International Community

Economic Decline and Its Social Costs

During the 1980s, and in particular under the "heterodox experiment" of the 1985–1990 APRA (American Popular Revolutionary Alliance) government, Peru experienced an unprecedented economic decline that, perhaps even more damaging, was accompanied by a virtual collapse of state institutions and public service delivery. Per capita GDP fell by 25 percent from 1988 to 1990 alone, and is now at 1950s levels. By 1990, meanwhile, real wages had fallen to below their 1970 levels. Under- and unemployment soared: in 1985, 60 percent of the population of the capital city of Lima were "adequately" employed; in 1990, less than 10 percent were.[1] Not surprisingly, these trends had severe and detrimental effects on poverty levels. From 1985 to 1990, poverty rates in the capital city rose from 14 percent to 54 percent of the population. Although countrywide data are unavailable, rural poverty levels have traditionally been far worse than urban ones and are likely to have increased with the steep decline in GDP of the late 1980s.[2] The impact of the August 1990 stabilization shocks, meanwhile, was regressive: while the middle income deciles experienced reduced consumption on the order of 53 percent, the lowest two income deciles—who spend a much higher proportion of their income on food—experienced declines of over 60 percent.[3] By

1992, estimates of total poverty rates were as high as 70 percent, with over one-third the population living in conditions of extreme poverty, defined as earning insufficient income to purchase a minimum food basket.

Perhaps even more damaging in the long term than the increase in poverty was the collapse of the state and a consequent reduction in basic public services such as education, health, and police protection. At $12 per person per year, the Peruvian government spent 30 percent less on health and education in 1990 than it had in 1980. And while GDP fell by 9 percent from 1986 to 1990, social expenditure fell by 22 percent.[4] The access of the average Peruvian citizen to police protection and judicial services, meanwhile, was virtually nonexistent by the late 1980s. These circumstances contributed to a lack of faith in the "system" and to an increase in support for insurrectionary groups.[5] The most vivid demonstration of the collapse of public services was the outbreak of cholera in 1991—a disease that had not been seen in Latin America since the previous century. In its initial year alone, the epidemic claimed over 150,000 victims in Peru, with over 1,000 deaths, and consequently spread to all other nations in the Southern Hemisphere.

Political Consequences

Severe economic decline, the collapse of the state, and the seeming helplessness of Peru's traditional politicians to provide an acceptable solution resulted in two rather contradictory but simultaneous phenomena. The first was a steady increase in the strength and support for Shining Path in the late 1980s and early 1990s. More than 24,000 people have died in battles between Shining Path and the armed forces since the revolutionary group launched its activities in 1980. And while five national provinces were under state of emergency in 1982, in 1991 there were eighty-seven. By 1992, Sendero was boasting of having achieved "strategic parity" with the Peruvian state.[6] The crisis culminated in waves of bombings and other violent activities—with hundreds of civilians killed—in central Lima in the middle of 1992. Shining Path's momentum came sharply to a halt, however, with the timely—and unexpected—capture of its leader and founder, Abimael Guzmán, as well as several other members of its directorate, by Peru's intelligence police in September 1992.

The second phenomenon, which has changed Peru's political spectrum like no other single event, was the June 1990 election of political unknown Alberto Fujimori as president. Fujimori's victory over Mario Vargas Llosa, more than anything else, reflected the average Peruvian's frustration with the "system": the state, established parties and politicians, and the economic situation. Vargas Llosa's aristocratic origins, his alliance with the traditional parties of the right and center, and his campaign platform, which openly advocated a harsh stabilization program, had little appeal to the average Peruvian. In contrast, Fujimori, who was of Japanese rather than elite Peruvian origins and used a vague campaign slogan—"Work, Honesty, and Technology"—capitalized on his lack of previous connections with the political system. Fujimori finished in second place behind Vargas Llosa in the first round of the election. In the second round, he was able to capture the vote of the centrist APRA and the parties of the left, as well as most independents, and was elected to the presidency with over 50 percent of the popular vote.

Once in power, Fujimori realized that in order to cope with the unsustainable fiscal deficits and hyperinflation inherited from the García administration and to generate the essential support of the international financial community, there was no alternative to orthodox stabilization. On 8 August 1990, the Fujimori government implemented a shock package harsher than anything advocated by the international organizations. Overnight, gasoline prices were raised by 3,000 percent and most basic foodstuffs by 500 percent. Since then, the government has put into place an impressive series of structural economic reforms with a commitment and speed that few outside observers would ever have thought possible: privatization of state industries, tax and tariff reform, incentives for foreign and private investment, and decentralization of some social services.[7] And despite the harsh nature of the stabilization shocks, there was virtually no popular protest. Instead, Fujimori retained extremely high popular approval ratings throughout the stabilization period and for several months afterward.

Several reasons explain the lack of popular protest against the shocks. The first was that a wide majority had voted for Fujimori; because most people had expected a dramatic economic package (*paquetazo*), it was politically more acceptable coming from him than from Vargas Llosa. And Fujimori initially was careful to build support among diverse political sectors. His first cabinet was composed of representatives from virtually all the major political tenets. The second reason was due to the general frustration with hyperinflation and economic decline and a willingness to suffer short-term losses for eventual stability and improvement.[8] A third reason for the lack of protest stemmed from the prevalence of political violence. People often associated street protests with terrorism and therefore were more likely to shy away from public dissent.

Last, and perhaps most important, was Prime Minister Juan Carlos Hurtado Miller's charismatic presentation and explanation of the economic measures and his promises that a broad-ranging social emergency program would cushion the poorest from the harsh effects of the shocks. Hurtado Miller's two-hour address to the nation emphasized the dramatic nature of the crisis, the inevitability of the measures, and a promised social emergency program. And despite the high costs of the reforms, and the government's failure to follow through on the promised social emergency program, Hurtado Miller was the most popular public official or politician in Peru in October 1990—with approval ratings even higher than Fujimori's, where they remained until his resignation in 1991.[9]

Despite Hurtado Miller's popularity—or perhaps because of it—Fujimori's style of government grew increasingly authoritarian, and he quickly alienated some of the most talented members of his cabinet, including Hurtado Miller. As he severed his links to various political sectors in Congress and lacked an organized party base of support, Fujimori relied increasingly on the military—one sector of the army in particular—to govern. By early 1992, faced with increasing congressional opposition to the social costs of his economic program on the one hand, and a growing presence of Shining Path in Lima on the other, Fujimori opted to institutionalize his support in the military.

The Autogolpe *and the International Response*

On 5 April 1992, the president, calling for a process of "national reconstruction," suspended the constitution, dissolved the Congress and the judiciary, placed several congressional leaders under house arrest, and imposed temporary but harsh censorship of the press. Fujimori subsequently launched a public relations campaign against all political parties and politicians, blaming them for everything from corruption to fiscal deficits to the existence of Shining Path. Popular unrest was minimal, and Fujimori's popularity rose dramatically in the weeks after the coup. In contrast, international reaction was extremely negative. Fujimori's actions quickly became known as an *autogolpe*, or self-coup.

There are several explanations for the coup. One is Fujimori's lack of an organized base in Congress. Until the coup, he had governed largely by executive decree. Of 109 decrees issued during his term, only 9 were evaluated by Congress and only 1 was vetoed.[10] When congressional opposition began to organize in early 1992, Fujimori was extremely vulnerable. He had alienated much of his original front of support, Change 90, with his turn toward orthodox economics. In the early days of his government, he had been able to strike political deals with the APRA party, such as the appointment of Jorge Chávez as the head of the Central Bank. But this changed in early 1992 when APRA elected former president Alan García, who had just emerged unscathed from an investigation into his questionable financial dealings, as secretary-general of the party. García, despite his disastrous administration, remained a charismatic populist and began to organize the opposition by attacking the government's "antipopular" economic strategies. With no social emergency program in place, Fujimori was particularly vulnerable to such criticisms.

Also undermining Fujimori's position was a highly publicized scandal in March 1992, in which the president's wife accused his brother, who was also his primary adviser, of mismanaging Japanese aid donations. Already besieged by an increasingly assertive Congress, the erosion of unity within Fujimori's close circle of advisers further weakened his political position. This incident occurred on the eve of the departure of Fujimori's influential adviser on drug policy, Hernando de Soto.

Further complicating matters was the increasing influence of Vladimir Montesinos, an adviser to Fujimori and a former officer with suspected links to drug traffickers. Montesinos was purportedly strongly in favor of a coup to prevent congressional investigations into corruption scandals in which he was implicated.[11]

Shining Path was yet another factor. Its visibility in and around Lima, especially in the shantytowns, had increased markedly in the six months before the coup. Shining Path's presence contributed to the pressure on Fujimori to show a strong hand in combating the insurgency, and therefore to popular support for the strong antiterrorist measures—which gave the military almost complete jurisdiction over all cases involving terrorist suspects—that were announced in conjunction with the self-coup.

Fujimori's popularity received a further and decisive Shining Path–related boost after the coup in September 1992, when the Peruvian national intelligence police captured Guzmán in a wealthy suburb of Lima. Shining Path's seemingly "all-powerful" leader was ridiculed for his bourgeois tastes and debauchery, and he received a life sentence in a military court. His capture was an important achievement and called into question Shining Path's ability to sustain a united strategy in the future. Yet it by no means indicated that the movement would disappear; nor would political violence, which is perpetrated in Peru by a variety of insurgent movements.

The *autogolpe* in Peru clearly presented a dilemma for the international community. Viewing recent incidents in the hemisphere, Fujimori may well have felt emboldened to make his move. The international response to the overthrow of the president of Haiti had not been particularly effective. Although a recent coup attempt in Venezuela had failed, it revealed a surprising degree of popular support and suggested that military intervention in Latin America was not as discredited as most observers had generally thought. And all three branches of the Peruvian armed forces stood behind Fujimori's measures.

Relations with the United States, furthermore, were far from comfortable. Fujimori had clashed publicly with President George Bush at the San Antonio drug summit in February 1992. His position, not an unreasonable one, was that Peru could not fight the drug war without adequate resources. In the current US political context, however, the United States could not provide any additional international aid. This, and the long duration of the arrears clearing process with the international financial institutions, may have led Fujimori to conclude that there was not much to be gained by cooperating with Washington. Some observers believe Fujimori, with members of the armed forces, conceived the coup much earlier. He correctly predicted that most Peruvians would support him, at least in the short term. The president enjoyed approval ratings of over 70 percent for several months after the coup.

There are two reasons for the Peruvian public's positive response. First, life in Peru was so desperate that popular support for a quick fix was unsurprising. As it became clear that the coup only worsened national troubles, however, Fujimori's ratings fell: by August 1992 they sank below his pre-April ratings of 50 percent. Second, opinion polls in Peru are traditionally volatile. Support for Alan García, for example, shifted from over 70 percent to less than 9 percent in less than three months in 1987. The credibility of polls, moreover, taken at a time of suspended constitutional guarantees and restricted press freedom, is questionable. It is telling that when respondents were asked if they also favored a return to democracy, most of them responded favorably.[12]

While Fujimori correctly predicted the national reaction, he totally misread the international one. The United States had recently decided to launch a new aid strategy based on support for democracy. Washington also made a priority of defeating Shining Path as opposed to fighting the war on drugs. After the coup, the United States suspended all but humanitarian aid to Peru, pending the return to consitutional democracy. Several nations, including Germany and Spain, and, after much hesitation, Japan, also withdrew their support. Although no single nation's aid program was determinant or particularly significant, the joint action jeopardized the reintegration of Peru into the international community, upon which Fujimori's entire economic program rested.

When it became clear how harsh the international response was, Fujimori took a step back from his measures. On 9 April, he announced a plan to hold a yes-or-no plebiscite on his measures and a vague timetable for returning to constitutional democracy. The United States, however, made clear it would not accept the plebiscite.[13] Fujimori then made a surprise visit to an Organization of American States meeting on Peru on 18 May. He presented a revised timetable, which included constituent assembly elections in November 1992,[14] as well as municipal elections that year. He also cancelled the plebiscite. While Fujimori laced his speach with vituperative attacks against the political parties, he had clearly changed his course.

Fujimori's apparent responsiveness to international pressure emphasized its enduring importance. After the coup, for example, most new decisions on loans by agencies like the World Bank, the International Monetary Fund (IMF), and US Agency for International Development (AID) were postponed until after the completion of constituent assembly elections.

Still, the president's commitment to democracy remained unclear, as was well demonstrated in June 1992 with his indefinite postponement of municipal elections, originally scheduled for November. Elections were finally held in January 1993, in response to international pressure. Dialogue with the opposition was still troubled. The government approached the "national dialogue" in the same authoritarian manner that it had implemented the coup and subsequent policy: Fujimori's arrests of APRA party members and his attempts to discredit parties in general were obstacles to productive discussions.[15]

Constituent Assembly Elections and the 1993 Referendum

The poor relations between government and opposition probably had some effect on the results of the constituent assembly elections, although the opposition parties were in general in an extremely weak organizational state and may have felt they had more to lose by participating in the elections. When the October deadline arrived for the parties' participation in the assembly elections, the three main political parties, APRA, Popular Action (AP), and Vargas Llosa's Liberty party, refused to register. The two main parties representing the left, the United Left and the Socialist Accord, failed to qualify because of Fujimori's ruling that parties had to have received more than 5 percent of the vote in the 1990 election.[16]

As a result of the limited nature of opposition participation, the constituent assembly that emerged was not broadly representative. Fujimori's supporters garnered 38 percent of the popular vote and forty-four of eighty congressional seats, giving him a clear majority in the Congress. This gave Fujimori a virtual free hand in the drafting of the constitution that was submitted to a national referendum in October 1993. Not surprisingly, then, the vote on the constitution hinged on two major issues promoted by the governing regime: Fujimori's reelection and the legalization of the death penalty. In addition, the new constitution institutionalized military jurisdiction over all trials involving suspects of terrorism.[17] It also included several clauses attempting to give permanence to Fujimori's economic reforms, such as one making the renationalization of privatized state industries impossible. Although such a provision may be an admirable objective, clauses about macroeconomic policy are inappropriate in national constitutions, and their inclusion reflects the equivalent ideological bias—on the opposite end of the political spectrum—as the clause in the 1988 Brazilian constitution limiting real interest rates to 12 percent.

In sharp contrast to the constituent assembly elections, in the municipal elections held on 29 January 1993, in which all parties participated and the vote hinged on local as well as national level issues, Fujimori's supporters fared far differently. Change 90 garnered only one municipality, for example. The traditional political parties received approximately 40 percent of the vote, with the majority of municipalities taken by independents.[18]

These divergent electoral results within a very brief period reflect the rapidly changing nature of Peru's political spectrum: although the opposition remained weak and divided, there were limits to the postcoup and capture-of-Guzmán political honeymoons. Established political parties remained discredited well after Fujimori's victory, as support for the self-coup and the election results indicate. Yet in the context of deep poststabilization recession and widespread poverty, there was also a limit to the sustained support Fujimori could garner from surprise measures such as the *autogolpe* or the capture of Guzmán. By March 1993, for example, recession and unemployment replaced terrorism as the nation's number one problem in national polls. Forty percent of the population polled said they approved of the economic program, while an equal percentage did not, with positive opinions directly correlated to higher income levels.[19] Yet the opposition remained notably short of credible economic plans. And no one person emerged as the leader of the opposition with the ability to challenge Fujimori. The result was a wide degree of de facto support for Fujimori, giving him an enormous amount of freedom in shaping the country's political institutions. This was clearly seen in the drafting of a new constitution by an assembly over which Fujimori had virtual veto power, and then in the results of the October 1993 referendum.

The results of the 31 October referendum, which the government won 53 percent to 47 percent, show Fujimori's clear advantages in securing access to the media and public resources, as well as his continued widespread popular support. At the same time, the opposition proved capable of far more unity and active campaigning than it had in any of the previous elections. Although a "no" vote implied considerable uncertainty, the "no" won in the provinces (Fujimori won only in Lima), and abstention rates were as high as 30 percent nationwide. The strong support for the "no" in the provinces most likely reflects the limited benefits that economic reforms have yielded to date for the nonurban sectors of Peruvian society. In addition, while support for Fujimori was strongest among the poorer Lima sectors in the 1990 elections, in the referendum it was much higher among wealthier income groups and it fell among the poor.[20] The outcome reflects the high social costs of the reforms for the urban poor and the lack of government attention to social and safety net policies, in contrast to the benefits that reforms have already yielded for higher-income groups.

One factor that helped produce a decline in support for Fujimori (prior to the vote the government was predicting a 70 to 30 victory) was his heavy-handed approach to public relations. Fujimori's overconfident predictions of victory were coupled with a caustic and uncompromising response to two public letters from Abimael Guzmán offering to negotiate a peaceful end to the Shining Path insurrection. Although Fujimori's authoritarian and underdog tactics had a great deal of appeal when he was in a disadvantaged position—trailing Vargas Llosa, badgered by an uncooperative Congress, or faced with an invincible challenge from Shining Path—they had far less appeal when he was in a position of strength that required more statesmanlike conduct. This, coupled with the sense that a Fujimori victory was guaranteed, may have encouraged some voters who would otherwise have voted "yes" to vote "no," and in part accounts for the surprisingly close vote.

The end result may have been the best possible outcome, given the circumstances. The opposition was increasingly organized by late 1993 but remained divided and without a viable leader or a credible economic program. Yet their organizational efforts and strong electoral showing demonstrated that they were indeed alive and a viable challenge and that Fujimori would *not* have a guaranteed electoral victory in 1995. The surprising degree of public support they garnered, meanwhile, may force Fujimori to pay more attention to issues such as social and safety net policy. Nevertheless, the results still give Fujimori and the military an enormous free hand on the political and juridical fronts, posing grave risks to human rights and civil liberties, and possibly presenting obstacles to the opposition in 1995.

It is in the arena of political democracy and civil liberties that international attention and cooperation will be essential. In the short term, the international community has little alternative but to accept Fujimori's government as legitimate: he presented an electoral timetable that was accepted by the international community, has abided by it, and emerged victorious. The international community, however, does have some leverage over Fujimori—via international financial support—as was demonstrated after the *autogolpe,* and should not hesitate to use that leverage if he diverges from democratic norms.

Unfortunately, short of another dramatic action such as the *autogolpe,* it is unlikely that enough international attention will be focused on Peru to generate a response from the international institutions. The most likely scenario is that Fujimori will have a relatively free hand over events, at least until 1995. Until then, a great deal of responsibility rests on a still-divided but strengthened opposition, which must provide an alternative to Fujimori that is capable of maintaining the economic reform program *and* of gradually reestablishing respect for democratic norms and institutions in Peru. Otherwise, it is likely that the 1995 elections will yield five more years of Fujimori, possibly resulting in further economic progress but also in continued deterioration of democratic institutions and a very unstable state of civil-military relations.

Organization of This Book

The chapters of this volume address three general areas: the prospects for democracy; the Shining Path insurgency, the role of the armed forces, and human rights; and the government's economic reform program.

In Chapter 1, Francisco Sagasti and Max Hernández describe the rapidly changing political-institutional framework in Peru. The principle theme of their work is that Peru faces a profound crisis of governance, as its formal institutional framework has been unable to keep up with four decades of rapid social change. The result has been a process of political "disintermediation," in which formal political institutions—parties, Congress, and the state more generally—neither represent nor are responsive to the needs of civil society.

According to Sagasti and Hernández, disintermediation has led to a general discrediting of formal institutions and the direct involvement of nonpoliticians, such as businesspeople, engineers (Fujimori), and writers (Mario Vargas Llosa), in political life. Fujimori's strategy of derogating institutions such as parties, the Congress, and the judiciary was an outgrowth rather than the cause of this process. As the political system in its present state lacks the checks and balances necessary to the functioning of a viable democracy, Fujimori has had an enormous amount of political freedom, which is based on a heavy reliance on the armed forces.

Generally, the two authors argue, the crisis of governance has created a tendency toward authoritarian solutions, a lack of an adaptive capacity to modify policies as needed to maintain stability, lack of channels for political mobility, and legitimization through results as opposed to institutional procedure and due process. Sagasti and Hernández feel that the international community does have an important role to play: it can condition aid on the maintenance of democratic norms, and it can attempt to counterbalance the unchecked power of the government by supporting local independent institutions and nongovernment organizations, which are the bases of the new democratic movement in Peru.

In Chapter 2, Fernando Rospigliosi is far less optimistic about the prospects for democracy. He attributes the failure to consolidate democracy in Peru to three factors: a lack of democratic tradition, chronic economic crises, and a legacy of oligarchic and patrimonial government.

Rospigliosi also touches on the failure of the political parties and democratic institutions to address Peru's two key problems: the insurgency and corruption. All of civil society—along with the politicians—failed to attribute enough importance to the insurgency early on. In the absence of a coherent or long-term strategy for combating it, the insurgency grew in strength and size. General "anxiety, insecurity, and short-sighted approaches" on the part of both civilian politicians and the military have been the results. Although corruption has been a persistent feature of Peru's political spectrum for decades, according to Rospigliosi, the public became far less tolerant as successive governments proved ineffective in the face of grave social and economic crises. The situation climaxed with the debacle of García's APRA government.

Rospigliosi, like Sagasti and Hernández, sees a role for the international community, albeit a limited one in light of widespread foreign aid budget cuts. He cites the OAS's role in the November 1992 constituent assembly elections as weak and unfortunate. Rospigliosi is also more pessimistic about the strength of grassroots groups. Although he sees these groups as important, he feels that they have been irreparably battered by Shining Path violence in the past few years.

In Chapter 3, the first of three chapters of commentary on the works by Sagasti and Hernández and Rospigliosi, Cynthia McClintock agrees that the Peruvian democracy begun in 1980, as conventionally defined in the United States, failed. The explanation for this failure lies, she argues, in a more precise examination of Peru's political party system during the 1980s. McClintock also agrees that since the *autogolpe* Peru has not been democratic and the chances for a return to democracy are bleak. The most difficult issue is what the international response should be. Fujimori's popularity has complicated the question, and because the international response has been unclear, Peruvian actors are left looking for signals. Finally, according to McClintock, although Peru should not be isolated economically, international pressure against human rights abuse has been important and should continue.

In Chapter 4, Manuel d'Ornellas comments that there is one main conclusion to be drawn from the current situation in Peru: the key political actor at present and for the foreseeable future is the military. The armed forces believe they are winning the war and that they are popular because of their social action programs. They feel untouchable following the passage of new laws supporting their role, and they are not disposed to integrating with the traditional power structure. Fujimori, d'Ornellas adds, must walk the tightrope between United States pressure to investigate human rights abuse and military pressure against such a step; he will have a difficult time finding a counterweight to United States influence. Moreover, d'Ornellas notes he is optimistic about the future of freedom of the press because the Fujimori government is not ideologically opposed to the media.

In Chapter 5, Carol Graham agrees with Rospigliosi that Fujimori is presenting a semblance of democracy for international consumption, while the political opposition has failed to provide an alternative. She disagrees, however, that Peru's elites or popular sectors lack democratic values. Rather, given their dire living conditions, Peruvians are naturally more concerned with easing the crisis at all costs, which is why Fujimori's drastic "solution" gained wide support. At the grassroots level especially, Peruvians act democratically. To restore faith in the democratic process, the economic reform program must prove successful and social service delivery must be restored. Fujimori's authoritarian tactics have eroded democratic institutions, Graham explains, but the erosion of state institutions prior to his arrival was equally damaging.

In Chapter 6, Carlos Iván Degregori focuses on Shining Path. Prior to Guzmán's capture, Shining Path was able to capitalize on a popular sense of crisis and pessimism, which had been deeply exacerbated by the APRA government and the virtual collapse of Peru's state institutions. Shining Path could make up for the lack of support in urban areas with the ideological cohesion of its cadres and increasing terror, as long as the political context proved favorable.

When Guzmán was taken prisoner, Degregori continues, that context changed dramatically: the "strategic equilibrium" pronounced by Shining Path in the middle of 1992 shifted dramatically in favor of the government. Shining Path was now faced with dealing with the loss of its all-powerful founder and leader as well as some of its top organization, avoiding divisions, and reorganizing its forces. Although it remained an impressive insurrectionary machine with a capacity to act, Degregori believes a juncture so unusually favorable as 1992 will be difficult to come by again. Shining Path's confusion was furthered by Guzmán's September 1993 letters offering to negotiate peace with the government. Degregori concludes that the movement's ultimate defeat will depend on whether Peruvians can construct a strategy for building a democratic government.

Degregori, like the previous authors, views civil-military relations as an obstacle to the development of democracy. The troika of command—Fujimori, the general commander of the armed forces, and the National Intelligence Service (SIN) as influenced by Vladimiro Monetesinos—are considered by much of the armed forces as an infringement on their professional institutional status. The November 1992 countercoup attempt was a direct outgrowth of this sentiment and reflects a dangerous instability within the military establishment.

In Chapter 7, Enrique Obando assesses systematically the political strength of the armed forces, using ten variables to measure the change in their power over time. In so doing, Obando is critical of the Belaúnde regime (1980–1985) for acting out of revenge against the military as opposed to trying to improve civil-military relations and for relinquishing the fight against Shining Path to the military.

President Belaúnde refrained from interfering in internal military affairs but also refused to cooperate in the necessary establishment of a national defense system. Alan García, by contrast, interfered in military affairs, according to Obando, and attempted to consolidate his control by establishing a single military command in the newly formed Ministry of Defense.

Alberto Fujimori subsequently pushed further ahead in establishing executive control over the armed forces command. Yet he also relied increasingly on the military as a base of support for governing. Under his government, the armed forces were, on the one hand, coopted through increased freedom and resources in exchange for support of the president and, on the other, institutionally divided into pro- and anti-Fujimori camps. The killings at La Cantuta University, for which nine military officers and enlisted men were convicted in February 1992, according to Obando, could have a major impact on Fujimori's government and future civil-military relations.

Obando concludes that the result of these diverse approaches is an armed forces whose power and impunity have increased dramatically at the local level, where it should not have, and decreased and fragmented at the national level, where coherent leadership is extremely important to political stability. Corruption, primarily related to drug trafficking, is also an issue that threatens an already-fragmented institutional leadership.

In Chapter 8, commentator Gustavo Gorriti argues that by preemptively declaring the success of an action, Shining Path attempts to gain a "strategic equilibrium," or advantage. Such a declaration creates pressure within the organization to advance toward that goal and also demonstrates the force of its conviction to the Peruvian population. Considering Peru's problems and that the government could increase repression if it runs into trouble—if political polarization continues and Shining Path can overcome Guzmán's capture—the group could become a major threat. A key to explaining the armed forces today, Gorriti adds, particularly in areas such as institutional division and corruption, lies in an analysis of the institutional developments of the 1970s, especially during the second military government of General Morales Bermúdez.

The political power of the military, argues Marcial Rubio in Chapter 9, should also be considered in the new international context. For example, he notes, the armed forces will be isolated by the United States and other nations if they institute a coup. The military remains a strong political force but in a more sophisticated way as the nation's more complex social structure has increasingly dispersed power. The military exercises political power through its monopolies on counterinsurgency plans and on the ability to maintain public order, which are especially important given Fujimori's lack of a supporting political apparatus. Rubio also notes that the military's power may have benefited from the average Peruvian's reluctant acceptance of protection against Shining Path.

In Chapter 10, David Scott Palmer raises several issues with his comments. First, given the extensive literature on the increased professionalization of the Peruvian armed forces since the 1950s, why do they allow themselves to be subjected to a cashiered army officer, Vladimiro Montesinos, operating out of the presidency? It may demonstrate the sharp division and demoralization of the institution. Second, what prevents the military from becoming more consistently involved economically and militarily in the counterinsurgency strategy? Regarding Shining Path, first, can the group overcome the capture of Guzmán and continue its orthodox strategy for taking power, or will it moderate its hard line? It now seems to be regenerating itself at a much lower level of activity. Finally, Palmer asks, how do Peru's economic and political crises affect Shining Path's long-run chances of success?

Chapters 11 and 12 focus on Peru's macroeconomy and economic development. In Chapter 11, Julio Velarde examines the economic stabilization and reform program of the Fujimori government. Although the results have not been as spectacular as expected, he writes, there is "a sense that the economy is on the right track" and that if some errors are promptly corrected, "the prospects for initiating a process of sustained growth are good." The current climate of political instability, however, may delay this process.

Velarde explains that the poststabilization period of December 1990 to February 1991 was rife with uncertainty due to policy disagreements among economic officials. Although the appointment of Carlos Boloña as minister of economics produced a period of more coherent management and a strong commitment to structural reforms, the subsequent pre*autogolpe* period was one of "fiscal disorder." Among the difficulties that emerged was a major rift between the president and Congress, which developed when Fujimori attempted to impose changes in the value-added tax.

The self-coup that followed, Velarde continues, had extremely negative effects on relations with international financial institutions and on the domestic financial sector. Economic policy under Jorge Camet, the minister of economics who has replaced Boloña, has demonstrated a high degree of policy continuity, including progress in negotiations with both international financial institutions and private banks.

As for the future, Velarde points to the need for, first, better policy management to spur entrepreneurial confidence. Second, a climate of increased political stability to inspire investor confidence would help ensure success. Given the recent return of foreign investment, if macroeconomic problems can be promptly addressed, economic recovery is a real possibility.

In Chapter 12, Efraín Gonzales de Olarte approaches Peru's economic difficulties from a developmental perspective, addressing the historical lack of productive investment, and offers a series of lessons for the future. He reviews the idea of the "Peruvian pendulum," or the oscillation of economic policy regimes and dramatic shifts brought about by the succession of civilian and military governments. For decades, policy has fluctuated between extremes of heterodoxy and orthodoxy, with greater focus on short-term adjustment than on development. The consequent instability of relative prices and the institutional framework have been the worst enemies of investment.

The adverse effects of the Peruvian pendulum in the areas of production, employment, and macroeconomic equilibrium have tended to persist long after the policies have changed. Moreover, Gonzales argues, the main revenue generating sectors, such as fisheries and mining, remain largely disconnected from the rest of the economy. They have had little impact on the kinds of investments that are made—or not made—in areas of the economy where there is a huge surplus of labor. The education system, meanwhile, is extensive but inappropriate for sustained growth. These two phenomena have produced a mass of "educated" and unemployed poor.

Gonzales concludes by addressing what needs to be done to return Peru to the path of development. Growth, he writes, will depend on investment, which will be determined by the levels of political and economic instability. And while investment, which is driven by foreign financing, has traditionally been higher during periods of military rule, in the current international context a climate of confidence and stability must be established under democratic rule.

Although there are positive aspects to the Fujimori economic program, John Sheahan comments in Chapter 13, it is neither well designed nor moving in the right direction. Rather, it is a terrible "strain-aggravating" program that must be changed to produce growth. Other stabilization programs show that Peru's is by far the most extreme—the least careful about the damage it is doing to society. According to Sheahan, Peru's export sector has suffered from currency overvaluation for twenty years. Yet Fujimori's tight monetary policy has pushed the exchange rate in the wrong direction—

toward further overvaluation. Dismal employment levels leave Peruvians feeling that they have no future, encouraging them to leave the country or turn to Shining Path.

In Chapter 14, Carol Wise explains in her comments that Peru has consistently performed poorly among major Latin American states in four areas: reliance on external debt and savings by the mid to late 1960s; reliance on state enterprise for ideological reasons, especially during the early 1970s; hostility between the public and private sectors, culminating in the late 1980s; and inability to coordinate social policy or redistributive measures. In addition, Peru's highly presidentialist political system, deterioration of financial and planning institutions, an underdeveloped bureaucracy, and weak state are impeding efforts at sound economic management.

Prospects for the Future

The future of democracy in Peru remains in question, although as most of the authors in this volume suggest, there is room for cautious optimism. Perhaps the most hopeful element is the extent to which democracy has taken hold at the grassroots level. Also important is the gradual strengthening of a democratic opposition that was, for all intents and purposes, nonexistent in April 1992. The weakening of Shining Path is critical, although political violence will remain a central issue for the foreseeable future.

Civil-military relations remains an arena of considerable uncertainty, and the problem of human rights has shown little improvement. The military's increased freedom and lack of accountability remains worrisome. The nature of the relationship between civilians and the armed forces clearly will be a determining factor in the development of Peru's democratic institutional framework.

On the economic front, a great deal has been achieved, but a great deal remains to be done, particularly concerning social policy and poverty alleviation. Achieving a climate of democratic stability, moreover, will be essential to future investment and economic growth.

International attention will remain critical to the course of the development of democracy in Peru. However, given the international community's propensity to respond to dramatic, headline-grabbing events as opposed to daily developments, it is unlikely that the sustained pressure necessary to influence substantially the changes in Peru will be brought to bear. Perhaps unfairly, but realistically, responsibility for democratic development will rest primarily with

Peru's nascent political opposition and with civil society at the grassroots level.

Notes

1. "Adequately employed" implies full employment: earning at least a minimum wage by working forty hours per week. Many Peruvians hold full- or part-time jobs in the formal sector and are forced to supplement their income with overtime work in the informal sector; the vast majority, meanwhile, work more than forty hours per week in the informal sector, yet still earn less than the minimum wage. For details, see *Ajuste y economía familiar* (Lima, Instituto Cuánto, 1991).

2. The rural poor tend to be far less directly affected by adjustment-related stabilization shocks than are the urban poor, however.

3. For details, see Paul Glewwe and Gillette Hall, "Unorthodox Adjustment and Poverty in Peru," *Finance and Development*, December 1992; and Carol Graham, *Safety Nets, Politics, and the Poor: Transitions to Market Economies* (Washington, DC, The Brookings Institution, 1994), chap. 4.

4. *Ajuste y economía familiar.*

5. For an example of this phenomenon in Peru's shantytowns, see Carol Graham, "Sendero's Law in Peru's Shantytowns," *The Wall Street Journal*, 7 June 1991.

6. Gustavo Gorriti, "Peru's Dictatorship Is Ridiculous But Real," *The New York Times*, 24 August 1992, p. A15.

7. Decentralization of basic services such as health and education has been attempted in Chile, which had a strong basic social infrastructure to begin with, with a great deal of variation in results among communities and income levels. Its potential for success is even less clear in a country like Peru, where the basic institutional structure either does not exist or has deteriorated dramatically in the past decade.

8. For the case of Peru, this conclusion is mainly drawn from the author's conversations with shantytown dwellers in the towns of Huascar, Bayovar, and Pamplona Alta in September–November 1990. More generally, the role of crisis in popular willingness to accept difficult economic reforms is discussed in Stephan Haggard and Stephen B. Webb, "What Do We Know About the Political Economy of Policy Reform," *The World Bank Research Observer*, vol. 8, no. 2 (July 1993), pp. 143–168.

9. "Celos?," *Caretas*, 24 September 1991. For a detailed account of the "failed" social emergency program, see Carol Graham, "Economic Austerity and the Peruvian Crisis: The Social Costs of Autocracy," *SAIS Review* (winter–spring 1993). For the important role that communication plays in making economic reform publically acceptable, see Carol Graham 1994, op. cit.

10. The vetoed decree proposed to place all trials for terrorism under the jurisdiction of military tribunals.

11. Gorriti, "Peru's Dictatorship Is Ridiculous But Real," *The New York Times*, 24 August 1992, p. A15.

12. *Caretas*, various issues, April–August 1992.

13. Plebiscites after coups have traditionally been tools used by dictators. Napoleon, Hitler, Mussolini, and Marcos obtained over 80 percent of popular

support in such plebiscites (Lima, Instituto Libertad y Democracia, 1992).

14. The Constituent Assembly will also have legislative powers through 1995, when new presidential and congressional elections will be held.

15. Such policies included the government establishing its control over the funds of nongovernment organizations, as well as several tough antiterrorism laws.

16. The left had split into moderate and more radical factions before the 1990 elections. The new coalition allowed for smaller parties to join only if they collected one hundred thousand signatures but gave parties little time to do so. Some leftist leaders did participate in the elections, either by forming new fronts and collecting signatures, or by running on the slates of other independent movements.

17. Appeal to the civilian courts is allowed only in cases where the death sentence is issued. Thus, there are countless cases where those suspected of terrorist activities can receive life sentences without access to a lawyer or other juridical guarantees.

18. *Caretas*, various issues, January–February 1993.

19. Polls taken by Apoyo S.A., one of the most reliable polling firms in Peru, cited by the president of Apoyo in a presentation to WOLA/George Washington University Conference on the Prospects for Peace and Democracy in Peru, Washington, DC, 28 April 1993.

20. "Geografía del voto," *Caretas*, 11 November 1993; "Lima: Cambio de clima," *Caretas*, 18 November 1993.

PART 1

Whither the Political System?

2

The Crisis of Governance

Francisco Sagasti and Max Hernández

Peru is experiencing one of the most complex processes of social transformation taking place in the Americas at the close of the twentieth century. Over hundreds of years, many cultures have interacted in one of the most diverse geographies of the region and have created a rather unique setting for the multiple manifestations of the crisis that exploded during the last decade.

The European conquest of the Inca empire was the traumatic foundation of Peru, a catastrophic event that established a definitive social rift between victor and vanquished. Three centuries of colonial rule defined the social, economic, and institutional order that consecrated the original division. One hundred and seventy-two years of republican life did not alter the social topography of the nation; only the colors of the demographic landscape changed slightly. Suddenly, during the last forty years, the pace of change began to accelerate: a number of crises, each starting at a different point in the nation's history, gained momentum and converged in a multiple crisis of near cataclysmic proportions, which came to a head during the 1980s and early 1990s. A demographic explosion and massive migrations from rural to urban areas shook the country's foundations, completely altering the apparent order that had prevailed for centuries.

The inventory of problems that accompany the most profound crisis Peru has experienced in more than a century is depressingly familiar. The economy has been stagnant for more than a decade,

---

Francisco Sagasti is a senior researcher with Lima's Development Analysis Group (GRADE); Max Hernández is a psychoanalyst based in Lima. Both are codirectors of AGENDA-Peru, a project sponsored by the FORO Nacional/ Internacional, Lima, Peru.

incomes in the Lima metropolitan area have been halved since 1985, and in early 1993 about 85 percent of the economically active population was unemployed or underemployed. After showing improvement during most of the 1980s, social indicators—including nutrition levels, school attendance rates, and the incidence of contagious diseases—began to lose ground in the late 1980s and early 1990s. In response to external demand and taking advantage of favorable agricultural conditions, drug traffic expanded rapidly, with its sequel of corruption, environmental damage, and economic distortions. The 1980s also saw the emergence of Shining Path, the most vicious terrorist group in the hemisphere and, in response, the rise of repressive violence by military and police forces.

Peruvian society has undergone such a profound transformation that the average citizen's perception and understanding of social reality is partial, fragmented, and distorted. Everyday violence has touched and shaken almost every Peruvian, badly affecting feelings of personal safety and emotional security. The rationality underlying economic reforms emphasizes impersonal market forces and requires a high degree of individual self-reliance to meet the demands of an increasingly competitive society. In a context of economic stagnation and widespread poverty, these two sets of conditions have unleashed contradictory forces that pull Peruvians apart: pressures toward individual and selfish behavior are poised against both the need to act in concert to improve the chances of survival and deep-rooted traditions of collective action.

For all practical purposes, the Weberian concept that the state has a monopoly on the legitimate exercise of political violence, primarily through the armed forces and the police, has been replaced in Peru by an "oligopoly" in which a variety of groups—Shining Path, Túpac Amaru Revolutionary Movement (MRTA), paramilitary death-squads, self-defense groups (*rondas campesinas, serenazgo*), private guards, and even drug traffickers—have joined the armed forces and the police in claiming, for a variety of different reasons, legitimacy in their resort to violence.

Peru has become a social laboratory in which the good, the bad, and the ugly coexist and contrast sharply, a country of paradoxes that defies conventional habits of thought. Peruvians have devised an enormous variety of creative responses to confront adversity. Community organizations, grassroot activism, and self-help movements show the resilience and ingenuity of those who have been most affected by the process of accelerated economic and social deterioration.

In the midst of the crisis, a stubborn streak of hope, together with a capacity for organization and expressions of solidarity, are transforming problems into challenges and opportunities. But this resilience cannot be taken for granted, nor can Peruvians withstand a continuous and precipitous decline in living standards without risking a total breakdown of the precarious social order now in place.

The Current Scene: A Crisis of Governance

At the root of this paradoxical combination of crisis and creative responses lies a fundamental fact of Peruvian political life: *the formal institutional framework of Peruvian society has been incapable of accommodating the accelerated process of social change that has taken place during the last four decades.* The explosion of social demands—a consequence of rapid population growth and of the increasing unwillingness to tolerate social injustice—overran the capacity of government organizations, legislative institutions, the legal framework, the judiciary system, political parties, private enterprises, trade unions, and many other entities that are part of the social fabric. Students of the Peruvian situation have variously described this phenomenon as "Popular Overflow and Crisis of the State," the "Rise of the Informal Sector," and a "Failure of the Elites."

As a result, the ways in which power and authority have been exercised in the conduct of economic and social affairs have broken down, and Peru faces a fundamental *crisis of governance.* The familiar inventory of social problems is but a symptom of such crisis. At the same time, the creative but fragile responses that have emerged to confront these problems suggest that the capacity and initiative shown by social movements, nurtured in a climate of openness and democratic freedom, may provide a way out of the crisis of governance.

The current political situation can be better understood against the background of the crisis. The inability of the political system, and of political parties in particular, to respond adequately to the growing need for jobs, social services, security, and a sense of order paved the way for *political disintermediation.* As a very visible part of an inadequate political system during the 1980s, when the multiplicity of crises converged, political parties became the obvious target for criticism. Their limited capacity to structure, process, and reconcile a variety of often contradictory demands from the population was thus reduced even further. As a result, political parties lost ground to a variety of pressure and interest groups that projected themselves directly on the national scene, and outsiders displaced traditional politicians.

The 1990 presidential election, in which two outsiders—Mario Vargas Llosa and Alberto Fujimori—faced each other in the second round, was a clear indication of the extent to which parties had lost legitimacy. Following Fujimori's election as president, the lack of viable political intermediaries in the executive and in Congress led to a cacophony of political demands (for resources, representation, recognition, influence, benefits), to rapidly shifting and unstable political alliances on specific issues, to improvisation and reactive political behavior, and to conflicts and inflexible positions. All of this made it extremely difficult to agree on policies and strategies to confront the explosive combination of problems faced by Peru at the beginning of the 1990s.

However, considering such a messy and volatile political context, Fujimori must be given credit for backing a series of economic reforms introduced by his ministers of economics and finance. Elected on a "no economic shock" platform, he revised drastically his electoral stance once he took office. He embraced an audacious program of reforms that began to stabilize the economy, although at the cost of a drastic reduction in incomes and a severe recession, which was compounded by drought during 1991–1992.

The government liberalized trade, cut government expenditures, improved tax collection, reformed customs, and resumed debt service to international financial institutions. As a result, hyperinflation was stopped, confidence was (precariously) restored, and the country returned to the international financial community in early 1993, after clearing its arrears with the IMF and the World Bank.

However, the improvised character of Fujimori's government, and its lack of a well-seasoned team of policymakers and managers, is leading to an impasse in economic policy: inflation persists (at the worrisome levels of around 4 percent per month), the country is still in a deep recession, and a variety of economic variables—exchange rate, public tariffs, interest rates—show rather unhealthy tendencies. Given the way in which Fujimori's government has managed the economy and its lack of a long-term perspective within which to place possible changes in economic policy, any significant departure from the established course may undermine confidence and thus end up making the problem worse.

In Peruvian politics, the traditional, knee-jerk reaction to perceived instability or political chaos has been the emergence of dictatorships or authoritarian governments. Alberto Fujimori proved to be no exception. His political inexperience and authoritarian instincts became a major liability in dealing with the turbulent world of internal politics and the rapidly changing international scene. A tendency to confuse "governing" with "giving orders" drew him close to the armed forces early in his tenure and laid the foundations for the coup of 5 April 1992.

While the military probably saw the coup as a means to improve its economic situation, gain a free hand to deal with terrorism, and obtain greater political influence, only a major miscalculation would make a democratically elected president add unconstitutional rule to a country already facing multiple crises. Moreover, as experience showed, the self-inflicted coup did not improve substantively the prospects for dealing with economic difficulties, terrorism, poverty, corruption, drug traffic, and political instability.

The capture of Abimael Guzmán, the Shining Path leader, in November 1992 gave a significant victory to the antiterrorist campaign of the government and helped to create a sense of greater security and optimism, particularly in the Lima metropolitan area. This presented a good opportunity for Peruvian society to begin exploring more consensual approaches to fighting terrorism. However, Fujimori did not take advantage of this opportunity to abandon his confrontational style of leadership and to foster a greater sense of national unity.

International pressure forced a series of changes in Fujimori's open-ended program of return to democracy. Elections for a Congress that combined legislative with constitutional reform duties were held in November 1992, in which candidates backed by Fujimori obtained 38 percent of the valid votes, enough to have a majority in the new Congress. After considerable protest from political parties and pressures from a variety of national and international groups, municipal elections were held on 29 January 1993. Candidates backed by the government and by established political parties suffered major setbacks, with independent candidates winning in many municipalities, including Lima.

Municipal and congressional elections, held under the supervision of the Organization of American States (OAS), gave a veneer of formal legitimacy to Fujimori's regime. The congressional election campaign showed evidence of gross imbalances in access to mass media, with government-backed candidates enjoying advantages—for instance, practically free access to several hours of prime-time daily television coverage in the week before the election—that were denied to the opposition.

At present, *the checks and balances that are essential to a viable and working democracy are not in place in Peru, and the prospects for improving democratic governance in Peru appear uncertain and problematic.* The judiciary is under the control of the executive, which decides on the appointment and removal of judges and prosecutors. In Congress a slim majority, elected with the backing of the president, exercises almost total control over legislative proceedings and has shown little inclination toward independence from the executive, or tolerance for the rights of the minority in opposition.

The set of incidents between Congress and the armed forces, (the La Cantuta case) stemming from denunciation of human rights violations by renegade paramilitary squads and confirmed by a former high-ranking general, has shown clearly the unwillingness of the government's majority to exert the full investigative powers of Congress. There is no desire whatsoever to trod an even slightly different path than that drawn by Fujimori and his appointees at the top level of the armed forces.

The constitution has been amended in a hurried way, without proper debate and with virtually no attempt at generating consensus on the changes proposed by the majority. Provisions that would allow Fujimori to run for immediate reelection and measures that would allow the president to dismiss Congress at his will are now under consideration and are most likely to be incorporated in the amended constitution.

Fujimori's self-inflicted coup, his confrontational style and authoritarian conduct, as well as the persistence of terrorism and other forms of violence, have exacerbated the polarization of Peruvian society, leaving little room for substantive and effective debates about the practice and the future of democracy in Peru. The political opposition has proven incapable, at least until now, of articulating a clear and strong set of positions that could resonate with the public at large. New initiatives, for example the Democratic Forum, are beginning to play a catalytic role in organizing the opposition to authoritarian rule.

In addition, it has become rather difficult to assess the roles actually being played by a variety of actors in a paradoxical, seemingly crowded and yet apparently empty national political scene. These actors include, among others, the central government, state corporations, local and regional governments, Congress, private enterprises, informal sector groups, community organizations, professional and business associations, academic institutions, religious groups, political parties, trade unions, the police, and the armed forces, as well as a variety of grassroots entities that have emerged as a response to the economic crisis and the disappearance of the state from many areas of Peruvian life.

In short, Peru faces a profound crisis of governance. The main current manifestations are the virtual disintegration of political structures, the inability of the government to deal with the prolonged economic recession, the deterioration of social conditions, the spread of an "epidemic of intolerance" at all levels of Peruvian society, and the persistence of criminal, terrorist, and repressive violence. This is complicated by the perception of many Peruvians that the only option to confront Shining Path and the MRTA is to support an authoritarian regime backed by the military, even though this will surely lead to wide-scale repression and human rights violations. Such perception is heightened by the government's appeals for continued support for its authoritarian actions to confront terrorism.

Deterioration of the Social Fabric and the Crisis of Governance

The profound crisis of governance that Peru is experiencing at the close of the twentieth century strongly conditions the prospects for political development. The broad historical processes outlined in the preceding sections, both with their long-term and short-term dimensions, have unleashed forces that must be taken into account in the design of strategies to improve the prospects for democratic governance in Peru.

An appropriate starting point may be an assessment of the degree of deterioration of the social fabric and its various manifestations. *A precarious social order* is now in place in which heterogeneity has become fragmentation, segmentation, and dissociation, and in which there is confusion, ambiguity, and uncertainty. The ground itself is in motion and there is no sense of clear limits or borders. There is a proliferation of partial perspectives and of aspirations to "special treatment," which impede concerted action and reinforce fragmentation. In turn, this leads to overlaps and friction between the different spheres of action of individuals, groups, organizations, and institutions, to which the growing response is some sort of segregation. Proximity and contact do not foster communication, but rather mistrust and rejection of "the other."

Impatience becomes generalized and leads to *demands for immediate gratification,* even if it is vicarious or imagined. Instant results are expected and "to act," in and of itself, is transformed into "to produce results," thus giving rise to a rapid sequence of actions that produce only effects—that often exist only in speeches or mass media reports—without regard for second-order consequences. Time lags between actions or interventions, on the one hand, and results or consequences, on the other, are ignored; the distinction between movement and action is blurred; and improvisation and superficiality become the norm, and even a virtue. This leads to a loss of the sense of history and of the perspective of the future; life becomes a series of isolated moments, of short terms without reference to what has been and what will be. Vision of the future and strategic thinking give way to reactive and short-sighted behaviors, which are dignified with the name of "pragmatism."

In such a social setting, *identities are constructed in a negative way:* because of *not* being this or that; because of *not* having done one thing or another. Positive referents for the construction of identities at the individual, group, organization, or institution level are very scarce, abstract, remote, and difficult to link to daily life. The lack of positive referents to identify with makes it difficult to engage with others in the pursuit of common objectives, reinforces the tendencies toward defining oneself by exclusion, and leads to a general loss of values—particularly among the young.

The loss of human, financial, physical, and organizational resources leads to *institutional disintegration,* which is accelerated because of the continuous modification of legal norms. In addition, few institutions have managerial and technical replacement teams, particularly in the public sector. As a consequence, a progressive and generalized reduction in performance standards takes place, mediocrity becomes acceptable and transforms itself into the norm, and excellence becomes something unreachable—and even dysfunctional—in group and individual behavior. Institutional weaknesses erode the sense of leadership, leaders are the object of envy and supposed to be "brought down and shown their place," and, without replacement teams, leadership in organizations and institutions becomes sporadic and intermittent.

However, together with all these manifestations of the deterioration of the social fabric, there is a multiplicity of positive responses—unstructured, amorphous, and even futile—that are struggling to be recognized, replicated, and expanded. Numerous acts of daily heroism in small scale suggest there is a latent potential of values and creativity that could and must be tapped. There is still a capacity to regenerate the Peruvian social fabric, which now lies in tatters.

In an attempt to avoid and elude the uncertainty, ambiguity, fragmentation, improvisation, and related manifestations of the deteriorating social fabric, individual and collective reactions are characterized by a flight to the normative domain, to what should be, to the realm of the prescriptive (which could perhaps be seen as a "sane" response to a "sick" situation, and as a defense mechanism to maintain sanity and self-esteem). Efforts to respond to the crisis of governance are directed toward the design of normative proposals, almost always disconnected from the messy and contradictory reality. The traditional preference for solving social problems through the enactment—or elimination—of laws and other legal devices reinforces the displacement of concerns toward the sphere of norms, precepts, prescriptions, and rules. This flight to the normative domain (often under the guise of concrete normative proposals) makes unnecessary the links with a turbulent and messy reality. In addition, it tends to put those who make normative statements on a "superior" plane, without the responsibility of putting them into practice.

Some Consequences for Governance Structures

These various aspects of the deterioration of the social fabric, together with the mismatch between social demands and the institutional capacity to respond to them—which is the hallmark of the Peruvian crisis of governance—lead to certain striking features of the structures through which power and authority are exercised in contemporary Peru. They are: the prevalence of authoritarian behavior, the lack of adaptive capabilities, the lack of channels for political mobility, and the legitimation of authority exclusively through results.

Authoritarian behavior. Authoritarianism permeates all the structures for the exercise of power (not only those of government). The capacity to respond to social demands is personified in the ruler at the highest level, and a pure, nonmediated relation is established between the ruler and the people, who are treated as a "mass." The political mediation process takes place through symbols, thus replacing mediation through institutions: the ruler "knows" what the people want and how to give it to them. Television and public opinion polls create the illusion of a direct connection between popular demands and the capacity of the ruler to satisfy aspirations and wishes; as a result, people tend to mortgage their hopes in the authoritarian figure, endowing the leader with supposedly extraordinary powers.

Such a context favors the functioning of "total institutions" that provide members with values, principles, guidelines for action, norms, and standards of behavior (the armed forces, Catholic church, Shining Path). In an authoritarian context, the diverse manifestations of the deterioration of the social fabric (corruption, drug traffic, crime, violence, repression) corrode and weaken even further the fragile structure of political intermediation, thus reinforcing authoritarianism.

Lack of adaptive capacities. The combined effect of the tendency to escape toward the normative domain, with the authoritarian character of power structures and the political disintermediation process described earlier, lead inevitably to the progressive isolation of the ruler and his or her close circle of associates. Signals are filtered and processed in a biased way, and the manipulation of indicators (approval levels in opinion polls, "spontaneous" gatherings of supporters) replaces the information obtained and processed through institutional channels.

As a consequence, there is no capacity to display adaptive behavior that could introduce partial changes to maintain the government along a stable course. Moreover, even if there is the intention to do so, there is a lack of institutional channels to introduce minor adaptive corrections. The final result is a total delinking of the power elite from the events on the ground (no reality check). Thus, there is no homeostatic feedback to maintain the system within certain parameters by means of partial adjustments, and change takes place only through catastrophic feedback in which there is a "total correction" that destroys the authoritarian system of government (but probably replaces it with a similar one).

Lack of channels for political mobility. Authoritarianism, the incapacity to adapt, and political disintermediation make access to the highest levels of government very difficult. Authoritarian rulers guard jealously their monopoly of linkages with the people, defending it from political rivals and from institutions that could provide channels for political mobility. Hence, the efforts to destroy institutions (political parties, government agencies, independent organizations) and, if this is not possible—as is the case of "total institutions" such as the armed forces and the church—at least to co-opt and manipulate them.

In this situation, political mobility takes place through periodic explosions (*huaycos* would be a better and more Peruvian word) that disarticulate the whole structure for the exercise of political power and push toward leadership positions whoever is in the right place at the right time. A second channel for political mobility consists of "capillary mechanisms," of uncertain effectiveness and slow filtration, that would permit a gradual political ascension that apparently does not threaten the authoritarian ruler.

Legitimation through results. Authoritarian rulers usually seek legitimation through the results they obtain, or claim to obtain. Without the legitimacy given by the respect for rules, procedures, and due process that characterize democracies, they appeal to the results produced by the authoritarian exercise of power: they substitute the "rule of outcomes" for "the rule of law."

However, because of the impossibility of producing satisfactory results on a permanent basis, and taking advantage of the demands for immediate gratification, the ruler tends to substitute the promise of results for a series of actions or movements, which acquire value on their own. This leads to some sort of Ponzi scheme of political promises, which is unsustainable in the medium term. Moreover, it amplifies the processes of catastrophic feedback and explosive political mobility.

Conclusion: A Role for the International Community

Fujimori's regime in the early 1990s conforms to the type of governance structure described in the preceding section. It has emerged against the background of the historical convergence of a multiplicity of crises that were incubated over long and varying periods. The prospects for political development and democratic governance depend on the extent to which it will be possible to address adequately the multiple manifestations of the crisis of governance, and of the deterioration of the social fabric.

The complex and paradoxical processes of social transformation under way in Peru will unfold at least until the end of the century. The primary tasks are to restore a fully working set of democratic institutions, reverse economic decline, improve social conditions, and defeat terrorism. In parallel, it will be necessary to begin the slow process of reconstituting the social fabric and of changing the conditions that have led to the establishment of authoritarian governance structures. These are tasks for Peruvians to accomplish. Other countries and international institutions have an important but supporting role in these processes.

The end of the cold war has altered fundamentally the parameters for evaluating national conduct and good international standing. In assessing how far to insist on policy changes in return for support and assistance, the international community must strike a difficult balance between respect for international standards of human rights and democratic practices on one side, and respect for national autonomy and sovereignty on the other.

The international community, and the United States in particular, has a vast array of options for providing development assistance, ranging from financial resources channeled through multilateral institutions, to direct assistance to local nongovernmental organizations, and to support for the provision of social services by the government. In exchange, it can expect the political and economic behavior of the recipient governments and institutions to be consistent with internationally accepted standards of human rights and democratic practices. Without interfering in the country's internal affairs, and taking into account its special characteristics, it should be possible to persevere in efforts to bring Peru closer to a fully working democracy in which human rights are scrupulously respected.

The international community can also expand its support of local independent institutions, seeking to counterbalance the concentration of power in government hands. This implies strengthening a variety of organizations—from community and grassroots movements to professional and business associations—that have become a clear expression of the creativity of Peruvian society.

Whether the years leading to the end of the century produce a more humane, secure, democratic, and prosperous society will depend, first, on the actions of Peruvians. The support that the international community can provide, and the requests it can make in exchange, will play a significant but subsidiary role. As the leading power in the Western Hemisphere, the United States is expected to wield influence and keep actively engaged in the economic, political, and social affairs of the region, especially in a country like Peru, where so much is at stake.

3

Democracy's Bleak Prospects

Fernando Rospigliosi

The prospects for democratization in Peru are weak and uncertain. President Alberto Fujimori's objective is to perpetuate an authoritarian government and to present the appearance of democracy so as to meet the demands of the international community. For its part, the democratic opposition is divided, with one sector trusting—paradoxically—in the military to remove Fujimori from government to return to representative democracy.

But at a more profound level, the difficulties in moving Peru onto the path of democracy lie in the extreme fragility of its institutions, in the process of disintegration the country has suffered over the last fifteen years, and in the limited extent to which democratic traditions and values are rooted in both the elite and the population at large.

The Institutions

O'Donnell (1990) has noted that building democratic institutions is the crucial issue for the "second transition" from an elected government to a democratic regime, that is, to an institutionalized and consolidated democracy.[1]

Why were such institutions, particularly political parties, not constructed in Peru following the restoration of democracy in 1980? Three contributing factors should be highlighted.

Fernando Rospigliosi is a researcher at the Institute for Peruvian Studies (IEP).

First, there are historical factors. In Peru the degree of institutionalization was very limited prior to the wave of modernization in the 1950s.[2] In contrast to more integrated and institutionalized countries such as Chile or Uruguay, Peru was fragmented. The military government (1968–1980) did not attain its objective of integration; to the contrary, modernization accelerated in some respects but did not create the institutions required to absorb the increased participation of the mobilized masses. The prolonged dictatorship crippled the development of political parties. The result was the typical picture of disintegration and instability analyzed by Samuel Huntington (1972).

Second, the economic crisis that began in the mid-1970s, complicated and prolonged by the debt crisis beginning in 1982, accentuated the processes of disintegration and social fragmentation. In this context, as characterized by growth of the so-called informal sector, the parties faced increasing difficulties aggregating the interests of different actors and classes (Grompone 1991:98).

Third, the persistence of a patrimonial regime, a legacy of the Peru of the oligarchic era, hindered the formation of a party system. This fostered the persistence of closed subcultures in which negotiation and tolerance are censured (Cotler 1993).

Democracy: Survival Is Not Enough

The (re)installation of representative democracy in 1980 did not meet citizens' expectations. When the military regime initiated the transition in mid-1977, economic growth had ground to a halt, the standard of living had begun to fall, and civil freedoms in effect up to 1975 were being increasingly cut back.[3] The aspirations of progress and societal integration of the recently urbanized popular classes, whose educational levels had mounted steadily in the two previous decades, began to be frustrated, and they turned against the government en masse. Entrepreneurs, the middle class, and the political parties, disaffected from the military from the outset, redoubled their calls for soldiers to return to the barracks. A spontaneous multiclass front formed in opposition to the dictatorship. The armed forces, conscious of the growth of widespread antimilitary sentiment among the population, and, perhaps more importantly, conscious that the politicization and factionalism within the armed forces threatened their institutional unity, decided to step down (Mauceri 1989).

Two points bear emphasizing here. First, siding with democracy was more utilitarian than a matter of principle for the popular sector, as well as for the middle and upper strata. That is, the economic crisis; declining wages, incomes, and profits; and the general drop in the standard of living were associated with the military dictatorship. Everyone thought that with democracy they would be better able to defend their interests and that the crisis would be overcome. Of course, utilitarian support for democracy is not out of the ordinary, nor is it necessarily bad. This happens in processes of transition, in countries in which there has been no prior history of stable democracy. The problem arises when democracy does not satisfy even the minimal expectations of the population and when it does not last long enough for citizens' values and patterns of behavior to begin to change.

Second, and linked to the foregoing, the advent of democracy was accompanied by excessive expectations[4] on the part of the population, especially the popular classes. Since those expectations were not met, over the years disenchantment began to undermine the appreciation of democracy,[5] which was considered ineffective in resolving the country's two major problems—economic crisis and terrorism—which dragged on as the decade continued.

Democracy, understood as political democracy,[6] does not necessarily imply an improvement in the population's standard of living, a more equitable distribution of wealth, or the long list of names that some theorists and political groups have assigned to it, according to taste: social democracy, participatory democracy, real democracy, and so forth. Yet there is undoubtedly a relationship between the achievements perceived by the population and its support or lack thereof for democracy. A democratic political regime in a country like Peru has a difficult time withstanding a prolonged economic crisis that steadily impoverishes the population and increases social inequality, especially if an already difficult situation is compounded by a phenomenon like armed subversion.

The result has been disaffection with democracy among broad sectors of the population, including people at both the top and the bottom. Surveys that periodically indicate that the majority favors a democratic regime should be read carefully and are inconsistent with support for the 5 April self-coup.

A recent study undertaken in poor neighborhoods of Lima demonstrates that 81 percent of the respondents agree with a "government not elected by the people if it is just and improves the situation" (Parodi and Twanama 1993:81). Along the same lines, a large majority (71 percent) prefers a "strong and just authority" to "broad political freedom" (29 percent). Basing their analysis on surveys and interviews, one conclusion the authors reach is that there is not much interest in political parties, but that there is interest in participating in the election of the government. From this it is deduced that there is a longing for a plebiscitarian democracy that establishes a direct nexus between the masses and the leader at the time of elections (Parodi and Twanama 1993:79).

The massive support for the self-coup among entrepreneurs appears to be motivated by the conviction that a get-tough policy is needed to eliminate the terrorist threat and by the belief that economic neoliberalism would favor their interests. Those of us who believed that the private sector's experiences with the regime of General Velasco (1968–1975) had taught entrepreneurs that a dictatorship can be very arbitrary and completely escape their control were mistaken. Likewise, those of us who thought that the private sector had learned that under democracy their interests could be better defended against arbitrary government, as occurred in 1987 with the failed attempt to nationalize the banking system, were also mistaken.

Support from business sectors was almost total, just as the entrepreneurs had massively backed candidate Mario Vargas Llosa and rejected Alberto Fujimori in 1990. Today, though shouts of anguish have been heard because the prolonged recession is asphyxiating them, business support for the government appears to be holding steady.

Ineffectiveness and Corruption

The political parties and the institutions of representative democracy have been discredited because of their inability to address the two problems that have afflicted the country in recent years: economic crisis and armed subversion.

The economic crisis can be traced back to 1975, when the country was under military rule. Peru has been in decline ever since. Certainly, the country has not taken a straight path downward, and there have been moments of recovery, but these have always been ephemeral interruptions of a general negative trend. Under democratic rule there have never been more than two consecutive years of growth, generally preceded and followed by abrupt decline.[7]

If we add to this the high levels of inflation that have characterized the Peruvian economy and that persist to this day, including the hyperinflation of the late 1980s,[8] we have a context that helps explain the political behavior of the various actors in this drama.

The armed insurgency, which began in 1980 and, although underestimated at first, quickly acquired alarming characteristics, began to affect the political behavior of the population and the institutions. Throughout the 1980s, political violence mounted and extended to ever larger parts of the national territory and the population.

All of this produced anxiety, insecurity, and short-sighted approaches, which stretches out the situation indefinitely. The long term is not taken into account, only the short term—how to survive until the next day.

The failure to solve these two problems was attributed by Peruvian citizens to the governments and institutions of representative democracy: the legislature and the political parties. In the eyes of the population, professional politicians are power-hungry people involved in petty power squabbles and are not concerned with the country's well-being. This perception is common to a greater or lesser extent in many developing countries and even in countries with consolidated democracies. But in Peru it reached unprecedented extremes precisely because of the tension, insecurity, and demoralization caused by prolonged economic crisis, the extended period of hyperinflation, and the savage actions of Shining Path.

Added to these factors is corruption, which is tolerated in times of abundance or when the government proves effective;[9] but it can become intolerable in times of a profound economic crisis affecting a great many people. The Peruvian population perceived that the APRA government (1985–1990), including President García and the main leaders of the party, especially in its last years, were extraordinarily corrupt.[10]

It was not just corruption but the impunity enjoyed by those presumed to be dishonest that irritated the population. In contrast to the cases of Fernando Collor in Brazil and Carlos Andrés Pérez in Venezuela, Alan García and his close associates were not tried in Peru while they held power.[11] During the Fujimori government, the parliament found sufficient grounds for removing García's immunity from prosecution and bringing charges against him before the Supreme Court. The court, however, decided that a trial was inappropriate and exonerated him of all charges. This decision had tremendous repercussions—and was cited by Fujimori as one of the reasons for the coup—ultimately discrediting the judiciary and pushing the population's patience to its limit.

Although the Fujimori government did nothing in two years to reform the judiciary, blame was laid on the party politicians, who failed to do what was needed in the 1980s to improve the administration of justice. The judiciary not only refrained from punishing corruption but also was extraordinarily tolerant of, or displayed complicity with, terrorists who were detained.

The fundamental problem of the Peruvian judiciary is the relationship between the administration of justice and political power (Pásara 1982:14). The subjection of the courts to political influence was not substantially modified with the shift to a democratically elected regime in 1980. The administrations of Belaúnde and García continued the traditional practice of trying to appoint their followers to the courts. Coupled with the aggravating factor of economic decline, which was impoverishing all state institutions, this practice systematically eroded the quality of judges and the efficiency of the administration of justice.

The situation continued during the first part of the Fujimori government. The only difference was that the president, reflecting the population's widespread discontent with the judicial branch, criticized it constantly—without making any effort to reform it. After the coup, hundreds of judges and judicial staff were removed from their posts, and others were appointed on a provisional basis by the government. The judges' dependence on political power was thus made absolute. Today, the perception is that the judiciary is no less corrupt and no more efficient than before, although it is clearly more dependent.

The Discrediting and Perplexity of the Political Parties

On 5 April 1992, President Alberto Fujimori took the political parties by surprise when he dissolved parliament and intervened in the judiciary. What the parties least expected was that the coup would be so strongly supported by the population, business elites, and, of course, the armed forces, which sustained Fujimori's action.

The leaders of the political parties considered this support for the interruption of democratic rule to be the result of government manipulation of public opinion, particularly by the intelligence services with the complicity of some of the major news media. According to this view, Fujimori's systematic campaigns since the beginning of his government to discredit the parliament, the judiciary, the political parties, and other institutions attained the objective of misleading the population.

While the foregoing may be true, such an analysis of these events is mistaken. First, the political parties, parliament, and the judiciary were already discredited before Fujimori came to power. He won the 1990 elections precisely because of the deep and widespread rejection of these institutions by a majority of the population.[12] The political elites neither perceived the extent to which they were isolated, nor learned the lessons of 1990 or 1989, when an independent was easily elected mayor of Lima.

Second, the political parties, precisely because they did not understand just how deeply isolated they were, did not do much to rebuild their ties with the electorate, modify their behavior, or democratize their institutional structures. (One must take into account the parties' inability to engage in self-criticism—their political *autism*—when analyzing the possibilities of a return to democracy.)

In addition, the parties did not present a clear image of themselves in this new context, in which for the first time since the restoration of democracy in 1980 the government did not hold a majority in the parliament.[13] As such, they were further discredited.

Even though they were not in the government, the parties were not part of the opposition either. With a fragmented parliament they generally acted in a responsible and moderate fashion, for several reasons. One was undoubtedly a dose of common sense: they understood that given the country's critical situation, obstructionist opposition could destroy democratic government. Another reason was a matter of political calculation: there was not much interest in discrediting the government's party because for all practical purposes it did not exist. If Fujimori were successful, the danger that his party might win the 1995 elections was much less likely. It would have been a personal success and the rules of the game then in force—which Fujimori could not change, because he did not have a majority in the legislature—prevented the president from running for reelection at the end of his term.

Finally, because of their basic agreement with Fujimori's economic liberalization policies, the parties that made up the now-dissolved Democratic Front (FREDEMO)—AP (Popular Action), PPC (the Popular Christian party), Libertad (the Liberty movement), and SODE (Solidarity and Democracy)—were brakes against more radical opposition. As for APRA, which supported Fujimori in the second round of elections, the party was tacitly allied with the government for the first year as a result of official backing for finding former President Alan García innocent of the charges against him. In addition, APRA's room for maneuvering was limited because it was greatly discredited, having been in power so recently that the bad memories had yet to subside. And the parties of the left, which also supported Fujimori in the June 1990 elections, were partly neutralized by the inclusion of three ministers from their ranks in Fujimori's first cabinet.

Given this complex and, from the population's perspective, confusing game, the parliament and political parties appeared opportunistic, irrelevant, and unnecessary.[14] That is, considering the depths of the prestige of the political institutions, the twenty months of democracy during the Fujimori government did not allow them to recover credibility. It was in this context that Fujimori's campaigns and intelligence service operations directed against the politicians and institutions—that is, against representative democracy—were successful.

If the situation were different, the behavior of the political parties would have been lauded as proper and exemplary. If Fujimori had agreed to engage in dialogue and negotiation, as representatives of various parties suggested to him many times, agreements possibly could have been reached that would have been to everyone's benefit. But Fujimori steadfastly refused to enter into any type of negotiation. One could have expected a favorable outcome if all or at least the main actors had been willing to play by the rules of democracy, but not if two of them—the president and the armed forces—wanted to discard those rules. Thus, the conciliatory conduct of the parties, which operated within a context of competition and cooperation, ultimately worked against them. (Although it is likely that the radical opposition would not have worked to preserve democracy either.)

It was not just a question of the president's refusal to follow the course that would be normal in any democracy but the inability of all the other actors to force him to accept the rules of the democratic game. The divisions among the parties—astutely fostered by Fujimori—around issues such as accusations of corruption against Alan García and his staff, or on economic policy, which brought neoliberals into conflict with populists, undoubtedly made pressuring Fujimori all the more difficult.

But the central problem, as noted above, was (and is) the weakness of institutions that could not withstand the authoritarian onslaught of a president ready to govern without the "bothersome details" (O'Donnell 1990:9) of the parliament and the judiciary.

Civil-Military Relations

Last but not least in importance is the problem of civil-military relations.[15] The armed forces developed a growing distaste for representative democracy and its institutions primarily because they felt abandoned in the struggle against the guerrilla forces. This was the main motive for their participation in the 5 April coup.

Alberto Fujimori, who came to power unexpectedly in 1990, disdains democracy. In this respect he found an essential affinity with the armed forces. Moreover, Fujimori, absent a proposal for dealing with one of the country's most pressing problems, the armed insurgency, turned to the military for advice, especially the intelligence services.[16] Thus the new president began assimilating military thinking in the area of counterinsurgency.[17] In this way, Fujimori came to embrace the thesis that the armed forces had been advocating for years, many aspects of which were not being heard by the civil authorities. He has become an exponent of sorts of military thinking, with which he gained the support of the institutions of the armed forces. In this way, the military obtained the political support it had been calling for, that is, official civilian support for the military's actions and civilian provision of a free rein in the fight against the subversives.

The military's disaffection for democracy grew throughout the 1980s. The primary responsibility for this falls on the Peruvian political elite. It should have addressed the problem of the armed insurgency by seriously considering the military's demands (which would not necessarily have meant accepting them) and setting out to train civilian experts in military matters. But it did nothing along these lines. This point is worth dwelling on for a moment. It explains why the armed forces so firmly supported the 5 April coup, why the Fujimori government today depends almost entirely on the support of the armed forces, and, furthermore, why the counterinsurgency strategy has become Fujimori's main justification for the 5 April coup and for his continuation at the helm of the government.[18]

The military's relationship with democracy and the political parties was marked by mutual distrust since the 1980 transition. The beginning of the war unleashed by Shining Path on 17 May 1980, even before the military government had ended, substantially contributed to the muddying of civil relations. Initially, the government of Fernando Belaúnde attempted to downplay the significance of the insurrection in Ayacucho. But this was a mistake not only on the part of the executive branch. The legislature, the judiciary, the political parties, the press, and society in general underestimated the phenomenon of Shining Path for at least the first three years (Gorriti 1990). No one paid attention to the warnings of the military that it, by virtue of its training, is extremely sensitive to any national security threat, to a threat to its monopoly on weapons, and to challenges to public order posed by Marxist groups seeking to establish a communist system.

From the outset, therefore, the armed forces distrusted a democracy that was incapable of taking a firm and decided stand against a threat such as Shining Path. Of course, the military was not in a position to apply much pressure so soon after returning power to civilian hands following twelve years of rule, at the end of which its prestige among the Peruvian population had declined considerably. The most important conflicts, however, began when the armed forces became directly involved in the war, taking charge of the emergency zones in late December 1982. By this point a great deal of tension had accumulated due to the position adopted by members of the parliament and the press vis-à-vis the insurgency, which focused on the violations of human rights by the police forces. The position taken by those political sectors was at least ambiguous; to the military, this bordered on treason. So there were two distinct approaches to the problem.

On the one hand, a sector of civilian society—politicians, journalists, intellectuals, and others—attempted to understand the insurgent phenomenon as the result of social inequalities, economic crisis, and lack of opportunities. They sought a *political solution* to the conflict, a response that would solve the economic and social problems that presumably were at the roots of the armed guerrilla movement and at the same time reduce the repression. In this way, they thought, it would be possible to deactivate the Shining Path insurgency little by little.

On the other hand, for the military the armed subversion of Shining Path fit squarely into the scheme of a typical communist movement endeavoring to destroy the state, society, and, of course, the armed forces in order to establish a radically different social order. For several decades the military institutions had been prepared for such a threat, and they had very well-developed ideas as to the need to confront such a movement forcefully.[19] While in the 1960s and 1970s Peruvian military officers certainly developed a national security doctrine distinct from those of the armies of the Southern Cone countries, emphasizing the need to undertake profound social reforms, the Peruvian armed forces also shared values and principles with their counterparts elsewhere in Latin America, including a conception of security that led them to consider the communist threat the principal enemy of the established order.

In summary, it appears that the armed forces, or at least a large part of them, considered Shining Path's insurrection as the product of a long-prepared and predetermined communist strategy to take power, and not as a consequence of particular political, economic, and social circumstances that led to its outbreak.[20]

The mutual distrust and lack of common understanding persisted. Neither military circles nor political and civil society made serious attempts even to understand the other group's thinking. Prejudices and preconceived notions predominated for more than a decade, until they found expression in the 5 April self-coup. The military was not only faced with the traditional opposition of radical or extremist sectors; they also felt abandoned by the entire society, including the civilian governments. In their view, the armed forces were adequately discharging their responsibility, but no one else was doing so. As General Luis Cisneros wrote: "Isn't it clear, perhaps, that reality is leading to the belief that nothing or very little has been done outside of the military to address the subversion?" (1990).[21] He then criticized explicitly the parliament, the judiciary, and the president.

There were not only conflicts between the military and the political sectors and press considered to be sympathetic to the guerrilla movement or to the opposition. There was also a division between the military and government institutions such as the parliament and the judiciary. During the 1980s, several investigative commissions were established in the parliament to inquire into human rights violations. In general, this only served to sharpen the conflicts, rather than to resolve them. No member of the military was ever tried and convicted by a civilian court for a single human rights violation. Nonetheless, the military's calls for "juridical security" have been continual, since the possibility of trial and punishment have remained open.

The mechanism of investigative commissions is dangerous and ineffective for two reasons, according to Alfred Stepan:

> First, and precisely because it is an ad hoc and not a standing committee, the legislative leaders do not have the support of a professional staff with expert knowledge of the details of the issue. Second, by its very nature, a special ad hoc investigative commission operates within a context of controversies and conflicts, which tends to increase the paranoia latent in most military organizations of the world with respect to political 'interference' in their professional activities (Stepan 1988:160).

In line with Stepan's analysis, the situation in Peru reached its limit. A high level of military prerogatives, coupled with a considerable degree of questioning of the legitimacy of democracy by the military, made a democratic regime unsustainable.

In summary, a consistent, appropriate relationship between the military and civilians was not established following the restoration of democracy. Successive governments for the most part ignored the problem of the war, which was the most pressing issue for the military. They left it in the hands of the armed forces without providing the resources and conditions they requested for carrying out their mission, and without proposing a broad strategy distinct from that put forth by the armed forces. As a result, the breach of trust continued to widen and relations grew worse.

Not until the months prior to the 5 April coup did the situation begin to change. This was due to: (1) the growing sense that Shining Path represented a threat; (2) crimes such as the killing of community leader María Elena Moyano, which had an enormous impact on society, and made it essential for the parties and mass-based organizations to coordinate with the security forces; and (3) the discussion of the November 1991 legislative decrees, which given the government's policy of presenting faits accomplis, made it necessary for the political parties to present more specific alternatives, consider some of the military concerns, and try to negotiate a consensus solution with the government and the military.[22] But this process was largely interrupted by the 5 April coup.

The Significance of the 1992 and 1993 Elections

Alberto Fujimori quickly adopted the idea, so common among the caudillos of Peru and Latin America generally, that he was a Messiah destined to transform radically the country's destiny. Therefore, he felt he had to govern with absolute powers and for a prolonged period of time, which, according to some of his close associates, ranges from fifteen years to the rest of his life. The models that inspired him most were those of Asia (South Korea, Taiwan, and Singapore) and Chile under Pinochet. That is, he was drawn to the combination of political authoritarianism and economic liberalism.[23]

Armed with simple ideas of the "common person," he embarked upon the process pompously dubbed "national reconstruction" on 5 April 1992. His speech the day of the coup made no mention of elections for a new Congress, only referendums in which the population would be called on periodically to respond to questions put to it by the government. But pressure from the international community forced Fujimori to change the scheme and convene the unanticipated elections for the Constituent Congress, to which he attached the adjective *Democratic.*

Actually, few people in the country were interested in those elections. Fujimori did not want them. The existence of a parliament bothers and irritates him, even if he has it completely controlled. An election under those circumstances did not suit the parties of the democratic opposition, as they knew they would be defeated. Their defeat was ensured not only because the elections were held without guarantees of impartiality—a result of the manipulation of the de facto government and because one could foresee that the Congress would lack autonomy and real power—but also because the parties themselves had become so profoundly discredited in the eyes of the population. The majority of the population was not very interested in the election of a new Congress, both because the previous parliament was discredited and because they knew that it would produce little change in the existing power relations and, therefore, government policies.

This disinterest and apathy were reflected in the extent of voter abstention and void and blank ballots, which were the highest in the last thirty years (voting is compulsory in Peru). They were also apparent with the unusual failure of any of the political groups to mount a large demonstration in Lima to conclude its campaign, as has been the practice in Peru for several decades (see Table 3.1).

In the elections the opposition parties split between "abstentionists" and "participationists." The coalitions that had held until then came apart. The choice between participating in the Democratic Constituent Congress (CCD) or boycotting it created divisions within the parties as well.

The government won a majority as a result, but not on the order that Fujimori and his allies apparently had hoped. The official slate won 37.5 percent of the votes cast and 49.3 percent of the valid votes (discounting void and blank ballots), which allowed it to garner forty-four of the eighty seats at stake. The pro-Fujimori candidates won the votes of 27.1 percent of the total electorate. This last statistic is useful, for Fujimori claims part of his legitimacy from polls showing him with a 60 percent approval rating. And it is assumed that the polls reflect the opinions of the entire population, not just the voters. The difference between 27 percent and 60 percent is, however, appreciable.[24]

Illustrating a distinct feature of the political situation in the country, in the municipal elections held two months later, the outlook for Peruvian politics changed radically. None of the parties that won on 22 November 1992 received favorable results on 29 January 1993. The government party, Change 90/New Majority, won only about 2.8 percent of all districts in the country.[25] In Lima, Fujimori withdrew his candidate when the polls indicated that he would lose by a wide margin. The other new parties that appeared for the CCD elections in 1992 (almost all were more electoral lists than political parties) were not a factor. None of them, including Change 90/New Majority, has a national structure to enable it to present candidates in the 1,800 electoral districts, or even in the 180 provincial capitals or 25 departmental capitals.

Table 3.1 Results of the Elections for the Democratic Constituent Congress (22 November 1992)

Party	Votes	% of Valid Votes Cast	% of Total Votes	% of Total Registered Voters	Number of Representatives
New Majority-Change 90	3,075,422	49.3	37.5	27.1	44
Popular Christian Party (PPC)	606,651	9.7	7.4	5.3	8
Independent Moralizing Front (FIM)	486,984	7.8	5.9	4.3	7
Renovation	440,314	7.1	5.4	3.9	6
Democratic Left Movement	341,646	5.5	4.2	3.0	4
Democratic Coordinator	328,153	5.3	4.0	2.9	4
Workers and Peasants National Front (FNTC)	237,977	3.8	2.9	2.1	3
Popular Agricultural Front of Peru	172,923	2.8	2.1	1.5	2
Solidarity and Democracy Party	126,822	2.0	1.5	1.1	1
Independent Agrarian Movement	107,543	1.7	1.3	0.9	1
Others (8 Groups)	313,247	5.0	3.8	2.8	0
Total Valid Votes Cast	6,237,682	100.0	76.1	55.0	80
Blank Votes	333,277		4.1	2.9	
Null Votes	1,620,887		19.8	14.3	
Registered Voters Who Voted	8,191,846		100.0		
Registered Voters Who Did Not Vote	3,151,363			27.8	
Total Number of Registered Voters	11,343,209			100.0	

Source: National Election Board of Peru

The so-called traditional parties, which placed their hopes in these elections since they could count on their party structure, did not fare as well as they had hoped. While together they won between 40 and 50 percent of the municipalities, they had expected to do much better. And in Lima an independent, whose first term was not exactly effective, was reelected with almost 50 percent of the vote, far in front of the vote of the political parties. One can conclude that this situation is highly volatile and unstable. As is said in Peru today: "Anything can happen."

The role of the OAS in the CCD elections was unfortunate. The regional body gave its blessing to the process and concluded that democracy had been reestablished in Peru. While no one could confirm massive fraud on the day of the elections—something that rarely occurs anywhere in Latin America in the current era—the context in which these elections were held left much to be desired.

First, the rules of the game were changed by Fujimori at his whim. The OAS recommendations, which were agreed upon by consensus with the opposition, were completely ignored. Second, those same rules were changed by the government on three occasions, creating a climate of instability.[26] Third, the president of the National Election Board (JNE) was removed by the government after the coup. The Supreme Court, as reconstituted by Fujimori, appointed the new president of the JNE, who, in turn, removed the highest-ranking administrative officer (the secretary general) and appointed someone else. Fourth, in Peru the armed forces play a decisive role in the organization and holding of elections due to the weakness, disorganization, and lack of resources of the JNE. Until 1990, the armed forces were impartial, but this has not been the case since the coup. In fact, several dissident members of the military later accused the army of actively collecting signatures for the government party's slate as required for ballot registration.[27] Fifth, the state's resources were openly put at the service of the government party candidates, despite explicit statutory prohibitions on such a practice.

Finally, and most important, the Congress born of these elections has not served to reestablish the balance of power among the branches of government in Peru. It is but a mockery of a parliament. It is totally subordinated to the president and armed forces, as has been demonstrated on several occasions, including the thwarted investigation of the disappearance and presumed assassination at the hands of the army of nine students and a professor from La Cantuta University.[28]

The OAS—in contrast to other specialized private organizations that regularly observe elections in Latin America, which on this occasion did not even send missions to Peru—nevertheless fully endorsed these elections.

Fujimori's Popularity

From the outset of his administration Alberto Fujimori enjoyed relatively high popularity. Initially the main reason appeared to be his success in halting the hyperinflation that hit the country during the last years of the García government.[29] But prior to the 5 April coup, one noticed a downward trend in price increases. With the self-coup, inflation shot thirty points upward. The following months saw a steady decline until 12 September 1992, when Abimael Guzmán was captured,[30] which brought a renewed upturn. Since then there has been another moderate downward trend (Apoyo 1993c).

These events have occurred in a context of increasing citizen apathy and popular alienation with politics, as reflected, for example, in the low participation in the CCD elections and in opinion polls, which show an increased lack of interest in politics. In April 1986, 35 percent of those surveyed responded that they were not interested in politics; by February 1993 this figure had increased to 63 percent (Apoyo 1993b).

This mix of desperation, in the face of such a prolonged crisis and disinterest in politics, brought on at least in part by the lack of confidence in the possibilities for change through collective action, has probably led large parts of the population to delegate to the "caudillo saviors" the power to govern authoritatively. But in that "democracy of saviors" (or dictatorship of saviors) "the path from great popularity to widespread abomination can be both swift and sudden" (O'Donnell 1992:81).

With respect to Alan García, who reached unattainable heights of popularity only to plummet into total disrepute, there was democratic legitimacy and the certainty that his administration would end on 28 July 1990, which allowed for hope and the possibility of change. Fujimori, however, broke the rules of the democratic game so as to keep himself in power and govern without constraint, thus no one knows when he will leave the government. The country's constitution has already been amended to allow for his reelection. But his continuance in power will depend not so much on reelection, but rather, primarily, on the control he is able to maintain over the armed forces and his usefulness to them. The favorable poll ratings are very important because they ensure that Fujimori is needed by the military. But to the extent that he loses popular support, his dependence on the armed forces will increase.

Finally, it is possible that Fujimori's relatively high popularity can be explained by the lack of a credible alternative. For example, from May to September 1992, when the terrorist offensive in Lima spread panic among the population, the polls indicated that a majority of the population disapproved of the government's economic and counterinsurgency policies. They disagreed with the way Fujimori was dealing with the two most important issues; he was still receiving approval from the majority of persons polled, although his rating was declining. One explanation of this curious phenomenon is that the population places its hopes on the president because it does not see any likelihood of a better government. This view is consistent with the low poll ratings of the political parties and their leaders.

Recently the possibility has emerged that Fujimori's rivals might rise from the ranks of the independents, who possess characteristics similar to his own: no political party affiliation, authoritarian, and an image of efficiency. Two examples are Ricardo Belmont, the current mayor of Lima, and Luis Cáceres, the former mayor of Arequipa. Nevertheless, in the hypothetical case of one of them replacing Fujimori, it is highly unlikely that the prospects for democracy will substantially improve. Another independent who has expressed interest in participating in politics is the former secretary general of the United Nations, Javier Pérez de Cuéllar, but it is too soon to assess his potential.

Obstacles to the Return of Democracy

The prospects for a return to democracy in the near future are bleak. Some opposition political groups are ready to play by Fujimori's rules; they are relying on erosion of his political strength and international pressure to lead to clean and fair elections in 1995, in which the president could be defeated. The possibility of this scenario occurring is more than doubtful. Fujimori is unlikely to step down as long as he maintains the support of the armed forces. And for now he has it.

How long will he keep it? It is very difficult to say, and it depends on several factors. The first is agreement among military officers that the counterinsurgency policy is being implemented successfully, as it is the policy that they themselves designed. Both *fujimoristas* and *antifujimoristas* agree on this point, and the president exploits it to the hilt.

Second, it will depend on the ability of Vladimiro Montesinos and the National Intelligence Service (SIN) to keep the system they have set up in place. This system is based on the manipulation of commanders and promotions by placing one's supporters in key positions; espionage, closely watching the high-ranking officers, offering incentives for informing on others, and creating a climate of paranoia; corruption, which ranges from cash payments from SIN funds, in a discretionary fashion and without controls, to the point of permitting bribes and robbery; blackmail, using the information they have, above all in corruption cases, to keep officers under control; separating those who are suspect, either retiring them or sending them to far-away places, within Peru or abroad; and the threat of reprisals, which can go as far as murder.[31]

The SIN is also important because it plays the role of a political party that Fujimori does not have. It collects information (from surveys to wiretaps); keeps Fujimori informed of the mood of the population and his adversaries' movements; and designs and executes government propaganda campaigns. In addition, the SIN has acquired exceptional legal prerogatives,[32] although many are still only theoretical. Most important, no outside force or agency controls it. Neither the Congress, the judiciary, nor any government agency, including the armed forces, supervises it.

Documents brought to light by the press[33] indicate that coup plans had been underway in the military since 1989; these plans were adapted to circumstances as they evolved. The coup leaders in the military, rooted primarily in the SIN, became allies of Fujimori and, as such, joined him in carrying out the 5 April coup. The military doctrine that guided these actions is basically the same as that that existed at the time of the 1968 coup, except that the socialist ideology in vogue at that time has been replaced by the neoliberalism in vogue today. Indeed, several of the men who work in the SIN today, both military and civilians, also held SIN posts during the 1968–1980 dictatorship, including Montesinos.

If this analysis is correct, and it seems plausible, the relationship between Fujimori and the military is not the one the president seeks to convey when he publicly affirms his control over the armed forces. In other words, the military group behind the coup is much more powerful than appears to be the case, and Fujimori holds less power than he claims. In this sense, one cannot discard the possibility that the authoritarian military leaders may at some point dispense with Fujimori, perhaps by a coup or by forcing him to relinquish power in elections, and entering an alliance with another civilian (or group of civilians) who accommodates their conditions. In any event, relations between Fujimori, the SIN, and the armed forces appear to be in constant flux and beset by tension.

Third is a factor that is not sufficiently discussed but is very important: the corruption of narcotics trafficking, which has grown especially since 1989, when the military had to assume control of the coca-growing zones in the face of inroads by the insurgents and drug traffickers. One cannot say precisely how large it has grown, but it is possible that it has reached the highest levels. The presence of Vladimiro Montesinos is not exactly a guarantee against its spread.[34] The problem is that if corruption reaches uncontrollable levels in the armed forces, it will become a very important hindrance to a return to democracy, as occurred in Bolivia, Panama, and Paraguay.

Yet, and fourth, this situation has sparked a response from "institutionalist" members of the military, indignant at the political manipulation and corruption spreading throughout the institution. The danger foreseen by several senior officers has materialized, and factionalism has taken root in the armed forces. Organizations of mid-level officers have been established, such as COMACA (Commanders, Majors, Captains).

What develops within the armed forces will be decisive for the future of democracy in Peru. But it is clear that the situation is very different from the late 1970s, when the transition to democracy occurred. Whatever form redemocratization takes, whether Fujimori steps down peacefully in 1995 or is overthrown by "democratic-minded" military officers who return power to civilians, who in turn hold free elections, the relationship with the military will be difficult. In any event, the armed forces will seek to maintain considerable prerogatives, which will be an obstacle to the advancement of any process of democratization.

The political parties are indispensable to a return to democracy, but their situation continues to be critical. Perhaps what is required first is that they understand the times they are living in—which is a prerequisite for any prospective process of renewal.

The Grassroots Organizations

Although Peruvian civil society has never been strong or integrated, in the last fifteen years both economic crisis and the war have caused it to weaken and erode. Some social scientists have insisted for some time that grassroots organizations have a resilience and extraordinary vitality that has helped build a strong social fabric. On this terrain one also finds new ways of participating in politics, alternatives to the traditional parties.

Nonetheless, observable reality is distant from these paradigmatic constructs. True, in the 1970s a great many popular organizations of various types were formed—trade unions, neighborhood organizations, peasant organizations—but it is clear that since the end of that decade they began to weaken with increasing speed due to the factors noted above: economic crisis and then the war.

In the first half of the 1980s new organizations of a different sort proliferated. This time, these were groups attempting to defend themselves from the havoc wreaked by the crisis, and not as much labor organizations seeking to recover economic losses. The Glass-of-Milk Committees, soup kitchens, mothers' clubs, and other groups spread, basically in an effort to bring families together to obtain what they needed most to survive from one day to the next, namely food. These organizations also moved beyond their immediate purpose and became important forums for socialization and interaction, especially in the poor neighborhoods. Yet, recent experience indicates that these organizations have also been hard hit by the prolongation of the crisis and intensification of the violence. Their vulnerability to outside pressure—from the state, foreign aid agencies, security forces, and terrorists—has curbed their role and limited their ability to organize and exert pressure.

During the 1980s, two locales in Peru stood out for the number and strength of their popular organizations, which helped the populations of these areas block the penetration of subversive organizations and the militarization experienced in other regions. They also organized solidarity organizations that served as a cushion against the growing poverty of the country. Villa El Salvador, a populous district of Lima, and Puno, an impoverished rural department in the southern Andes, were the outstanding examples. But today, unfortunately, there is much evidence that the autonomous organizations in these areas have been greatly weakened or destroyed.

The outlook is no more encouraging in the rest of the country. This does not mean that it will not be possible to reconstruct these types of autonomous organizations in the future. But it appears clear today that one cannot expect consistent resistance to authoritarianism, the development of new ways of practicing politics, or the emergence of bastions of democracy in such organizations.

One recently formed group is the Democratic Forum, which brings together several hundred intellectuals, professionals, young politicians from several parties, journalists, and some businesspeople and retired military officers. The forum considers itself a nonpartisan group struggling for democracy and against authoritarianism. It could perhaps become a core group that helps to build a democratic alternative, but it is still in its formative stages.

The Role of the International Community

Given Peru's precarious economic situation and its dependence on the multilateral lending agencies (IMF, IDB, World Bank), the influence that foreign governments and institutions can exercise over Peru today is enormous. This influence has been apparent on many occasions in recent years, particularly concerning human rights violations by the security forces, which have diminished almost exclusively as a result of international pressure. The elections for the CCD, as noted above, were also held because the international community demanded it. The preservation of democratic freedoms at present is possible thanks largely to the vigilance and continued warnings of foreign governments and international organizations.

In summary, in my view, international pressure, in the new international context following the collapse of communism, has kept Peru from falling into the hands of a highly authoritarian and repressive government. But these pressures have their limits, and they can neither regenerate democracy, strengthen institutions, nor halt the process of disintegration. They can help by supporting internal efforts in these directions, but they cannot replace the efforts of Peruvians themselves. If the democratic elements of Peruvian society do not recover, little can be expected in the way of results from external pressures.

There are extreme cases of intervention, such as in El Salvador and Kampuchea, where the international community has almost constituted a parallel government. At least in the case of El Salvador, such a role has been extraordinarily useful to date in allowing the development of the peace process, but it is still too early to evaluate the long-term effects. In any event, the pressures on and oversight of the Fujimori government should be maintained so as to continue to reduce human rights abuse and to guarantee the maintenance of democratic freedoms.

One crucial issue that the United States in particular should not abandon is narcotics trafficking. US involvement in Peru has been very limited to date, and it appears that the tendency for the future is to reduce it further. This would be a grave error, and it would compromise, for the reasons discussed above, the prospects for redemocratization as well as the institutional integrity of the armed forces.

The international community should be attentive to the possibility of a new military rebellion and should evaluate it carefully. A coup by military officers with links to drug trafficking is not the same, for example, as a coup by "institutionalist" military officers seeking to prevent the armed forces from meddling in politics and therefore promote a return to representative democracy (as was the stated intention of the conspiracy of General Salinas and other officers in November 1992). The differences in the nature of any rebellion need to be established, although military intervention always entails unforeseen dangers. Furthermore, the international community must unequivocally signal that it will not accept the perpetuation of military rule under any guise. This stance is necessary given that some members of the military believe that international actors will be permissive and/or that Peru can survive even if marginalized by one part of the world community because, they believe, another part—specifically Japan—will support them regardless of what happens. (This perception may be mistaken, but it is held by some military officers, and they act according to that perception.)

The role of the OAS in the CCD elections was unfortunate. Apparently little can be expected of the regional organization. Nevertheless, immediately after the 5 April coup the OAS did play a role that limited the most authoritarian aspects of Fujimori's project. Perhaps if some of its most important members assume a firmer position, the OAS could contribute to the task of steering Peru toward democracy, rather than serve to conceal and remake the image of an authoritarian government.

Notes

Note: The paper as presented in the conference benefited from comments by Cynthia McClintock, Carol Graham, and Manuel d'Ornellas, the presentation by Francisco Sagasti, and the ensuing discussion. Any errors are my responsibility.

1. "The crucial element in determining the outcome of the second transition is the degree of success or failure in the building of a set of democratic institutions that become important decisional points in the flow of political power" (1990:3).

2. See Cotler 1978.

3. Even though it was a military dictatorship, the number of unions in the countryside and cities, for example, skyrocketed, as did the number of strikes. Relative freedom of the press continued until 1974.

4. High expectations are characteristic of the present in Latin America and Eastern Europe. This was not the case with the wave of democratization that followed World War II (O'Donnell 1992:77).

5. Seymour Lipset states that "the groups that have to force their way into politics are inclined to exaggerate the possibilities of political participation" (1987:69). This applies to the Peruvian popular classes.

6. As Sartori says, "political democracy as a method or procedure should precede any substantive achievement that we ask of democracy," although its importance may lie in its nonpolitical by-products (1988:32).

7. If we measure them by per capita GDP, to use one indicator, we have the following for 1980 to 1992:

1980	2.8%
1981	2.8%
1982	-2.3%
1983	-15.2%
1984	-2.3%
1985	-0.5%
1986	8.5%
1987	8.1%
1988	-10.0%
1989	-14.9%
1990	-6.4%
1991	0.0%

Source: Webb and Fernández Baca 1992:591. In 1992, GDP was approximately -4.7 percent.

8. From 1978 to 1982, cumulative annual inflation fluctuated between 60 percent and 7 percent. From 1983 to 1987, it fluctuated between 110 percent to 160 percent (with one exception), exploding to 1,700 percent in 1988, 2,700 percent in 1989, and 7,600 percent in 1990 (Webb and Fernández Baca 1992:551), falling to 140 percent and 60 percent the following two years.

9. For example, in the first years of the dictatorship of General Manuel Odría (1948–1956), the economic boom mitigated the effects of corruption. More recently in Arequipa, and on a smaller scale, Mayor Luis Cáceres (1987–1992) was reputed to be corrupt, but was reelected and received popular support because he was effective and built public works projects. He was runner-up in the Lima municipal election in 1993.

10. In a survey completed in the last days of the administration, in which the participants were asked if they believed that any of eight prominent figures had committed any act of corruption, the majority answered affirmatively in seven cases, including the president, a vice-president, three cabinet members, and several ministers (Grupo Apoyo survey, in *Perú Económico,* vol. XIII, no. 8, 1990).

11. The president could not be tried for corruption during his term, according to the 1979 constitution, but could be once his term had ended.

12. For more information on the discrediting of the parties and other institutions vis-à-vis the outcome of the 1990 elections, see Rospigliosi 1991: 417ff.

13. Change 90, Fujimori's movement, initially had fourteen senators and thirty-two deputies, representing 22.3 percent and 17.8 percent of each chamber, respectively. These numbers have declined since the beginning of his government due to members leaving and being expelled.

14. The fluidity of situations involving these shifting coalitions "also creates an image of instability, lack of principles, dependence of the political

parties on interest groups, opportunism, and struggle between leaders for personal power" (Linz 1987:123).

15. This subject has been developed in a research project underway at the Institute for Peruvian Studies (IEP) (Rospigliosi 1992).

16. During the election campaign, Fujimori set forth some vague ideas regarding the struggle against subversion, which, to a degree, were similar to those offered by APRA and leftist parties. But he did not really believe in them, nor did he have a consistent proposal on the issue (or on any other). After winning the elections he searched in the marketplace of ideas, so to speak, for those he deemed most appropriate, and found them in his immediate surroundings: former Captain Vladimiro Montesinos. Montesinos, who had come to him as a lawyer well known for his ability to "fix anything" following his resolution of the problem of undervaluation of tax liabilities, was familiar with military thinking, and he had a proposal. This plan was essentially the one the military had been supporting, certainly in the form articulated by Montesinos.

17. These are the predominant views on everything in the army. It is obvious that not all members of the military think alike, nor do all of the institutes have the same approach to the subversive movement, but there are commonalities and dominant ideas.

18. In his 5 April 1993 speech marking the first anniversary of the coup, Fujimori referred almost exclusively to the successes of the counterinsurgency policy, leaving aside the long list of motives for the coup he had declared one year earlier.

19. "The subversive war was designed by experts on political violence as the principal instrument of the revolutionary war at the service of the international communist movement. . . . This political violence is practiced . . . by the communist parties during this century in almost all the nations of our continent in accord with the permanent and universal global strategy of the international communist movement" (Noel y Moral 1989:9).

20. "Many attribute the cause of that attitude (the violence) to the serious economic crisis that affects the majority of Peruvians." Nevertheless, "the response must be found in the ideological influence. . . . The terrorist attitude derives from the Marxist ideological conception" ("Actitud ideológica del terrorismo," in *Actualidad Militar,* July 1986).

21. General Luis Cisneros was minister of interior during the military government and minister of war in the second government of Fernando Belaúnde.

22. For the government, Prime Minister Alfonso de lo Heros participated in the negotiations; he reached agreement on almost all points with the delegates of the parliament. It was later discovered that the negotiation had been no more than a Fujimori stratagem to preoccupy the parliamentarians and prevent them from derogating his decrees as he prepared the coup. The prime minister played an unwitting role in this game. He found out about the coup on the day it occurred, whereupon he immediately resigned from the cabinet.

23. This is a very common *image* in Peru of those countries; it does not reflect reality, particularly with regard to their economic policies.

24. One explanation may be that Fujimori cannot transmit his popularity to other candidates. A second, not contrary to the first, is that the polls reflect the opinion of only part of the population. One element that appears

to be having a decisive bias on their validity is the very high percentage of refusals—people who refuse to respond to the interviewer's question. According to some interviewers, the rate of refusals can reach as high as 50 percent of the people they contact.

25. Apoyo 1993a. There are no published results of the national vote because the National Election Board, the only body that might have them, has not made them available. Actually, it has not made public any consolidated results (number of districts won by each party, results by department and province, etc.). The data provided therefore are only approximations based on electoral districts, not actual votes.

26. The elections were convened by the government for 18 October and then changed to 22 November. The decree-law convening the elections (No. 25684) of 22 August was amended 25 August (DL No. 25686) and changed once again on 1 September (DL No. 25701).

27. These members include: Division General Rodolfo Robles, today exiled in Argentina, and Colonel Jorge Noblecilla, sentenced to seven years in prison for participating in the 13 November conspiracy.

28. On 21 February 1994, responding to growing domestic and international pressure for a resolution of the case, a military court sentenced nine army officers and enlisted men to military prison for the murders at La Cantuta University. A secret military court tried the case after legislation was pushed through the Congress, in a move that produced substantial criticism of the government and eroded Fujimori's popularity, to ensure that the case would be removed from civilian jurisdiction by a decision of the Supreme Court. To many political observers, Fujimori's handling of the case confirmed his dependence on the military.

When an investigation was begun at the initiative of the opposition in April 1993, General Hermoza, general commander of the army, read a written statement upon leaving the Congress affirming that he would not tolerate the parliament's intervention. In subsequent days, he ordered tanks to parade through the streets of Lima. The progovernment majority did not allow the investigative commission to summon implicated military officers or undertake an authentic investigation. It later approved a report exonerating the military officers. The Defense Committee has approved a bill that prohibits the Congress from investigating members of the military as long as the war continues. Although as of this writing the law has yet to be passed by the CCD, it is already being applied in practice.

29. See, for example, *Caretas*, 30 December 1991, beginning on page 16. But as noted there, the nature of his popularity is changing, becoming similar to the support for Mario Vargas Llosa in 1990: more support from the upper-income class and less from low-income Peruvians.

30. Guzmán's capture was presented by Fujimori as proof of the success of "his" counterinsurgency strategy. Actually it was the work of the DINCOTE (National Anti-Terrorism Directorate), the specialized police. And within the DINCOTE, the GEIN (Special National Intelligence Group), which had long been pursuing the Shining Path chief and which came close to capturing him in January 1990 and in mid-1991, was the main player. Fujimori was fishing in a remote lake in the Peruvian jungle and the minister of Interior, an army general, was at a diplomatic reception when the capture occurred. The military attempted to take Guzmán to the DINCOTE offices the same night he was detained, but the chief of that office, Police General Antonio Vidal,

kept them from doing so. Vidal, since this event considered a national hero, was reassigned to a bureaucratic post in December 1992 and replaced by an officer who, as of today, works in the National Intelligence Service (SIN) under Vladimiro Montesinos.

31. All this has been denounced by generals such as Jaime Salinas Sedó, Alberto Arciniega, Luis Cisneros Vizquerra, Rodolfo Robles (all in prison, in exile, or being tried by military tribunals), and other officers.

32. Legislative Decree 746 of November 1991.

33. *Oiga* magazine, 12 July 1993 and 19 July 1993.

34. Former Captain Montesinos was expelled from the army and sentenced to prison in 1976. Upon release, he became a lawyer and took up the profitable business of defending narcotics traffickers, an activity he pursued, as has been verified, from 1979 to 1986. According to some sources, he continued to do such work after 1986, but did not sign any of his written material until 1990, when he became the de facto director of the SIN and a key player in the Fujimori government. In the last Survey of Power by the magazine *Debate*, of one thousand Peruvian elites, Montesinos, who according to official accounts is an unpaid adviser to the SIN, appears as the second most powerful person in Peru, after Alberto Fujimori, and ahead of General Nicolás Hermoza, general commander of the army and president of the Armed Forces Joint Command (Debate, No. 73, August 1993), who occupies third place.

References

Apoyo S.A.
1993a *Resultados de las elecciones municipales. Informe de Opinión.* February.
1993b *Informe de Opinión.* February.
1993c *Informe de Opinión.* May.

Cisneros, General Luis
1990 "Enrique López Albujar." In *Actualidad Militar* No. 361. March–April.

Cotler, Julio
1978 *Clases, estado y nación en el Perú.* IEP, Lima.
1993 "Descomposición política y autoritarismo en el Perú." Paper presented at the "Andean Conference on Comparative Perspectives for the Resolution of the Democratic Crisis in the Region." Universidad de los Andes, Bogotá, February.

Gorriti, Gustavo
1990 *Sendero. Historia de la guerra milenaria en el Perú.* Lima: Apoyo S.A.

Grompone, Romeo
1991 *El velero en el viento. Política y sociedad en Lima.* IEP, Lima: IEP.

Huntington, Samuel
1972 *El orden político en las sociedades en cambio.* Buenos Aires: Paidós.

Linz, Juan
1987 *La quiebra de las democracias.* Madrid: Alianza Editorial.

Lipset, Seymour Martin
1987 *El hombre político. Las bases sociales de la política.* Madrid: Tecnos.

Mauceri, Philip
1989 *Militares: insurgencia y democratización en el Perú 1980–1988.* Lima: IEP.

Mercado Jarrin, General Edgardo
1988 "Subversión y democracia." *Defensa Nacional,* CAEM Magazine. Vol. VII, no. 8.

Noel y Moral, General Clemente.
1989 *Ayacucho: testimonio de un soldado.* Lima: Publinor.

O'Donnell, Guillermo
1990 "Delegative Democracy?" Draft paper for the meeting of the East and South System Transformation. Budapest (December).
1992 "El dilema de las transiciones." *Nuestra América* (January–February). São Paulo, Brasil.

Pásara, Luis
1982 *Jueces, justicia y poder en el Perú.* Lima: Cedys.

Parodi, Jorge and Walter Twanama
1993 "Los pobladores, la ciudad y la política: Un estudio de actitudes," in Jorge Parodi, ed., *Los pobres, la ciudad y la política.* Lima: Cedys.

Perú Económico
1990 "Carta de Opinión," survey by Grupo Apoyo. Vol. XIII, no. 8 (August), p. 39.

Rospigliosi, Fernando
1991 "Polarización social y desprestigio de los partidos políticos: Los sorprendentes resultados de las elecciones peruanas de 1990," in Rosario Espinal et al., *Análisis de los procesos electorales en América Latina,* IV. San José, Costa Rica: IIDH-CAPEL.
1992 "Las fuerzas armadas y el 5 de abril. La percepción de la amenaza subversiva como una motivación golpista." Manuscript. Lima: IEP.

Sartori, Giovanni
1988 *Teoría de la democracia. 1. El debate contemporáneo.* Madrid: Alianza Editorial.

Stepan, Alfred
1988 *Repensando a los militares en política. Cono Sur: Un análisis comparado.* Buenos Aires: Planeta.

Webb, Richard and Graciela Fernández Baca
1992 *Perú en Números 1992. Anuario estadístico.* Lima: Cuánto S.A.

4

Commentary

Cynthia McClintock

Fernando Rospigliosi's chapter is an outstanding, thoughtful analysis, and I agree with his conclusions. I want to reiterate the two key general points he makes and use them as the basis for my comments. First, between 1980 and 5 April 1992, Peru was democratic in the conventional US sense of the term. Elections were open and intensely competitive, and the civilian presidents were able to make crucial decisions on counterinsurgency policy and the role of the military, for better or worse. Yet that democracy failed; the system did not fulfill the goals that were expected of it. Second, Rospigliosi also makes it clear that since 5 April 1992 Peru has not been democratic and that the prospects for a return to democracy are bleak.

The failure of the 1980–1992 democratic regime, as Rospigliosi highlights, was essentially a failure of political institutions in general and political parties in particular. In addressing this issue, I believe we must examine Peru's party system with greater precision so as to determine its exact nature and explain why it weakened. Peru's party system was not as weak as Ecuador's or Bolivia's in the conventional sense, for example. Some parties did not have completely personalistic leaders. Peru did not have the huge range of parties that characterize countries like Ecuador. The more institutionalized parties in Peru were APRA, of course, and the Marxist left that was participating in electoral politics.

What did this mean? One must note first that the 1980s was not a good decade for the left or leftist parties to be in power; this proved especially true for APRA and Alan García between 1985 and

Cynthia McClintock is a professor of political science at George Washington University.

1990. The international economic context made it very difficult for the political ideologies that were prevailing in Peru at the time. Of course, the leaders made poor decisions, and no one should absolve García of responsibility for what happened during the 1980s. But one also must acknowledge that in contrast to Ecuador, Bolivia, and Brazil, Peru was a country in which the center-left was very strong. Peruvians identified with the left more than virtually any other population in the region did with its leftist parties. They were able to express that preference electorally, and unfortunately for Peru, given the international economic context, the prevailing circumstances for that expression were not fortuitous.

Which Peruvian political parties were weakly institutionalized in the early 1980s? They were the parties on the political right, as has been documented in depth. Again, this contrasted with most of Latin America. In my view, *Acción Popular* (AP) was not a rightist party; it was populist. Why was the right so weak in Peru? I feel this was due partly to the experience of the Velasco years and partly to historical factors. There never really has been a strong political right in Peru, which is perhaps related to the traditional diversity of the Peruvian economic base. It has not been the case that a couple of key products have dominated the economy over a long period of time. A wide range of goods have been produced, which has meant that economic interests within the Peruvian right have varied widely, tending to weaken it as a political force.

I slightly disagree with Fernando Rospigliosi's work on another point. The 1990 election was certainly about popular opposition to traditional politicians. But it was also about something more, namely, the economy. One must not forget that Mario Vargas Llosa was the candidate of the economic shock program, while candidate Alberto Fujimori stood in opposition to a shock. Peruvians again voted for a leftist alternative as opposed to a political right that remained pretty feeble. The right had a great chance to win in 1990, and it lost, in part because it was not in touch with its bases and in part because it could not express its message in an appealing fashion. Fujimori followed the pattern of many Latin American leaders during the 1980s by adopting a more leftist political line during the campaign and then moving quickly to the right after his election, which, of course, does not do much to promote party consolidation either. In short, we need to examine closely the political context of the 1980s to understand why the political parties, especially those of the left and the center, grew weaker in Peru.

We should also consider how the parties could have been strengthened. There is much discussion in the United States today about the parliamentary style of government. I do not believe parliamentarism would be appropriate for Peru today, but I do agree that some constitutional changes would have helped Peru during the 1980s. For example, the convening of midterm congressional elections and changes in some of the provisions in the 1979 constitution that reduced the power of the Congress, which meant that the parties had fewer functions and were less able to exercise accountability over the national leadership, probably would have had a positive impact.

In addition, it is difficult in the environment of the 1980s and 1990s to strengthen political parties, as we have witnessed in the United States. Because of the prominence of television, it is easy for a personalistic leader to make appeals to the public without the use of a party apparatus. I tend to believe that few countries, if any, witnessed the strengthening of their political parties in the 1980s.

Issues involving the post*autogolpe* period are much more controversial and much more difficult to assess. The points made by Rospigliosi in this regard are interesting, but I would like see greater elaboration of them, one in particular. He suggests in a footnote that in the polls that have been indicating 60 to 70 percent support for Fujimori since the *autogolpe,* the rate of people refusing to participate in the surveys has been as high as 50 percent. It is not entirely clear to me how common this pattern is, but if the refusal rate is that high, it deserves greater explanation. Fujimori's apparent high level of popular support, of course, has been a crucial influence on the international response. If the opinion polls really are much less or no longer valid because of high refusal rates by the respondents, that fact should be highlighted.

Another crucial question requiring greater elaboration is: who precisely should receive the credit for the capture of Guzmán? As Fernando Rospigliosi emphasizes, Guzmán's capture was the major reason Fujimori was able to maintain his support through the end of 1992. Should democratic institutions be credited for achieving this objective? Or did Fujimori do something after the *autogolpe* that allowed it to occur? What were the real reasons that enabled the DINCOTE to make the capture? Or was it just luck? Was the DINCOTE, in fact, fairly successfully moving toward making the capture during the 1980s, and should it be viewed as a victory for that particular institution? This issue is particularly important in shaping how Peru's journalists and intellectuals discuss the achievements or lack thereof of the various Peruvian governments. Will such a debate alter the general view that García was a disaster and that Belaúnde was not much better? To the extent that there is not much discussion about what actually went right and what went wrong, about whether or not Fujimori deserves the credit, and about possible achievements earlier that may have contributed to the capture, critical information is missing.

The most difficult question—one that I been wrestling with since 5 April 1992—is what the international response to the Peruvian situation should be. This is a highly complicated issue, in part because Peru is so complicated, in part because Fujimori has enjoyed political support, at least as far as one can tell from the polls, and in part because the opposition has been weak. Moreover, as the international response is ambiguous, Peruvian political actors do not know what to do either, and they are looking for signals. No one is quite sure how to approach the situation.

Rospigliosi's chapter also demonstrates a lot of ambiguity. He suggests, and I agree, that the international community's response immediately after the *autogolpe* was very important in Fujimori's decision to hold the elections, in ensuring freedom of the press, and so forth. Yet he is also much more critical of the international community's role during the elections for the CCD. I very much agree with this position. The intellectual community has not sufficiently stressed the problems with the November 1992 CCD election. Rospigliosi mentions a couple of the problems, such as the scheduling delays, which meant international observer teams other than the OAS did not monitor the vote. If it is not known when elections are going to be held, groups do not organize delegations, and the result is a lack of diversity of monitoring organizations.

This election followed a very short two-week campaign, which began once the required signatures had been fielded. In the midst of this, the attempt at a countercoup was made, which essentially monopolized attention for a significant period. There were also problems of polling table monitors and so forth. I believe that the international community should have sufficiently progressed by this point to have better monitored the elections. We should be able to do a better job at rejecting an election that does not meet international criteria. If there had been greater pressure for a free and fair election in the month or so prior to the CCD elections, the outcome would have been different; Fujimori would not have received a majority in the Congress, and we would have quite a different situation today.

Rospigliosi suggests a need for the international community to monitor the Peruvian military. This raises ethical and practical questions; that is, it would be extremely difficult to do. I agree that international pressure has been crucial to press freedom and to the prevention of further deterioration of the human rights situation. At the same time, there are concerns about how long international pressure can work. This issue was raised during the attempted *autogolpe* by President Jorge Serrano of Guatemala in May 1993, and one cannot predict events or how the Clinton administration will react to the Peruvian situation in the future.

In my view, US policy should be to attempt to prevent a delay of Peru's reinsertion into the international financial community. Peru deserves acceptance on economic grounds, as the suffering that would result from continued isolation is simply unacceptable. It makes no sense to punish Peru economically for political crimes. At the same time, in allowing Peru's reinsertion, the world community must not fail to continue to exert pressure for the improvement of the human rights situation. Serious human rights questions remain, and although they are extremely difficult to monitor, efforts should be made to resolve the problem. The number of disappearances has fallen, but extrajudicial executions have increased and the number of Peruvians falsely imprisoned also has risen. Is this improvement or not? It is often difficult to make an assessment based on a single criterion. The United States must not end up rubber stamping the human rights situation for reasons that have nothing to do with human rights.

5

Commentary

Manuel d'Ornellas

If we are draw one conclusion from the work of Fernando Rospigliosi and of Francisco Sagasti and Max Hernández, it is that the key actors in Peruvian politics at present and for the foreseeable future are the armed forces. Everything depends on them. The military is the reality of Peru today. Members of the military are confident of their position, they feel that they are winning the war, and that they are popular because they are waging civic action campaigns. They therefore believe that they are untouchable.

An example is the April 1993 incident in which the military surrounded the Congress with tanks, a move that has been deemed a legal insubordination as a result of a law passed by the CCD. The incident was a warning by the military that it is not disposed to join in the traditional power games. In this sense, the government of Peru, either Fujimori or whoever is in the national palace, is between a rock and a hard place. *Newsweek* (the Spanish version) summed it up very well: the dilemma for Fujimori, or whoever may be in his place, is that, on the one hand, the United States exerts pressure for the investigation of human rights abuses in Peru and, on the other hand, the military exerts pressure to ensure that human rights cases are not investigated. Caught in this situation, the government is walking on a tightrope, because it needs both US support and the support of the military.

This means that one way or another, as Rospigliosi notes, Fujimori will have to develop a counterweight to US influence. Could it be Japan and other Asian countries? Japan continues to be supportive

Manuel d'Ornellas is director of the Lima dailies *Expreso* and *Extra*.

of Fujimori; he already has been received several times by the Japanese in an evident demonstration of sympathy and support. But it is also true, as is well known, that Japan does not take independent positions in international policy, other than in highly exceptional circumstances. Generally, Japan will endorse the position of the US government, even though it may provide less assistance in some cases. As such, the idea that Japan will be a counterweight to the United States is for the most part invalid, and the pressure of the United States continues to be very strong.

Getting the military to change its attitude appears to me to be a very difficult proposition. General Robles, who rebelled against the army by denouncing a number of human rights cases and who is presently in self-exile in Buenos Aires, made a comment in *La República* a short time ago that is fundamentally important. He confirmed that he had provided support to the *autogolpe* of 5 April 1992. And he made another key comment: "We felt that they were losing [the war] against subversion and we decided that we needed a civilian dictator." It makes one think that the self-coup was something that was negotiated and worked out, and much less Bordaberry-like than what we had thought. (Juan M. Bordaberry, elected president of Uruguay for the term beginning in March 1972 and facing political division and the Tupamaro insurgency, was quickly forced to cede control of the government to the military in a "soft coup." He remained the titular head of the regime until late 1975.)

Apparently, according to General Robles, a military council decided to establish a civilian dictatorship. Then it approached Fujimori and said: Look, we can do it with you or without you. This, of course, is what occurred in Uruguay in 1972. In any case, Robles expresses the point of view of the military, the accuracy of which continues to hold, despite the discrepancy now with the position taken by General Hermoza at the time. And this view probably reflects the ideology of 90 percent of the armed forces. We have no way of knowing for sure what occurred, but this explanation appears logical in view of events.

The paradox is that the changes within the armed forces and the politicization of the military institution grew out of a decision made by Fujimori a year prior to the *autogolpe,* due to a modification of a law on the status of the military ("Ley de la Situación Militar"). The decision was very important because since the 1960s, as of Prado's second government, the armed forces had a measure of autonomy. Promotions were approved by the parliament, but the military proposed the promotions. And commander generals passed into retirement such that that position was filled by an officer designated by the military. Aside from the ratification of promotions, civilians played no role in the management of changes within the armed forces.

Once a promotion was considered, it gathered a momentum of its own. In 1968, for example, President Belaúnde could not remove General Velasco, whom he knew was conspiring against him. When Belaúnde's ministers told him to fire Velasco, he responded that he could not do so because he did not have concrete proof that Velasco was conspiring to carry out a coup and that the autonomous management of the general command prevented him from doing so. We all know what happened afterward.

What has happened today is that Peru has returned to the traditional scheme of civil-military relations. In the past, be it a civilian or military government, the minister of war had the complete trust of the president. The minister, in turn, would place people he himself trusted in key positions. The system functioned relatively well. As noted above, it was dismantled during the Prado years. Prado was politically weak vis-à-vis the military because he had reached an accord with APRA in 1956. APRA had been the military's number-one enemy since before the Rodriga dictatorship. The weak Prado acceded to the creation of this totally autonomous military joint command.

Today we are returning to that old system. However, again paradoxically, instead of strengthening Fujimori, he may actually be getting weaker. Commander General Hermoza, knowing that he could maintain his position, purged all of the dissident elements of the armed forces, therefore converting himself into the person who makes the decisions within the armed forces. Fujimori is thus left without a counterweight. If Fujimori were to fire Hermoza today, he would not have anyone to replace him because all of the remaining officers would be supporters of Hermoza, such that the process of replacement would simply become a power struggle. So the apparent strengthening of civilian power over military power that has meant the elimination of this system of automatic promotions also may be weakening the power of the president himself.

In the view of the military, it is winning the war not only because it believes that the work of Antonio Ketín Vidal, who captured Guzmán, was guided by the intelligence divisions. Above all, what most people know and what is most important, is that today when the leaders of Shining Path are arrested, they are no longer set free soon afterward.

Statistics apparently based on independent calculations indicate that 75 percent of the terrorists who were imprisoned between 1980 and 1991 were released because of lack of evidence. This occurred because the repentence law, which grants amnesty to individuals who provide information on the insurgents, did not function as planned. No one would provide information out of fear of being killed later in reprisal. Today, apparently, there are more accusations, more people willing to serve as informants, and evidently more security to the extent that at times even innocent people are being imprisoned. The situation has moved to the other extreme with respect to the imprisonment of suspected terrorists. But I believe this has led to a change in popular perception; that is, Peruvians feel they are winning the war not only because there are prisoners, but also because what they have won is concretely evident.

So the danger of greater military pressure being translated into greater disrespect for human rights is real; this danger is directly related to the military. I agree completely with Rospigliosi's emphasis on the importance of international pressure, exerted not only by governments but also by the media, so that disrespect for human rights can be exposed within Peru by the free press. International pressure and a free press in Peru have to work hand-in-hand. There has to be close exchange and communication between the two.

I am much more optimistic about freedom of the press than others for a simple reason. In another era, on 3 October 1968, when General Velasco entered the national palace, he was already talking about the free press. He was already indoctrinated with an ideology regarding the media. Everything he did in the following years, all of his repression of the media through the 1970s, emerged from a preconceived plan, an ideology that guided his acts like a machine, gradually increasing the attacks until there was nothing left. This was the ideology of the Velasco government. In Peru today, I see no government ideology with regard to freedom of the press. There may be statements by elements of the military, but I do not perceive any type of doctrine regarding the media, or any belief that the press is intrinsically perverse or nonrepresentative, as was claimed by the Velasco government. So I remain optimistic. With a little international pressure, a free press can be maintained, and no one will be able to indoctrinate the government with ideas about the media.

6

Commentary

Carol Graham

I very much agree with Fernando Rospigliosi's depiction of the status of Peruvian democracy today. On the one hand, Fujimori is basically maintaining a semblance of democracy to appease the international community; on the other hand, the political opposition is divided and not presenting a credible alternative to the Fujiumori government. The situation leaves individuals in Peru and the international community in a dilemma; that is, it is difficult to know exactly how to respond to Fujimori and his popularity. I believe much of this dilemma is due to a lack of credible alternatives *at this point.*

Rospigliosi subsequently states that the main problem with Peruvian democracy is the country's fragile institutions, a point with which I also very much agree. But I slightly disagree with his emphasis on the lack of democratic values among both elites and the popular sectors. I feel democracy at the grassroots level is surprisingly vibrant, given conditions under which people are living. Rospigliosi cites a poll in which 81 percent of those surveyed would prefer non-elected government if they were guaranteed that conditions would improve. Such polls do *not* mean that the Peruvians' values are less democratic than the values of, say, North Americans, the French, or Venezuelans. Rather, the results reflect the severe conditions most Peruvians must endure each day. If one is poor in Peru, which characterizes well over two-thirds of the population, if one lives in a *pueblo joven* without running water, without access to other basic services, without protection against crime, and without access to employment, is it a surprise that the main concern is feeding one's family rather than who is running the government or how it is being run?

Carol Graham is a visiting fellow at the World Bank.

The message of these polls is that Peruvians are more concerned with substance than process. Democratic values are not necessarily less important to Peruvians; it is just that in the short term, the dire nature of the crisis they are facing is all-consuming. This situation also leads to a desire for dramatic solutions. The strong popular support for Fujimori's *autogolpe* is a case in point. His support very much reflected the desire for a quick and dramatic solution to an extreme crisis.

I thus view the issue of democratic values in a slightly different fashion. Democracy does function at the grassroots level. Almost every neighborhood in the urban slums of Lima, for example, is organized at the neighborhood committee level. All kinds of group initiatives, especially self-survival initiatives, are developed by people operating in a democratic manner.

Two factors are key to restoring faith in the democratic process in Peru, factors that are not emphasized by either Fernando Rospigliosi or Francisco Sagasti and Max Hernández. First, there must be a successful outcome in the process of economic reform. In a country in which there is no growth and in which over 75 percent of the population is unemployed, again it is no surprise that the democratic process is not the primary concern of the populace. People need to eat before they can worry about how they are being governed.

Second, and very much related to the success of economic reform, social service delivery must be restored. I note that Fujimori's authoritarian tactics are having an extremely negative effect on the development of democracy; they have eroded democratic institutions. I also believe, however, that the deterioration of the economy and state structures that preceded Fujimori, particularly during the APRA government, were equally damaging to the democratic process—having totally eroded the state's capacity to function. One cannot have faith in the democratic process if there is no underlying consensus on the legitimacy of the state, which desperately needs to be restored in Peru.

I do not see popular frustration with the process per se as necessarily surprising. Nor is it surprising that the process is associated with inefficiency and corruption, given the recent record of state institutions in Peru. And this situation is not unique to Peru. If one considers what has been occurring in Brazil, Venezuela, and most recently, Guatemala, popular frustration with the democratic process—a search for alternatives, and not necessarily authoritarian alternatives—is evident regionwide. It clearly points to a desperate need for reform of state institutions to enhance their capacity to deliver services and for the restoration of economic growth through the eventual success of adjustment.

Rospigliosi depicts the 1992 elections very nicely as elections that nobody wanted to convene. Fujimori himself did not want them. The opposition did not want them because it was not particularly well organized. And Peruvians generally did not want a new congress; they were quite supportive of the old one having been thrown out. So, who wanted to hold these elections? Clearly, the OAS wanted them, so much so that it declared that they were legitimate, even though all kinds of indicators pointed to the contrary. I agree with Cynthia McClintock that there is a need to examine closely that electoral process.

Nevertheless, I would argue that the results of the elections were very important. First, Fujimori received a majority, but he clearly did not achieve as large a majority as he wanted or expected, especially if one considers that there was not really a credible alternative for which Peruvians could cast their votes. The opposition was hopelessly divided. Second, in the subsequent elections, the January 1993 municipal elections, there was an enormous rise in the election of independents. Rospigliosi points to this as a reflection of the volatility of the Peruvian political situation. I agree, but I also see a slightly positive result in that Peruvians are ready and willing to exercise their capacity to choose among candidates if they see an alternative to a single progovernment candidate. The electoral process in Peru today is imperfect, but there are still positive elements to it, and it remains an important aspect of Peru's political life.

A point that is mentioned in both Rospigliosi's work and the work of Sagasti and Hernández is the erosion of faith in collective action in Peru. I believe this is a result of the erosion of faith in the state, on the one hand, and of the informalization or disintermediation of politics that the Sagasti and Hernández chapter discusses, on the other. Because there is an absence of faith in state institutions and political parties, Peruvians are acting on an individual level, and there consequently has been a reduction in collective action at the macro level. Yet again, I believe there is still strong faith in collective action. Neighborhood organizations, grassroots organizations, and nongovernmental organizations are extremely strong and vibrant in Peru today.

Rospigliosi correctly notes that the role of parties is the key in the evolution of Peruvian democracy—if it is to be restored. I would like to see, however, more suggestions about how to go about reforming political parties. How do parties need to change to move away from their current state, which clearly is not particularly effective? Rospigliosi also calls for the United States to increase, not decrease, its role in fighting drug trafficking. My question is: how should this be done, given that, in my view, the US's past role has been negative?

Finally, I fully agree with Rospigliosi's mention of the importance of the role of the international community, especially following the *autogolpe*. He rightly notes that the work of the international community cannot replace an internal process of democratization, that Peru's political leaders at all levels—local and national—must recognize what they themselves need to do to assist in the development of Peruvian democracy. There is a limit to what the international community can do.

Turning to the work of Sagasti and Hernández, I also agree with their general description of the Peruvian situation, in particular, the focus on the erosion of the state's monopoly on political violence and on the negative impact that that erosion has had on faith in democratic institutions generally. I very much agree with their description of political disintermediation: the channels between state and society through which demands are communicated and addressed, which are integral to democracies everywhere, are absent.

In Peru, it is not just the economy that is overwhelmingly informal; the entire political system has become informal in nature. Peruvians are participating in all kinds of nontraditional, informal channels. In his earlier work, less than in this chapter, Sagasti has noted the positive aspects of disintermediation, such as the energy and strength of democracy that exists at the grassroots level. Moreover, he has noted the new kinds of political participation developing at that level and described how these new forms of participation may provide answers to the question of the future development of Peruvian democracy. As I have indicated above, I very much agree with this point.

I further agree that democracy not only has inherent value but also is a better instrument for implementing reform, especially in the economic sphere. Recent empirical evidence indicates that authoritarian and democratic regimes have fairly equivalent records at initiating democratic reform, but that democracy is a better tool if the goal is consolidating economic adjustment and economic reform.

In conclusion, I return to the two conditions that I believe are necessary for the restoration of democracy that are not mentioned by the authors. First, restoration of economic growth is vital, and the successful completion of the economic reform program is an integral part of this objective. Despite its flaws, the economy is heading in the correct direction. Second, there must be reform of the social sectors and the creation of state capacity to deliver basic services. Social service delivery is crucial to restoring the public's faith in the state, and therefore democracy, and to the development of human capital. But again, without a measure of consensus on the legitmacy of the state, it is difficult to have faith in the democratic process, or any system of government.

The restoration of faith in the state in the short run, while Fujimori is in power, can be accomplished on two levels, the macrolevel and the microlevel. At the macrolevel, continued international vigilance and pressure is important. In view of the events following the *autogolpe,* international pressure can play a critical role; it should play a larger role in areas such as human rights and freedom of the press. The international community can pressure the Fujimori government to move beyond the veneer of democracy.

At the microlevel, the effective provision of social services is important to the restoration of faith in the state. This objective can be achieved in two ways. In the long term, political parties must be reformed. A major problem today is that many political parties are out of touch with the poor of Peru, with what is happening at the grassroots level. Parties have become highly centralized institutions with very weak ties to their constituents, which Fujimori quickly realized and easily took advantage of in the 1990 elections.

In the short term, one instrument that could be used to provide a channel between the state and the poor is a demand-based social fund. Such funds have been used successfully in several different countries, from Bolivia to El Salvador. In Peru, the National Compensation and Social Development Fund (FONCODES) is a weak attempt at creating a program. But if it does develop in a broader fashion, if it is genuinely based on communities organizing among themselves to secure access to state services, and if the state can deliver those services, the fund would be an important step forward for democracy as well as social welfare.

Finally, Cynthia McClintock and I have an on-going debate on the role of international aid. I very much agree with her in principle, that is, in not linking the provision of economic and political aid. It is not fair to punish Peruvians on the economic front for abuses or delinquencies on the political front. Unfortunately, in practice, given the small size of the US aid program in other areas—less than $40 million for 1993, for example—I believe the only real instrument presently available to pressure the Fujimori government is the threat of withdrawal of the international community's support for the reform program. I am not arguing that the United States should be micromanaging the operation of the reform program or linking economic progress to progress on human rights issues. But as far as the larger issues are concerned, such as those that emerged with the *autogolpe,* when a stronger instrument is needed the only real tool we have is the level of support we can refuse to provide for Peru's economic reinsertion process. There may again be a time when we will have to use that instrument.

PART 2

Achieving Social Peace

7

Shining Path and Counterinsurgency Strategy Since the Arrest of Abimael Guzmán

Carlos Iván Degregori

After the *paro armado,* or armed strike, that shook Lima on 22 and 23 July 1992, it was said that all the cells of the Communist Party of Peru–Sendero Luminoso (Shining Path) toasted consolidation of the "strategic equilibrium" in their war. In Europe, Luis Arce Borja, director of the pro–Shining Path *El Diario Internacional,* euphorically told the German weekly *Der Spiegel:* "We are on the verge of taking power, the enemy is demoralized . . . [and] on the run. There is no option but unconditional surrender."

The mood in Senderista ranks could not have been better. In actuality "the strategic equilibrium was shaking up the country," as their slogans boasted, especially in Lima, which awaited the new offensive set for October and November in a sort of fatalistic paralysis. Apocalyptic scenes were invoked with greater frequency. The bloody stalemate in Lebanon was most often evoked. Lima's weekly newspapers began to publish maps with arrows pointing out by what routes the armies of neighboring countries and the United States could enter Peru. This was also the preferred scenario for Shining Path, which had adopted the slogan "Yankee go home" even before the Yankees were supposed to arrive.

The perception that the Peruvian situation was becoming impossible to sustain reached beyond the country's borders. In March 1992, in US congressional hearings on Peru, Assistant Secretary of State for Inter-American Affairs Bernard Aronson warned about the possible third genocide of the century if Shining Path emerged victorious. Shortly thereafter a report from the Rand Corporation

---

Carlos Iván Degregori is director of the Institute for Peruvian Studies (IEP).

announced the possibility that a cordon might be established around Lima and the government might collapse.[1]

Suddenly, on 12 September 1992, Abimael Guzmán, the leader of Shining Path, was arrested. The entire country, all areas and social sectors, breathed a sigh of relief equal to the fear and demoralization felt the day before. It has been almost one year since the arrest, and despite the government objective of weakening Shining Path and its triumphalist public discourse, the war continues. The purpose of this article is to assess the current situation and prospective developments among the main actors in the conflict: Shining Path, the government, and the armed forces.

* * *

A complete analysis of Shining Path would be beyond the scope of this chapter.[2] Suffice it to note that its growth in the 1980s was facilitated by a crisis that was not just economic, but also moral and political, particularly in the area of political representation. But these problems alone would not have been sufficient without the tremendous political will of the Senderistas, which contrasts with the inability of the other actors to advance in their aims, and the glaring absence of a government pacification strategy. From 1980 to 1982, Shining Path defeated the police forces in Ayacucho, making it necessary for the armed forces to step in.[3] In 1983 and 1984, the armed forces carried out a counteroffensive that resulted in more than five thousand dead, mostly civilians, in an area of just over half a million inhabitants. Nonetheless, Shining Path survived, broke the cordon, and proceeded to establish other fronts, particularly in the central highlands and the Huallaga Valley, the premier center of coca leaf production in the world, and in Lima, which holds one-third of the country's population. In 1988, Shining Path held its first National Congress; on 27 July 1988 its underground leader had a lengthy interview with *El Diario* (Guzmán 1988). A few months later, Shining Path documents began to speak of a qualitative leap forward in the war, the "transition to a strategic equilibrium."[4]

On the military front, this transition meant moving from columns, detachments, and companies engaged in guerrilla warfare to battalions capable of waging a war with continually shifting front lines. To bolster its battalions, Shining Path needed more combatants, who were recruited among youth, the organization's seedbed, and through force in some rural regions. Shining Path needed more and better arms, which it could also obtain through its base in the Huallaga Valley and its connections with narcotics traffickers. But as the Maoist saying goes, "the guerrilla army must move among the masses like a fish in water." Therefore, Shining Path needed not only to ensure the neutrality or passive consent of important sectors of the population, but also their active support.

And so Shining Path's problems with the rural population mounted. The group's demands increased and tended to undermine the fragile balance of "adaptation-in-resistance" (Stern 1987) that the peasants had attained in the previous years. Shining Path demanded more recruits, more supplies, and participation of the masses in military actions. The Senderistas increased discipline and were inclined to resort summarily to the death penalty for violators. These new requirements made adaptation difficult and favored resistance. Shining Path responded by carrying out many more massacres of peasants. Nonetheless, the result was the mass proliferation in the late 1980s of "self-defense" groups, which the armed forces had tried unsuccessfully to impose by force in 1983 and 1984.

Furthermore, in an effort to shorten its timeline, Shining Path turned the cities, especially Lima, into the principal targets of its actions. In Lima, Shining Path first worked in the factories, with few results. By 1989, the focus of its actions shifted to the poorest neighborhoods, where it established footholds in certain impoverished settlement communities that had mushroomed amid the full-blown crisis of the 1980s.

Several factors contributed to Shining Path's advance in Lima. First, Shining Path's role as a source of *order*, which helped it so much in its first years in the countryside, created possibilities in the urban pockets of extreme poverty, in many cases inhabited by persons who had been displaced from their places of origin by the violence. Furthermore, Shining Path's "war communism," with its emphasis on ensuring equality from top to bottom, collectivism, and the belligerent rejection of the state became attractive to groups that have been excluded and have little hope of inclusion.

But outside the pockets of extreme poverty Shining Path found a heterogeneous situation that was difficult to fit into its schemes. It made headway among a minority of radicalized youth from the national universities and secondary schools, but most of the population continued to want to participate economically in the market and in national political life. The social fabric, despite being weakened by fifteen years of crisis, stood in the way of Shining Path's effort to establish its totalitarian order. As in the rural areas, the Maoist group responded with violence against grassroots leaders and terror against the general population.

Shining Path was able to make up for the lack of support with the ideological cohesion of its cadres and a growing recourse to terror *so long as it enjoyed a favorable political context.* In this sense, the scenario created as of 1990 with the Fujimori presidency is ambiguous. On the one hand, the very harsh economic adjustment and recession appeared to favor Shining Path's growth, as did Fujimori's departure from the constitutional order with the *autogolpe,* or self-coup, of 5 April 1992. Nonetheless, the economic crisis and misgovernment of the last part of the Alan García administration (1985–1990) as well as the sustained escalation of terrorist acts created an urgent popular demand for order. In this regard, Shining Path's war helped pave the way for an *autogolpe* that enjoyed popular support. More paradoxical still, the crisis and misgovernment that enabled Shining Path to advance through terror also gave the organization a false sense of invincibility that made it vulnerable to the patient work of the National Anti-Terrorism Directorate (DINCOTE). Before looking at the current counterinsurgency strategy, however, let us review how it evolved in the first ten years of the war.

* * *

Beginning in 1983, when the armed forces went to combat Shining Path in Ayacucho, the civilian governments, in the words of Americas Watch in 1984, "abdicated democratic authority." They turned leadership of the war over to the military, which de facto assumed very broad powers in the growing number of provinces declared to be in a state of emergency. Tension mounted between the prerogatives that the 1979 constitution gave the armed forces and their growing political responsibilities.[5]

Without a clear strategy defined by themselves or the successive governments, the armed forces felt they were bearing the brunt of a conflict that was becoming bloodier without the support of "the politicians," who failed to appreciate the full scope of the terrorist challenge. By 1990, with 32 percent of the national territory and 49 percent of the population under military control (Senado de la República 1992) and with Shining Path increasing the pressure on Lima, the contradiction between prerogatives and responsibilities reached its high point. Worse, hyperinflation was marching along sometimes at more than 60 percent monthly, in effect shrinking the military budget and officers' salaries, which were by far the lowest in the region.[6] Requests for retirement multiplied at an alarming pace. Mediocrity and the temptations of narcotics trafficking threatened the institution of the armed forces.

Yet, at the same time, other events pointed in another direction. Most important was the proliferation of the "civil defense committees" in Ayacucho and then in the central highlands in the late 1980s. Since 1983 the armed forces had wanted to organize such committees in a vertical fashion, similar to Guatemala's civil patrols (Americas Watch 1986). In the context of the indiscriminate repression visited upon the rural population in those years, however, the armed forces ran up against the stubborn resistance of the majority of the rural population.

Five years later, large sectors of the campesino population had changed their attitude. This was a result in part of some change in the approach of the armed forces. Their initial distrust of the population tended to be replaced by a paternalistic and populist rapprochement which, in another context, had been one of the features of the twelve years of military rule from 1968 to 1980. But, with respect to decisionmaking of campesinos, at least as influential as the changes in the armed forces was Shining Path's growing brutality and direct contradiction of their medium-term interests. The armed forces began to appear as the lesser of two evils.[7]

Around 1990 the armed forces finally delineated a strategy to combat Shining Path. Left to its own devices by the political class, the armed forces took charge of directing the war, eliminating any significant role for the civilians, whose involvement was construed as meddling by the politicians. They also stubbornly defended and distorted the prerogative of the military courts as the exclusive forum for trying cases of human rights violations. In other words, instead of politicizing the war, the armed forces militarized society and politics. Nevertheless, though authoritarian, it was not a genocidal strategy, despite provocations by Shining Path, which needed an even more brutal military response than that in Ayacucho from 1983 to 1984 in order to continue its advance.

Around 1990, amid hyperinflation that dramatically reduced the military budget in real terms, a political crisis emerged that delegitimized all of the parties and appeared to provide Shining Path an opportunity to advance. The declining gap between constitutional prerogatives and political responsibilities tended to become incompatible with the persistence of a democratic regime, although this was not clearly perceived by public opinion or the political class. There were, thus, two possibilities. Either the civilian government would assume leadership of the war, or the government itself or the military would bestow legal and constitutional validity on these lofty responsibilities, transforming them into real prerogatives.

It was in this context, taking advantage of the attrition afflicting the political parties, that Alberto Fujimori won the 1990 elections.

He was an outsider, with no party or program, who from the first moment uncritically accepted the armed forces' counterinsurgency strategy.[8] And Fujimori's victory was most opportune for the military, which lacked political leadership and favorable public opinion but did have a strategy.

Whether the 5 April *autogolpe* had been planned over a long period is still a mystery. But it is clear that some moves began to be made very early on. Fujimori named an active-duty general as minister of interior in his first cabinet, the first time an active-duty officer had been appointed to the cabinet in twelve years. In the following months the amount of arms given to the civil defense committees increased rapidly. In addition, the armed forces began to intervene, with no legal authority, in several national universities they considered foci of subversion, as well as in the prisons with the largest number of persons accused of terrorism. At the same time, the president leveled ever harsher criticism at the parliament, the *cúpulas partidarias,* or small groups of political party leaders, and at corruption in the judiciary. Given the advances of Shining Path and the passivity displayed up to that time by the state, both the new military powers and the presidential criticisms of the other branches of government were well received by public opinion.

From November 1991 to March 1992 the destiny of the democratic regime was at stake, yet none of the parties in conflict realized that this was the case. In effect, in November 1991 the executive, which had been delegated legislative powers by the parliament, promulgated more than twenty legislative decrees on pacification and national defense, which demonstrated the hegemonic desires of some sectors of the armed forces. Among the most important are the Law on the National Defense System (Legislative Decree 743), which redefined the structure of the state in relation to internal defense matters. The previous structures of the National Defense System related primarily to the possibility of an external conflict. Legislative Decree 743 redefined those structures to bring the state apparatus into line with the confrontation with the insurgent forces. While it is true that under this decree the president formally directs the National Defense System, the real power for planning and execution of political and military actions is in the hands of the armed forces.

Laws were also promulgated to legalize expanding the armed forces' powers. Thus, they were authorized to enter areas not declared to be under a state of emergency under certain circumstances, as well as prisons and universities, where they had already intervened. Likewise, the arming of civil defense committees as self-defense committees and their participation in countersubversive activities was legalized.

The decrees were forwarded to the parliament for review. But all of the parties discussed the proposal from the executive and surprisingly agreed on a set of changes that emphasized the role of civilian authorities in the emergency zones and civilian leadership of the war. The changes were approved in a special legislative session in February 1992. But by that time the parties had lost credibility with the armed forces. The mutual distrust between the political parties and the armed forces was perhaps at its highest level, while Fujimori, with extraordinary skill and patience, cultivated a network of alliances within the military institution.

The possibility that this alternative strategy might be ratified by the parliament in the next legislative session, which was to begin 6 April 1992, was one of the main causes of the *autogolpe* the day before. From that moment on, Fujimori began to issue the decrees drawn up by the executive that the parliament had sought to amend. There was broad popular support for the executive's strategy, which included regaining control of the prisons, where those accused of terrorism had created veritable "liberated zones," as well as the removal of hundreds of magistrates from the judiciary. This support appears to be the postscript to twelve years of abdication by civilian governments and political parties of their responsibility to develop a democratic strategy for pacification. The need for order was a pressing demand, and just as much a source of concern, if not more so, than economic necessity. Given the inability of the political parties to consolidate a democratic order, the majority of Peruvians accepted an authoritarian order.

The victory of progovernment candidates in the elections to the new Democratic Constituent Congress (CCD) on 22 November 1992 opened the doors for Fujimori and the armed forces to incorporate the new military prerogatives and functions within a new authoritarian, ultrapresidentialist constitutional framework before the end of 1993. But while the tension between constitutional prerogatives and political responsibilities was handled in this fashion, new tensions arose. The most dangerous was the politicization of the armed forces in a direction directly opposite the "hypothermia" that Rial (1992) speaks of to describe the low profile assumed by the armed forces in other Latin American countries with the end of the internal conflicts and the cold war. Even though these measures were taken by Fujimori, a civilian, the armed forces have become, for all practical purposes, the government party, or to be more accurate, its main base of support, and are assuming political functions to the detriment of the elected civilian authorities.

Even worse, the type of relations established between the government and the armed forces fosters instability as long as they are personalized rather than institutional. The president co-opts one sector of officials and asserts control over the rest. Two of the many presidential prerogatives are particularly important in this regard. One is the power to name the general commander of the armed forces and decide that this lead officer should remain in the post as long as the president deems advisable, even beyond the general's date of retirement. The second is making the National Intelligence Service (SIN) autonomous; with the new laws that govern the National Defense System, it is not subject to control by civilian authorities or even the institution of the armed forces. Indeed, the SIN is now expending much of its effort on detecting any evidence of discontent within the armed forces.

The resulting model is highly unstable. It will last only as long as the troika lasts. The troika comprises the president, the general commander of the armed forces, General Hermoza, and Vladimiro Montesinos, the éminence grise of the SIN. To tighten their control over the government, the three have infringed on the *professional* institutional status of the armed forces and have forcibly retired several officers who were highly regarded in the military. All three troika members have, in turn, become targets of military discontent.

Just when the president was consolidating his victory on all fronts after the capture of Guzmán and when his victory in the elections for the CCD was beyond challenge, the instability of his main ally began to come to light. On 13 November 1992, General Salinas Sedó led a "constitutionalist" coup attempt. Since then, tensions have persisted. When the CCD named a commission in April 1993 to investigate the July 1992 disappearance of nine students and one professor from the national university of La Cantuta, General Hermoza sent tanks through the streets of Lima for several days to remind the Congress and the president that the independence of military courts is a nonnegotiable prerogative.[9] In May, when General Rodolfo Robles, third in the military hierarchy, was removed from his career track of becoming a general commander and sent into "golden exile" in Washington, he took refuge in the US Embassy and denounced the complicity of Hermoza and other top officers in the disappearances of La Cantuta and in several other massacres.[10]

* * *

It is in this context of military and police victories and political and institutional fragility that one must assess the current counterinsurgency strategy, as well as Shining Path's evolution since the fall of its leader. The backdrop to this strategy is the personal leadership of the chief executive, who is seeking to win over the civilian population in order to increase dramatically the number of combatants in the countryside and improve intelligence work in the cities. This plan is complemented with effective control of the prisons, greater severity in judicial sentences, and an improved international image for Peru. I will now examine each of these areas.

The Civil Defense Committees

These committees constitute the state's greatest success in the war. In strategic zones of the Andes, Shining Path was bogged down in a war of attrition against the organized peasants. According to the head of the joint command of the armed forces, in April 1993 there were more than 4,000 committees with approximately 300,000 *ronderos*. Of these, approximately 10,000 probably had rifles.

The emergence of the committees became widespread in the late 1980s. The current government increased its support and provided them some weapons in an effort to ensure strict control over their activities. Fear in the military that the committees might grow independent is well founded. Some groups could become assassination squads for drug traffickers or use their arms in a war among peasant groups. Yet, to date, the main tendency has been for the committees to become the main axis around which social life is reconstructed in communities devastated by the dirty war of the preceding years.[11] But instead of promoting the reconstruction of the social fabric and the rise of a minimally democratic institutional order with the aim of reabsorbing that potential for violence by the armed peasants, it was decided to militarize rural society.

One congressional bill stipulates that the committees will become part of the National Defense System and that the *ronderos* will be part of the military reserves nationwide, not just in war zones. A recent supreme decree requires that the hundreds of *rondas* that were formed more than ten years ago in the northern highlands for self-defense from cattle rustlers and corrupt authorities—which ultimately formed an alternative system of justice and self-defense (see Starn 1991)—fall into line with the militarized organization and functions of the self-defense committees that are operating in war zones. Political and military authorities, as well as local authorities, have thus found a legal mechanism for unleashing an offensive in the north against the *rondas,* which constitute one of the few institutions of civil society that subsists amid the crisis. Several leaders have already been accused of subversion and put in jail.

Sweeps and Civic Action

In the cities, the armed forces surround impoverished settlement communities and search house-to-house for presumed terrorists. At the end of such operations they distribute food and provide primary medical care. In other words, the operations entail a combination of selective repression and social welfare assistance. This tactic has created a new presence of the state in the peripheral neighborhoods, but it is an intermittent one due to the erosion of the social organizations, municipal governments, political parties, and even the progressive church, which traditionally has been present in such areas. Once the armed forces pull out, the vacuum returns.

In recent months there have been efforts to ensure a more permanent state presence. This has included initiating projects that have been financed by the National Compensation and Social Development Fund (FONCODES) since the end of 1992 and having the president appear in such areas on a regular basis. In contrast with earlier presidents, Fujimori visits communities that have been attacked, distributes arms to the *ronderos,* goes to impoverished settlement communities, and travels through the city when Shining Path decrees armed strikes or forced work stoppages. But his is the presence of a protective *caudillo,* given that it is not linked with grassroots leaders, especially if they appear to be associated somehow with the opposition. Several leaders, especially women, stalked by Shining Path and absent state protection, have had to leave the country.

Intelligence

Advances in this area are unquestionable, but the situation is complex and controversial. On the one hand, the impeccable capture of Guzmán was the work of a police intelligence body, the DINCOTE, and not of the SIN, which has become so powerful. Moreover, petty politics could be interfering with intelligence work. In late 1992 General Antonio Ketín Vidal, chief of DINCOTE and head of the team that captured Guzmán, was moved to the harmless post of inspector of the National Police. The president argued that the struggle against subversion required teamwork: strategies matter, not individuals. This is exactly the opposite of what he said when asked, at home and abroad, why General Hermoza and security adviser Montesinos were being kept in their posts: "They are doing an excellent job and there is no reason to change them." It would appear that the president places a greater value on consolidating his personal power and the power of the group around him, a mission in which SIN plays a pivotal role, than on effectiveness in the work of pacification.

The capture of voluminous files undoubtedly has enabled the state intelligence services to continue striking against disconcerted Senderistas. Yet in recent months it seems as though quality is being sacrificed for quantity, again because of short-term political considerations. Instead of concentrating on getting as close as possible to the vortex of the Senderista hierarchy presently reconstructing itself, forces are being diverted to capture grassroots militants, peripheral individuals, and even innocent people, detained to meet the needs of the "psychological war," another pillar of the counterinsurgency strategy. "Subversive criminals" in striped prison garb and leaders enclosed in cages have been shown on prime-time television and on the front pages of the daily papers. Although this removes the terrorists' air of invincibility, it is a violation of human rights and becomes a sort of drug. The government needs it to win points in the polls, its main source of legitimacy, especially in light of the difficulties it has had engineering an economic recovery. In April, the public approval rating of the antisubversive policy was about 70 percent in the polls, while the approval rating for economic policy was just over 30 percent.

Prisons

A net gain for the government has been ending Senderista control over cell blocks. While in the 1970s some universities became seedbeds for Shining Path, in the 1980s the prisons became the main centers for ideological training. The clandestine organization had massive and permanent cadre schools in the prisons, where it could test, as if in a nutshell, its model of a "new society." This has ended, and the prisons have become once again one of Shining Path's main targets. Shining Path has freed jailed militants on two occasions, one in Cuzco and the other in Huaraz.

Judicial Power and Antiterrorist Legislation

Prior to 5 April the courts and prisons were a sieve. Today the pendulum has swung to the other extreme. The new antiterrorist law, issued in May 1992, established sentences of twenty and thirty years and incorporated into the penal code life imprisonment for terrorist leaders and members of "annihilation squads." The judgment is in the hands of faceless courts and judges. In August 1992, another decree-law (25659) made treason a crime to be tried in military courts.[12]

According to human rights organizations, the virtual summary character of these trials leads to the imprisonment of innocent persons, and the collaborators or rank and file members of the terrorist organizations receive disproportionate sentences. Their only recourse is a plea-bargaining law by which they have little to gain if they do not have valuable information to offer. Nonetheless, this law, which reduces or voids sentences in exchange for information, has facilitated arrests and dismantled Shining Path cells, although in other cases it has been used to accuse innocent persons and to settle private scores.[13]

Human Rights

Violations of human rights continue to be the Achilles' heel of the antisubversive strategy. Indiscriminate repression has diminished significantly, but disappearances and extrajudicial executions have continued. From 1988 to 1991, of all the countries in the world, Peru experienced the greatest number of cases of people detained who then disappeared. Nonetheless, the figure has fallen from 549 in 1988 to less than 100 in the first six months of 1993. But what persists is what several analysts call the systematic failure to punish official forces responsible for human rights violations (see Degregori 1993). Twenty-one cases in which the person presumably responsible and fifty-seven cases against persons found responsible for human rights violations are currently before the military courts; some of them have been pending for more than six years. Four cases have ended in an *auto de sobreseimiento,* or dismissal. The contrast with the rapidity in the treatment of individuals charged with terrorism is notable. In February 1993, in the face of international pressure, for the first time in thirteen years an officer was found guilty of a human rights violation. Two more were found guilty in subsequent weeks.

The case of the disappeared from La Cantuta became a litmus test of how far the regime is capable of advancing with respect to human rights. As of this writing, the results of the case have been mixed.[14] The government does not accept the idea that respect for human rights is not only a moral principle and a requirement for Peru's reinsertion into the international community, but also an important practical component of any victorious—and democratic—antiterrorist strategy.

Unfortunately, in this area the government meets with the indifference or support of most of public opinion. There are many reasons for this. I will mention only one: the fear and indignation that Shining Path produces. Shining Path's "river of blood" has paved the way for consolidation of an authoritarian commonality in which the defense of human rights is viewed as complicity with terrorism.

International Image

In the 1980s Shining Path became the central protagonist of the Internationalist Revolutionary Movement, a group of small Maoist parties from various parts of the world. At the same time, it tried to build Committees for Support of the Peruvian Revolution (CARP) in Colombia, Bolivia, and Ecuador. Given the failure of previous governments to act, the main obstacle Shining Path found in mobilizing sympathy abroad was the discrediting of communism, as well as its own brutality. The current government has created a commission to improve the country's international image, but Fujimori's break with the constitutional order in 1992, as well as his confrontations with human rights organizations and journalists and with politicians and military officers choosing exile, frustrate the success of any such campaign.

In view of the above, after the *autogolpe* the government achieved a series of victories in the war against Shining Path. But definitive victory is not guaranteed, for the government strategy militarizes society instead of politicizing the war. It thus destroys or at least fails to renew the institutional fabric and the party system. This blocks the development of a massive, citizen-based political and ideological response to the terror of Shining Path. While the lack of an antisubversive strategy helped Shining Path grow in the 1980s, the mistakes of the current strategy could save it from total defeat in the 1990s, making political violence an endemic, long-term phenomenon.

* * *

A set of aggravating factors made the capture of Abimael Guzmán a devastating blow for the Maoists. One is that Guzmán had been elevated to Godlike status, which is unprecedented in revolutionary movements.[15] Gorriti (1992) ironically calls it the "capture of the queen bee." Other aggravating factors included the time and manner in which Guzmán fell prisoner: on the eve of the major offensive on Lima, and without a single shot being fired. In October 1992, the Sixth Great Military Plan was to be launched under the slogan, "Build the conquest of power throughout the country!" The plan was aimed at reaching the political objective of achieving equilibrium: making the country ungovernable. On that occasion the armed strikes were to include mass mobilizations in those pockets in which Shining Path maintained a presence. Units of the People's Guerrilla Army (EGP) were to mix in, unnoticed, with the population and to be well armed so as to decimate any police unit sent to put down the demonstrations.[16] The objective was to provoke a response by the armed forces, which, being unable to concentrate its efforts on the EGP units, would repress the entire population. This would be the longed-for genocide that Guzmán believed was necessary to achieve strategic equilibrium, make the country ungovernable, and provoke US intervention.[17]

Since the Second Plenum of the Central Committee of February 1991, when the idea was first announced, Shining Path has been anticipating the transition from "civil war to anti-imperialist war" (see PCP 1991). Actually, they needed foreign intervention to attempt to reproduce nationwide their feat of 1983–1984, when they broke through the military cordon in Ayacucho and expanded throughout the country. Guzmán predicted that foreign intervention would initially cause a brief setback but then lay the conditions for the great offensive. Indoctrinating its militant activists with this perspective, the EGP changed its name to the National Liberation Army. At the same time, Shining Path sought to build a People's Liberation Front (*El Diario*, Dec. 1992/Jan. 1993).

Along with Guzmán, other high-ranking leaders from the Political Bureau of the Central Committee were also taken prisoner, captured with detailed records on Shining Path's organization. At that point the state regained the tactical initiative for the first time since 1983. In effect, Shining Path's main advantage was its ability to decide when and where to attack. After 12 September 1992, the Senderistas did not know how many other names were kept in the computers captured along with the high-level bureaucracy of their "new state," which operated in the middle-class neighborhoods of Lima. Shining Path was put on the tactical defensive and had also regressed to a defensive position strategically.

One can distinguish two stages in this process. The first began when Guzmán, already captured, ordered his followers via television to "carry out what was agreed upon," that is, to begin the Sixth Plan. That mandate gave this first stage a time frame, since carrying out what had been agreed upon meant disturbing the constituent elections set for 22 November. While the number of Senderista actions increased after Guzmán fell prisoner, they were not as well coordinated as before. In addition, the number of frustrated attacks increased, indicating that contingents with less military experience were going into action. Finally, the armed strikes called in the days before the 22 November elections failed. Nonetheless, on 3 December, Guzmán's birthday, Shining Path paralyzed Ayacucho. The warning was clear: we are not totally defeated. A significant part of the leadership of the Metropolitan Committee of Lima—the hardest hit—and of the so-called *Socorro Popular*, a logistical support group, was taken prisoner, but in the provinces the regional leadership bodies had not been as affected.

The second stage began with what appears to be the rebuilding of a national leadership apparatus of Shining Path. In December 1992, the Central Committee met with the chiefs of the various regional committees and issued a "historic resolution" in which they made a highly revealing commitment. They reaffirmed the fulfillment of the Sixth Military Plan—dubbed "Building the conquest of power!"—but baptized the First Campaign of that plan "In defense of the leadership. Against the genocidal dictatorship!" They recognized de facto that they had to undertake a defensive campaign, which is far from what they had imagined before Guzmán was captured.

This new stage has witnessed more military activity in the regional committees less affected by the repression. Actions have stepped up in the north: in the highlands of Ancash and La Libertad (Huamachuco–Santiago de Chuco), in the Piura highlands (Huancabamba and Ayabaca), and in northern Cajamarca (Jaén). According to statements by Carlos Tapia (*Sí,* May 17, 1993), this appears to indicate that the hardest hit has been the "Chanka faction," that is, the old guard from Ayacucho, close to Guzmán, whose approach may have been questioned within Shining Path.[18] Whether or not this is true, internal contradictions in Shining Path will undoubtedly mount. For a party unaccustomed to doubting its course, a series of dilemmas arise regarding, for example: what role should Guzmán and "Gonzalo thought" have?[19] Should peasant work be a priority or should an urban emphasis be maintained? Should more extensive work with the masses be done, or should the use of terror relative to the population be augmented?

The armed strike called for 17, 18, and 19 May 1993, in commemoration of the thirteenth anniversary of the beginning of the war, can be taken as a yardstick. It meant that Shining Path still placed priority on urban work. The outcome of the strike can be described by reference to the classic image of a glass half full. Compared to the

1992 armed strikes, it was a failure. But taking into account the setbacks Shining Path had suffered, the result was not so disastrous.

The strike was felt in Lima, especially the first day, and was successful to varying degrees in cities such as Ayacucho and Huaraz. It left Huancayo and Arequipa without power. Shining Path displayed a national presence that serves as a warning to the government and public opinion, but above all the organization lifted the spirits of its demoralized militants. Recall that according to Fujimori, 98 percent of the Shining Path leadership is in prison. According to more moderate assessments of *Sí* (May 17, 1993), approximately eight cadres directly under the central leadership were taken prisoner, along with one to two hundred from zonal commands, and a few thousand grassroots forces, or individuals who are not party members but collaborators or sympathizers who have recently been won over to the cause.

The fact that Shining Path maintains its capacity for action despite the wide-ranging government offensive has to do with, among other things, a quantitative factor. According to general consensus estimates, the party had some three thousand members and the EGP from five thousand to eight thousand fighters, including local militias. But captured documents that have circulated among journalists suggest that these figures should be almost doubled. There is also a qualitative factor: Shining Path was able to build a solid organization. It is vertical, totalitarian, and terrorist. All these characterizations are accurate, but Shining Path is also an institution, something to which the current government fails to give much importance.

Nonetheless, it would be a mistake to overestimate Shining Path's current potential. Its activities after the strike indicate that it has opted to work along two already well-known lines of action, but which in the new situation may lead to unmanageable internal contradictions in the medium term. Shining Path is increasing the terror to try to recover lost ground in a population that has lost some of its fear of the organization. In the days after the strike, Shining Path dynamited buses that had continued to run during the strike, assassinated merchants who had opened their stores, and even killed the mayor of Tocache, in the Upper Huallaga, who opposed the strike. These were punishments meted out to teach a lesson, methods Shining Path had already used at its discretion prior to the capture of Guzmán.[20]

Parallel to the terror, the organization appears to be focusing its efforts on developing work with the masses, especially in its original seedbed: among teachers and university and secondary students, seeking to keep alive the call of "Gonzalo thought," recruiting new cadres, and waiting for the chance to grow once again. In broader perspective, without Guzmán, who acted as the final arbiter in earlier internal struggles, recourse to terror and work with the masses may become incompatible.

Even if Shining Path is able to overcome its current dilemmas—coming to grips with what Guzmán represents, avoiding divisions, and reorganizing its forces for 1994–1995—the country will no longer be the same. Despite the authoritarianism, social disorganization, and weakness of the democratic political alternatives, a juncture so unusually favorable to Shining Path as was 1992 will be difficult to come by again. Strategic equilibrium is a dynamic concept in which even the frame of mind of the population can play an important role. While it is risky to make predictions about any part of the world today, it is most likely that Shining Path will develop over the coming long years a dirty war that bloodies the country, fed by and at the same time feeding authoritarianism. Whether Shining Path is defeated for good will depend on whether Peruvians are capable of finally constructing a democratic strategy for the country.

Notes

1. The report concluded by noting: "Whether the movement succeeds or fails in this effort will hinge more on SL as an organization than on any realistic set of responses from the government of Peru, which has shown little understanding of the insurgency and even less ability to stop it" (McCormick 1992:78).

2. More or less comprehensive descriptions and analyses can be found in Favre 1984; Degregori 1985, 1989, 1990; and Gorriti 1990.

3. For more on those years, see Gorriti 1990.

4. According to Mao (1954) the "prolonged war" consists of three major strategic phases: defensive, equilibrium, and offensive.

5. On military prerogatives and democratic regimes, see Stepan 1988.

6. Basic pay for a division general in June 1991 was equivalent to US$ 210, far below what their peers were receiving in neighboring countries: Ecuador, $558; Bolivia, $910; Colombia, $915; Chile, $1,115; Brazil, $3,700 (*Sí* weekly, Lima, 9 June 1991, p. 15).

7. The decision by peasants to join the civil defense committees accelerated the changes in the armed forces but has not brought an end to human rights violations. Repression is becoming more selective. Indiscriminate massacres are declining, but from 1988 to 1991 Peru occupied first place among all the world's countries in number of persons detained and then disappeared (see, for example, Instituto de Defensa Legal 1990).

8. In the weeks after his election and prior to assuming the presidency, Fujimori went to live for a time at the *Círculo Militar*, or the military's social club. Beginning at that time he built a special relationship with the armed forces, especially the army. Vladimiro Montesinos, a former military officer

who was forced out of the institution in the 1970s for supposed ties to the CIA and since then Fujimori's adviser, appears to have played a major role in fostering close relations between Fujimori and the military.

9. Twelve days after the CCD appointed an investigative commission, the military initiated its own investigation into the case. Invoking the exclusivity of military jurisdiction, the officers implicated in the case refused to make statements to the commission from the CCD.

10. In July 1993, maps sent anonymously to *Sí* led to the discovery of graves with human remains that, according to many indications, belonged to some of the disappeared students.

When the journalists from *Sí* found mass graves with charred human remains in a valley near La Cantuta, the attorney general accused the magazine of interfering in the administration of justice and refused to accept foreign forensic support to identify the remains. A delegation from Amnesty International was not received by any government representative. Shortly thereafter, some keys found in one of the graves opened the door of the dorm room of one of the disappeared students.

On 21 February 1994, responding to growing domestic and international pressure for a resolution of the case, a military court sentenced nine army officers and enlisted men to military prison for the murders at La Cantuta University. A secret military court tried the case after legislation was pushed through the Congress, in a move that produced substantial criticism of the government and eroded Fujimori's popularity, to ensure that the case would be removed from civilian jurisdiction by a decision of the Supreme Court. To many political observers, Fujimori's handling of the case confirmed his dependence on the military.

11. On the complex nature of the *rondas,* or committees, and their role in the new rural society, see Coronel and Loayza 1992 and del Pino 1992.

12. In his 28 July 1993 message to the nation the president reiterated his plan to establish the death penalty for crimes of terrorism and reported that from 1981 to 1991, 575 people accused of terrorism had been convicted, while in the fifteen months since the *autogolpe,* 589 had been convicted. Two days later the public prosecutor for terrorism cases boosted those figures by reporting that in the two weeks before the presidential address, 57 more terrorists were convicted and 18 of them were sentenced to life imprisonment.

13. According to the prosecutor for terrorism cases, as of July 1993, four hundred terrorists had availed themselves of this law, three hundred of them in the upper Huallaga Valley. The vast majority of persons turning themselves in through plea bargain arrangements belong to the Túpac Amaru Revolutionary Movement (MRTA).

14. See note 10 above.

15. Recall that the personality cult of Stalin and Mao did not occur until *after* they came to power. Pol Pot, with whom Guzmán has often been compared, always kept a low profile (see Hinojosa 1992).

16. This information is based on personal conversations with Carlos Tapia.

17. When SL set out to attain strategic equilibrium, Guzmán began to speak of one million dead and the possible advantage of genocide to attain that equilibrium (Guzmán 1988). "The revolutionary triumph will cost one million lives," he affirmed when he appeared on television after his capture.

18. Even before the First Congress of SL in 1988, Guzmán had been considered internally as a *hoxhista,* or follower of Enver Hoxha, for shifting

the emphasis to urban work. In light of events, these criticisms may be voiced once again.

19. "Presidente Gonzalo" is Abimael Guzmán's nom de guerre. "Gonzalo thought" is his doctrine, which for Senderistas represents the creative development of Marx, Lenin, and Mao. Therefore, as they see it, Gonzalo is the "fourth sword of Marxism."

20. In August 1993, a Shining Path column unleashed a series of attacks on *ronderos* in the central jungle region, which culminated in the massacre of more than sixty colonists and members of the Asháninka ethnic group.

References

Americas Watch

1984 "Peru: Abdicating Democratic Authority." New York: Human Rights Watch.

1986 "Civil Patrols in Guatemala." New York/Washington, DC: Human Rights Watch.

Coronel, José, and Carlos Loayza

1992 "Violencia política: Formas de repuesta comunera en Ayacucho." *Perú: El problema agrario en debate.* SEPIA IV. C. I. Degregori, J. Escobal, and B. Marticorena, eds. Lima: UNAP/SEPIA.

Degregori, Carlos Iván

1985 "Sendero Luminoso: Los hondos y mortales desencuentros" and "Lucha armada y utopía autoritaria." Working papers 4 and 6. Lima: Institute for Peruvian Studies (IEP).

1989 "How difficult it is to be God: Ideology and political violence in Sendero Luminoso." *Critique of Anthropology.* Vol. 11 (33):233–250.

1990 *El surgimiento de Sendero Luminoso: Ayacucho 1969–1979.* Lima: IEP.

1993 "Derechos humanos: Debate tenso y decisivo." *Argumentos.* No. 5:10–14. Lima: IEP.

del Pino, Ponciano

1992 "Los campesinos en la guerra. O de cómo la gente comienza a ponerse macho." *Perú: El problema agrario en debate.* SEPIA IV. C. I. Degregori, J. Escobal, and B. Marticorena, eds. Lima: UNAP/SEPIA.

Favre, Henri

1984 "Sendero Luminoso: Horizontes oscuros." *Que Hacer.* No. 31:25–34. DESCO. Lima, October.

Gorriti, Gustavo

1990 *Sendero: Historia de la guerra milenaria en el Perú.* Vol. 1. Lima: Apoyo Editores.

1992 "El arrebatamiento de la cuarta espada." *Ideele.* No. 45–46:39–41. Lima, December.

Guzmán, Abimael

1988 "Presidente Gonzalo rompe el silencio: Entrevista en la clandestinidad." *El Diario.* Special edition, 24 July 1988.

Hinojosa, Iván
1992 "Entre el poder y la ilusión: Pol Pot, Sendero y las utopías campesinas." *Debate Agrario.* No. 15:69–94. Lima: CEPES.

Instituto de Defensa Legal
1990 *Perú 1990: La oportunidad perdida.* Lima: IDL.

Mao Zedong
1954 *On the Protracted War.* Peking: Foreign Language Press.

McCormick, Gordon
1992 *From the Sierra to the Cities: The Urban Campaign of the Shining Path.* Santa Monica, CA: Rand Corporation.

Partido Comunista del Perú
1991 "Construir la conquista del poder en medio de la guerra popular!" Mimeo. Unpublished.

Rial, Juan
1992 "Las relaciones cívico militares en la transición y consolidación democrática en América Latina." Paper presented at the seminar "Crisis política y reformas institutionales en América Latina y el Perú." Lima: IEP (October).

Revista Sí
1993 "Sendero Luminoso: Cambio de guardia." Lima, (17 May), pp. 34–35.

Senado de la República
1992 *Violencia política en el Perú.* Lima: Ediciones del Senado.

Starn, Orin
1991 *Con llanques todo barro: Reflexiones sobre rondas campesinas y nuevos movimientos sociales.* Lima: IEP.

Stepan, Alfred
1988 *Rethinking Military Politics: Brazil and the Southern Cone.* Princeton: Princeton University Press.

Stern, Steve (ed.)
1987 *Resistance, Rebellion and Consciousness in the Andean Peasant World: 18th to 20th Centuries.* Madison: University of Wisconsin Press.

8

The Power of Peru's Armed Forces

Enrique Obando

Believing that the role of the Peruvian armed forces is critical to the future of democracy in Peru, I will analyze and attempt to measure their influence on the state and society. And believing that it is impossible to comprehend the current situation without a historical perspective on how that situation took shape, I address a rather long period in Peruvian politics. I begin with the military government (1968–1980) and continue through three civilian governments: Fernando Belaúnde's second presidential period (1980–1985), Alan García's term (1985–1990), and Alberto Fujimori's presidency (1990 to date). Moreover, studying the political influence of the military and its institutional prerogatives requires a point of comparison. I use the period of military government, during which I argue that the power of the armed forces over the state and society was at its height, for this purpose.

How does one measure the power of the military during this twenty-five year period? I quantify and then analyze the change over time using a number of key variables. Such quantification, of course, can be viewed only in relative terms; that is, military prerogatives or influence can be measured at levels—high, medium, or low—only relative to a point of reference. As I mentioned, the point of reference will be the military government of 1968 to 1980. My use of the term "power" refers to political strength, and not to military firepower.

For this study I use the following ten variables, which seem to me to be most clearly presented as questions.

Enrique Obando is a senior researcher at the Peruvian Center for International Studies (CEPEI).

Who decides how the national defense system is organized?

I assume that the military, as one pressure group of the state, is interested in creating a defense system organized as it sees properly fit. The extent to which the defense system is organized by the military is an indicator of the political power of the armed forces. The imposition of the system by a civilian government without taking military criteria into consideration would demonstrate weak capacity of the armed forces to exert pressure on the government.

Has the national defense system been implemented, and does it function?

Here I again assume the military is interested in designing and implementing a national defense system. This objective implies the creation of a large defense-related bureaucracy as well as the institutionalization of a complex state system of coordination between civilian and military agencies, which civilian governments are not always willing to develop. Given the economic cost of such a defense system, the extent to which it has been created and is operational indicates the military's political power. If the system is not operational because the government has failed to implement the defense plan, one can conclude that the armed forces' capacity to exert pressure within the state is low.

Who appoints the high command of the armed forces? Who determines the nominations and promotions to important positions?

Armed forces that autonomously appoint the high command would signal their strength. But intervention by the civilian government or Congress in these decisions would signal a low level of power.

Who decides who the enemies of the country are? Who develops the potential war scenarios?

If the military can attain government acceptance of its views of who the enemy is, one can posit that it has garnered a high degree of political power. By contrast, if the government decides who the potential enemies are without taking into account the military perspective, one can conclude that the armed forces hold a low degree of political influence.

What is the power and the scope of action of the intelligence services?

Is the power of the intelligence services unrestricted, such that they monitor not only the enemy as generally accepted, but civil society as well? Or are they a nonfunctioning bureaucratic instrument? In the first case the military is politically powerful, while in the second case it is politically weak.

How successful is the military in obtaining government approval of its defense budgets and arms acquisition programs?

Are the budget and acquisition programs usually accepted as presented or with minor changes? Or is the government able to reduce the military budget and reduce or halt an arms acquisition program? Once again, on the one extreme the military is highly politically influential, while on the other it is politically weak.

Does the military maintain privileges?

To the extent that the armed forces hold privileges, they have political power. If their privileges are extensive, their power is strong; if their privileges are few, their power is weak.

What is the level of military income?

A relatively high income could denote a high level of political power, whereas a low income would undoubtedly signify a low level of political power.

Is the military able to protect the members of the armed forces from investigation and/or prosecution by civilian courts for human rights violations and economic mismanagement of state funds?

An answer of yes indicates military power; an answer of no indicates political weakness.

To what degree does the military exert power over the local and regional governments?

Once again, a high level will denote a politically influential military. A low level could denote a politically weak military.

These ten variables are the tools with which I will attempt to measure the political power of the armed forces. This approach is, of course, theoretical. To fully understand the reality one must also consider the political and economic context from which the variables are measured. For instance, a situation in which the government halts military arms acquisitions at a time of economic prosperity is quite different from one in which the government acts similarly during an economic crisis. The same can be said about military income. Assessing the political power of the military requires taking all of these variables into account.

Finally, one must consider the relative importance to assign to each of these variables. Should each carry the same weight? I tend to think not, and therefore divide the first nine variables into three main groups. The first group includes all the elements related to the satisfaction of the military's personal needs (income, protection from civilian prosecution, and privilege); the second group includes elements related to the satisfaction of institutional needs (a national defense system of its own creation, designation of its own command, approval of the defense budget, and acquisition programs); and the third group comprises elements related to the satisfaction of the need to exercise influence on civilian government and civil society (the power to define who the enemy of the country is, the use of intelligence to monitor civil society, and the implementation of a national defense system that includes the civilian agencies of the state). I do not classify the last variable (the incidence of military power over the local and regional governments), as it is the result of the exceptional circumstances of the counterinsurgency war. As such, the military power achieved at the regional and local level can be considered exceptional as well. Moreover, the military itself does not want it to become permanent. Regional and local military power is related to the war and will decline when it ends.

Based on my analysis of the Peruvian armed forces (see Figure 8.1), I rank the importance of each group of variables (or prerogatives) in inverse relation to the order in which they were eliminated with the return in 1980 of a democratically elected government. During the Belaúnde presidency, the military lost the ability to exercise influence first. The armed forces subsequently began losing their institutional prerogatives. During the García government, they lost the only remaining prerogative of influence, as well as two institutional prerogatives and the personal prerogative of income maintenance. During the Fujimori regime, the armed forces lost the only institutional prerogative remaining: the autonomous appointment of the high command. With the exception of income, the military has maintained its personal prerogatives to the present. Hence, I assume that the variables related to group one (personal needs of the military) are most important to the military. Second in importance are the elements of group two (institutional needs of the military). Group three (the need to exercise influence) ranks third.

Figure 8.1 Loss of Prerogatives by the Peruvian Military

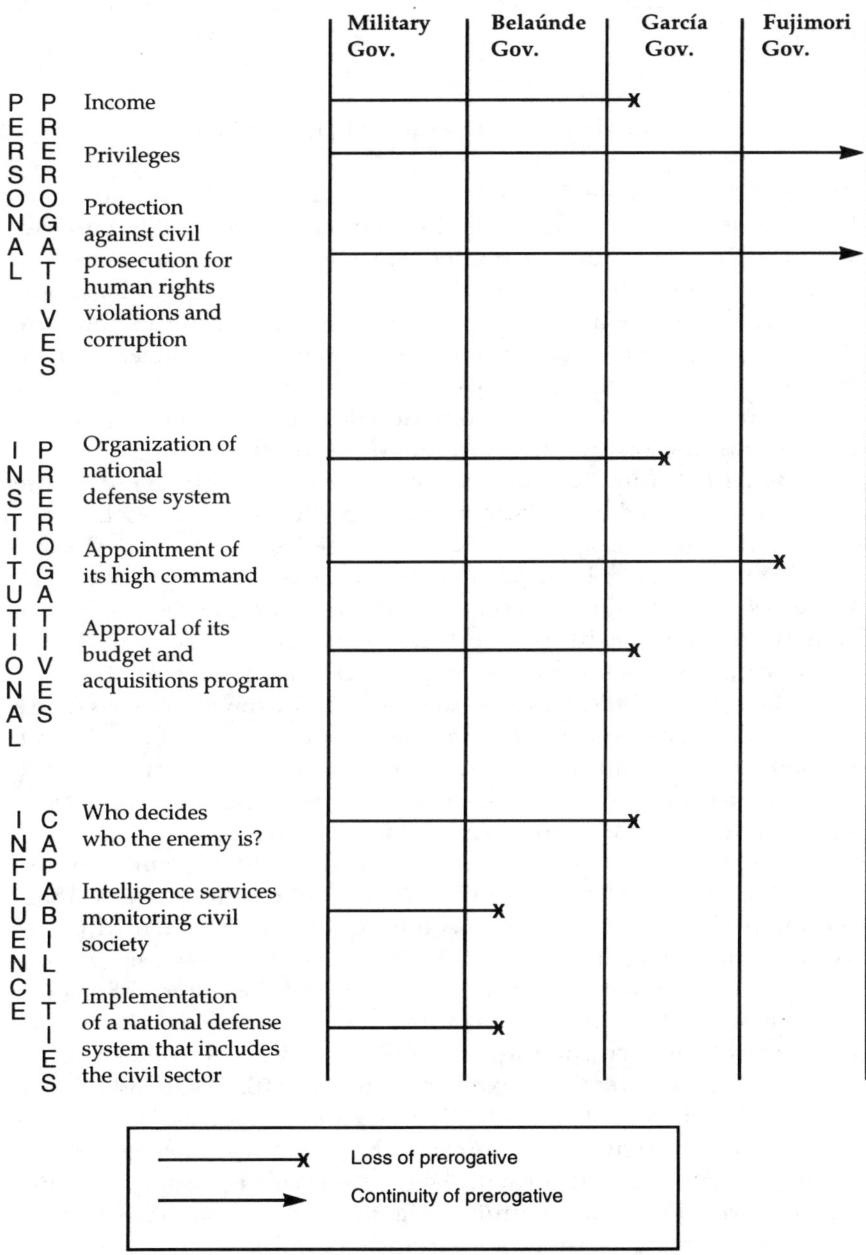

This ranking is drawn from the Peruvian experience, but it may be of interest to determine whether it holds for other Latin American militaries.

The Military Government (1968–1980)

As noted above, the ten variables demonstrate that the military's political power was at its maximum during this period. The defense system, which at the time was called the High Command of the National Defense (Organismos Altos de la Defensa Nacional), was conceived of by the armed forces.[1] In theory, it did not include the entire state apparatus, only some of its specialized agencies. In fact, however, given that the military was the government, it could use any government agency to serve the national defense if considered necessary. And this was the situation for twelve years.

As of 1979, when the military returned the government to the civilians, it created a new defense system that guarantees that the ministries and state agencies could be used if needed for the national defense. They incorporated the civilian agencies into the defense system; through the creation of a new law, the system institutionalized what had been a de facto reality for twelve years.[2] This would cause problems with subsequent civilian governments. However, the idea behind this step—that defense of the nation was a task for all Peruvians, not just the military[3]—was correct. Even so, the civilian view was entirely different: they saw the incorporation of the civilian government agencies into the defense system as an attempt by the military to interfere throughout the state apparatus.[4]

During this period, the designation of the high command and the nominations and promotions to high-level positions were carried out by the armed forces with absolute autonomy. The armed forces decided who the enemies of the country were. Two potential war scenarios were accepted, one related to Chile and the other to Ecuador. One must recall, however, that these scenarios were made by seriously taking into consideration the international environment of those years; they were not excuses to justify military arms acquisitions. Relations with Chile and Ecuador were especially tense, first because of ideological differences with the Chilean government of General Augusto Pinochet, and later as a result of geopolitical differences with Chile and boundary claims by the Ecuadorans.

The military government constantly monitored the activities of political parties as well as political leaders, union leaders and activists, the peasant movement, university students, and so on. The intelligence system not only kept a close watch on civil society, but also created union and peasant federations that were used to build political support for the military regime. The intelligence services dominated the media as well. They also developed a habit, as a result of the ideological differences within the armed forces, that may well prove fatal in the future, however: they began to spy on each other.[5] Since the armed forces and government were one and the same, the most important arms purchases in Peruvian history were made during this period.[6]

The military benefited from the privileges gained during previous military governments, especially the regime of General Manuel A. Odría (1948–1956). But from 1968 to 1980 they were notably increased. As a result, the armed forces today have special hospitals, special schools for their children, special shopping centers, special clubs, a special housing program, and so on. Although they pay for these services (except in hospitals where services are free), they are heavily subsidized. Moreover, the privileges of the high-ranking officers (the rank of colonel and above) included cars (they did not own them, but could use them, and then purchase them at subsidized prices upon retirement), chauffeurs, gasoline, spare car parts, stewards, and the like. Military income was at its highest level during these years.[7]

It was unnecessary to exert pressure to protect members of the armed forces against prosecution and investigation by civilian courts. During the military government, the violation of human rights was very limited. Nor was corruption in the high-ranking military an important problem, except in the later years of the government of General Morales Bermúdez when some officials, such as Minister of Interior General Fernando Velit and the president's son were suspected of illegal enrichment. Human rights was thus not an issue at all when the civilian politicians returned to govern, and corruption was a relatively minor problem. The guerrilla war in 1980, however, involved human rights violations by the army. The drastic reduction of military income because of the economic crisis soon generated corruption within the armed forces. The ability to cover up these abuses, however, is a good indicator of the political power of the military.

Finally, the armed forces had absolute control over the local and regional governments. Mayors were designated by the military and the heads of the regional development organs (Organismos de Desarollo, or ORDES) were members of the armed forces. Again, during this era, military power was at its highest level.

The Belaúnde Government (1980–1985)

The Belaúnde government brought about a reduction of the power of the military relative to the preceding period. The problem is that this did not occur as a consequence of the reinsertion of the armed forces into a new constitutional order that restricted their role to national defense. Rather, it was an antimilitary reaction by the new civilian government—the same government that was overthrown in 1968—that neither took into account the considerably harmful impact it had on the national defense nor properly considered the defense of the nation to be an objective of all Peruvians, as opposed to just the military.

The Belaúnde government did not in any way modify the structure of the national defense system so as not to alienate the armed forces. But the system was a paper tiger because the civilian arm of the government did not work to implement it. As a result, the defense system failed to operate at the very moment Shining Path was launching its insurgency.[8] With respect to the appointment of the high command, the military maintained its autonomy. But the new government did produce the constitutional requirement that Congress ratify the promotions of generals and admirals.[9]

The intelligence system was weakened. Members of the Belaúnde government, as well as other political parties, were particularly sensitive to the surveillance to which they had been subjected by the intelligence services, which in some cases led to deportations.[10] The government not only deactivated the elements of the system used to monitor civil society; it significantly reduced its budget in an effort to limit its effectiveness. Once more the civilian government acted out of political revenge and in response to the conflict in civil-military relations. It failed to consider the needs of the national defense at a moment when the most bloody and dangerous insurgency in Peruvian history was growing.

Believing them to be the most sensitive military issues of all, the Belaúnde government left the defense budget and arms acquisitions processes alone. The armed forces thus received as large or larger a budget during the first years of the Belaúnde presidency as they did during the military regime. The acquisition program designed during the military regime was accepted in its entirety by the civilian government, which contributed to the significant increase in Peru's external debt witnessed during this period.[11]

Not one personal privilege was affected. The apparent objective of the government was to keep the military happy by preserving its privileges and acquisitions, again, as seen in the treatment of the defense and intelligence systems, to the neglect of the impact on the operation of the defense system. One can see a similar lack of defense planning and consistency in the government's acceptance of the military's potential war scenarios. The scenarios related to Chile and to Ecuador were both ostensibly accepted without change. But the government did not help coordinate civilian and military agencies as required by the plans that emerged from such scenarios. Not even a military incident with Ecuador, at the border in Falso Paquisha in 1981, made the government more cooperative in the implementation of the defense plans.

The government's lack of coherent policies—the acceptance of the need for arms acquisitions and defense scenarios coupled with the failure to act on such plans—continued in addressing the Shining Path insurgency. The armed forces had developed a potential insurgency scenario, and during the Belaúnde government it became a tragic reality. The government—calling for a military solution to the crisis—left the entire problem in the hands of the military without providing the support required for the defense system to operate. When military officers such as General Adrián Huamán pointed out that the solution could be achieved only through a policy of repression, that social and economic support also was required to gain popular support, the government disagreed. A social and economic response demanded a level of expenditure that the government, already immersed in economic crisis, did not want to support. When General Huamán publicly objected, the government replaced him with someone more supportive of a purely military solution. In short, the armed forces had complete freedom to decide how to fight the subversives, as long as it did not require increased expenditure.

Two factors were behind the change from a policy of allowing the armed forces to purchase myriad conventional weapons to one of refusing to accept the costs of a social and economic campaign against the insurgency. First, by 1983, the economic crisis was a palpable reality[12] and did not permit increased spending on defense. Second, the implementation of a policy of socioeconomic support for the zones affected by insurgency would have signified the subordination of civilian ministers to a strategy designed by the military. And this the civilian politicians were not ready to accept.

The counterinsurgency war carried a great contradiction. The armed forces that were losing political power at the national level were increasing their strength at the regional and local levels. This was a consequence of the appointment of a political-military chief in Ayacucho, in the south-central Andes, to control the insurgency. The appointment was an army general who controlled the military forces as well as the police and was authorized to develop counterinsurgency operations in the zone. The remainder of the civilian state apparatus in the Ayacucho area (mayors, development corporations, bureaus of the ministries) continued to exercise authority. Ultimately, the counterinsurgency war led to excesses. A "dirty war" was carried out in Ayacucho. There, the civilian government did support the military to the utmost, as President Belaúnde indicated when he stated that he threw Amnesty International's reports on human rights violations in Peru into the garbage.

In summary, the Belaúnde government signals a significant reduction of military power in a state and society with unique characteristics. A reduction of military involvement in the state was a natural consequence of the country's return to democracy. However, the military did not occupy a position appropriate to a democratic state. In some respects, the armed forces' power was more limited than necessary for the fulfillment of their national defense duties. In other respects, their power was greater than what it should have been in a democratic regime. The military did not have increased capacity to implement the national defense system because of lack of cooperation on the part of the government. But at the same time the military had special power in the region of Ayacucho, apparently carte blanche to carry out a dirty war against subversive activity. Curiously enough, this was not the result of military pressure on a weak government, but rather of a coincidence of civilian government and military methods in the fight against Shining Path.

During the Belaúnde period, the armed forces did not have enough power where they should have, and they had excess power where they should not have had it. The power of the armed forces was incompatible both with democracy and with an effective, professional military.

Military Power Under Alan García's Government (1985–1990)

Fearing a coup, the main objective of President García relative to the armed forces was to control them. If Belaúnde tried to control the armed forces by not interfering in their internal processes (while refusing to cooperate in the implementation of the national defense system), García sought to control them by intervening actively in their internal operations. That meant an even greater reduction in the power of the armed forces at the national level. Yet because of the increase in intensity and territorial expansion of the Shining

Path and Túpac Amaru Revolutionary Movement (MRTA) guerrillas, the armed forces witnessed an important increase in their power at the local and regional levels.[13]

Although Belaúnde did not allow the implementation of the national defense system, he at least left the determination of its structure in the hands of the military. The García government modified the structure of the system against the wishes of the armed forces. A new ministry of defense was created, combining three military ministries (war, navy, and air force) with the National Secretariat of Defense and the Joint Chiefs of Staff.[14] The idea of creating a single ministry was not a bad one. The problem was that it was not implemented as a technical measure to rationalize the defense structure, but as a political measure to control the military.

This was not to be the only problem the military faced. The armed forces' prerogative of determining (through the war scenarios) who the enemies of the country were also was diminished. Whereas Belaúnde had approved the Chile and Ecuador scenarios but did not support the implementation of the resultant defense plans, García went a step further and rejected the Chile scenario. Moreover, the military's autonomy in designating their command was threatened by the García policy of government co-optation of the high command. The government secured the political support of high-ranking military officers in exchange for important state appointments, such as minister of defense, minister of interior, ambassadors, and so forth.

The intelligence service, weakened by Belaúnde, was now strengthened. It was used by the government to monitor the military itself, to tap the telephones of the high command in an effort to ensure their loyalty. To carry out his plans, García relied on co-opted military officers or officers with ideological affinity, which created internal divisions and the destructive politicization of the institution.

Given the economic crisis and the co-optation of the high command, the ability of the armed forces to press for the approval of the military budget and acquisitions diminished almost completely. The income of the military fell so dramatically that it severely affected morale, producing a great number of retirements within the officer corps and even some desertions.[15] Under the Belaúnde government the military enjoyed the autonomy to fight the counterinsurgency war; Alan García attempted to put a stop to human rights violations. He fired a president of the Joint Chiefs of Staff, a commander of the Second Military Region, and a political-military chief in Ayacucho on human rights grounds. Judicial proceedings were begun against members of the armed forces for human rights abuses. Nevertheless, as the García government came to an end, the military was continuing these abuses, which indicates that this was the only area in which military prerogatives managed to prevail.[16]

Finally, García respected the privileges the military carried over from the Belaúnde years, but because of the economic crisis and the military's extremely low income, these privileges were no longer symbols of status. Rather, they highlighted the incongruence between military status and the reality of the situation. For example, a high-ranking officer with a car provided by the army would, rather than drive, sell the gasoline[17] or spare parts to feed his family. He often had to let his miserably paid chauffeur work part-time so that the chauffeur could take another job for his own well-being. Also, the services available to the officer corps—hospitals, schools for their children, clubs, etc.—declined in quality because of budgetary problems.

All of these conditions combined to produce great dissension within the armed forces and led some officers to begin planning to overthrow the government. At least two coups were being planned by the end of the García period.[18] Low- and medium-ranking officers, had they moved ahead with their plan, would have directed the coup against not only the president, but also the high command because they considered its members to be traitors for not having defended the institutional interests of the military. Another coup was being planned by the high command itself to preempt the young officer's coup, because the high-ranking officers knew the coup planned by the junior faction would also be aimed at them.

If the armed forces lost political power over the state and civil society at the national level, they increasingly acquired strength regionally and locally. As a result of the growth of the insurgency, the government declared new zones to be states of emergency and more political-military chiefs were appointed to these areas.[19] Consequently, the armed forces took charge of almost one-third of the territory of the country. Since Shining Path and the MRTA had assassinated or threatened away the civilian authorities in these zones, in most places the only state authority was the army. This power was not, however, total. The military commanded only their own forces and the police; where it still existed, the military did not control civilian authority.[20] The García government never acceded to the military's request for control over civilian officials.

The armed forces' power at the regional and local levels was also incoherent. The military did not have even the minimal tools required to accomplish its mission. The forces that had helicopters often did not have gasoline to operate them. They did not have spare parts for vehicles, or sufficient food, ammunition, boots, and uniforms. In many cases, instead of taking control of a zone, garrisons were put on the defensive, attempting to survive not only the guerrilla attacks, but also the lack of government support. This situation led to many excesses, such as troops plundering for food, and created an environment conducive to human rights abuse during the counterinsurgency war.[21]

In summary, the armed forces lost nearly all of their capacity to exert pressure on the Peruvian state during the García period, except when it came to protecting its cadres from investigation for human rights violations and for corruption, which the government happily used as a tool for co-optation. The civilian government selected the most corrupt members of the armed forces for important positions,[22] recognizing that the threat of publicly exposing their illegal acts could easily be used to control them. In short, as for the subordination of the armed forces to the civilians, the García government sought only to control the armed forces, not to develop an efficient institution or provide the military with the tools needed to accomplish its mission.

Military Power During the Fujimori Government

Some of the features in civil-military relations under García have continued under Fujimori, but the current government has brought important changes as well. The co-optation policy has not only been continued but intensified. While García's only objective was to control the armed forces, Fujimori—because he does not have a political party backing him—wants to use them or to rely on them to implement his political project. To achieve this objective, and marking a major difference from the Belaúnde and García years, Fujimori has provided the armed forces a legal framework with which to prosecute the counterinsurgency war more efficiently. For the first time in the conflict, the government has designed a national counterinsurgency strategy.[23] The result has been a further decline in the institutional power of the armed forces to levels even lower than those reached during the García presidency. At the same time, however, the effectiveness and operative capacity of the armed forces has increased.

Witness, for example, the new structure of the defense system and the legislative decrees of November 1991.[24] Both measures were designed not by the military, but by a group of civilian presidential advisers who work at the National Intelligence Service (SIN), which is under the direct supervision of Fujimori. And they were readily accepted by the military. These measures allowed a much more efficient fight against the insurgents, but they were also designed to give the government greater control over the military and civil society. Fujimori was unable, however, to secure increased control over civil society. First, Congress strongly opposed such a move. Second, following the dissolution of the legislature with the *autogolpe* of 5 April 1992, international pressure against it was too strong. Nevertheless, SIN keeps an eye on the activities of the political opposition and the press.

The military no longer has the autonomy to appoint the high command of the armed forces (which includes the highest-ranking officer, or "commander general," the chief of staff, and the inspector general from each of the three services: army, air force, and navy). In this regard, Fujimori has moved further than García ever dreamed of doing. García co-opted the high command, but it was the armed forces who appointed its members. Fujimori, however, with the help of the new law of November 1991 (Legislative Decree 752),[25] the president now makes the appointments from among the high-ranking generals and admirals (see Article 5 of the decree). Those selected do not have limited terms of service on the command, after which they retire (see Article 55). Rather, they can maintain their posts for the duration of the presidency. It is no longer necessary to co-opt a new member of the command each year once the president finds a general or admiral who is completely loyal. Hence, the selection of the generals on the high command has became politicized.

On the one hand, this new situation has advantages. A commander general now can gain experience by remaining in the position for several years, which was very difficult when the generals were shifted annually. It also gives the president absolute control over the armed forces. On the other hand, the disadvantages are great. In the election of the commander general, political loyalty is now more important than professional capability. This can be a serious problem for a country at war with an insurgency. In addition, the civilian government controls the armed forces, but the government does not have a democratic program, as was seen with Fujimori's *autogolpe.* Control of the armed forces through co-optation absent deep democratic conviction can be a serious problem. The co-opted generals are not loyal to the constitution as they should be, but rather to the president. Again, this was clear with the *autogolpe.* As such, co-optation can work in favor of authoritarian presidents, who can use the armed forces to threaten or dominate the Congress and civil society.[26] Finally, the president's power over the armed forces extends even further. The new constitution (Article 172) gives the president the power to grant promotions for admirals and generals.

The intelligence service is probably at its most powerful since the military government. This is a positive development for the counterinsurgency war. On the negative side, the service's antennas are directed not only against subversion, but also civil society and the military itself. As of the November 1992 attempted coup against Fujimori, all officers are being closely watched.

Clearly the co-optation of the military has not been accomplished without opposition. It has been, in fact, costly and traumatic. The army is divided between the institutionalist officers and the co-opted officers, a split that opened wide with the institutionalist officers' attempted coup against Fujimori and the co-opted high command in November 1992. The internecine struggle continued with the prosecution of the officers involved in the coup. Subsequently, nineteen former commander generals of the army wrote two letters criticizing the present commander general, Nicolás Hermoza. Many generals who did not have the confidence of General Hermoza or Fujimori were forced to retire. Two retired generals who publicly criticized the current commander general were prosecuted for doing so.

In 1993, documents revealing human rights violations by a special commando unit of the army, in which several co-opted officers, including General Hermoza, were named, were leaked to the press and to an opposition member of Congress. The political warfare continued with a direct accusation by General Rodolfo Robles, who was number three in the military hierarchy, that presidential adviser Vladimiro Montesinos and General Hermoza were involved in several cases of human rights violations, including the disappearance of several students and a professor at La Cantuta University and the killings in Barrios Altos, a district of Lima. Then emerged the anonymous note, apparently from within the army, which revealed to the media the burial site of the disappeared students of La Cantuta.[27]

The emergence of evidence in human rights cases as a result of the struggle within the army leaves open the possibility that more evidence will be forthcoming. The bitter division between the institutionalists and the pro-Fujimori officers is likely to continue and is a source of ongoing instability for the government.

What is curious is why this division has occurred at all. Fujimori could have had the support of the army at no political cost to him because he has not intervened in ways that usually alienate military support. A president can alienate the military in two ways. The first is political, by being a communist or Aprista (a member of APRA, or the American Popular Revolutionary Alliance party), for instance. The second is by being grossly ineffective. Fujimori is none of these. He is not ideologically oriented, but rather a pragmatist who cannot be considered ineffective. His counterinsurgency strategy as well as his economic policy have the approval of the military. The military also approves of the president's criticism of the traditional political parties and the judiciary. And it approved of the president's April 1992 self-coup ostensibly to preserve the counterinsurgency policy and reform the judicial system. The high price paid for co-optation, therefore, has been unwarranted, and its consequences—unease within the armed forces—could provide the president with more than one bad surprise in the future.

Nearly all of the other variables I have used to measure the power of the military are at very low levels today; they indicate very weak armed forces relative to the state and Peruvian society as a whole. But all of this can be attributed to the economic crisis. Military acquisitions are very limited. The income of the military remains incredibly low. At the high end of the scale, a division general receives a monthly salary of 589.52 soles (US$283.42) and at the low end, a second lieutenant receives 442.59 soles (US$212.78). The salaries of all other ranks are between these levels.[28] Military pressure for the approval of their budget is almost nonexistent. The privileges of the higher ranks still exist, but except for cars, they do not carry the value they did in the past. They have chauffeurs and stewards but would prefer a better salary. If an officer chooses not to take a chauffeur and steward, he or she will receive their salaries instead, which amounts to 110 soles each (US$56.12). It is important to recognize that Lima is as expensive a place to live as Washington, DC, and many areas of Peru, such as cities located in jungle regions, can be even more expensive. The hospitals used by the military remain free but lack medicines, and patients must pay full price for those that they buy. The schools for their children are poor, and so on.

Yet, it is important to note that even if the armed forces were well paid and even if an important arms acquisition program existed, the military's power would not be enhanced. These variables are not incompatible with a system of co-optation. In fact, if the economy improves, salaries and arms supplies will likely increase—promoting further co-optation, rather than producing an increase in the autonomy of the military. In a system of co-optation, what is important is who appoints the commander general, who decides the promotions, and who determines who gets which position. Except for the prerogative of protecting their members from civilian investigation and courts in cases of human rights violations and corruption, other variables are secondary.

To date, the armed forces have been successful in protecting their cadres from Congress and civilian judicial investigations. Not only does the military retain the power to block them, but the president is not terribly interested in investigating human rights abuses, although he repeatedly tells the media that he is. More problematic still is that the institutionalist officers have used these issues—human rights violations and corruption—as a tool to discredit the co-opted high command of the armed forces.

In the army, through General Robles, the institutionalists have accused General Hermoza of human rights violations, and they have accused the pro-Fujimori commander general of the navy, Admiral Arnaiz, of corruption. President Fujimori has defended both commanders. In the instance of Robles' accusations against Hermoza and others, the commander general of the army himself brought the case to the military tribunal so as to prevent the civilian courts and Congress from investigating. The Fujimori government argued that Congress could not investigate the case because it would duplicate the efforts of the military judge. The Peruvian constitution guarantees the exclusivity of jurisdiction in the administration of justice. This point is understood by the government to mean that nobody, not even Congress, can intervene in a case a military judge is preparing. The congressional opposition maintains that the constitution allows Congress to create a committee to investigate any issue. A committee was created to investigate the charges of human rights violations made by General Robles, but the military, with the consent of the government, refused to testify when it was called to appear by the panel.

The case of La Cantuta is a clear example. A group of journalists were informed by an anonymous dissident within the army of the site where the missing students of La Cantuta were buried. They found bones at the site and presented the evidence to a civilian attorney. The government claimed that the map used to discover the graves was part of Shining Path strategy to discredit the army, that the journalists were being used by the subversives. Moreover, the government rejected the assistance of anthropologists from Amnesty International who offered to lend their expertise in the identification of the bones. Facing great pressure and in some cases being removed from their jobs, the civilian attorneys on the case continued their work and discovered that a set of keys found in the graves opened the door to the home of one of the missing La Cantuta students and his locker at the university. The civilian court has begun prosecuting the military officers accused by General Robles of having participated in the killings, and there is a jurisdictional dispute between the civil and military courts that the Supreme Court must resolve.

The La Cantuta case will be a test of the independence and autonomy of the newly restructured judiciary—a system restructured on the orders of the president. If the Supreme Court grants jurisdiction to the civilian court, the military will be forced to choose between cooperating and turning to open insubordination against the new constitution. If the Supreme Court denies civilian jurisdiction, it will become obvious that the military court has no intention of reaching a verdict, and the independence of the judiciary will be thrown into doubt.[29]

These are not the only military-related cases that have not been investigated by the Fujimori government. Corruption due to narcotics trafficking is also a serious problem within the armed forces. This is not to argue that the army as an institution has ties to narcotraffickers, but many low- and middle-ranking officers, and some of high rank as well, have been corrupted in the coca-producing areas. Although the problem has long been evident, there have not been many investigations in recent years.

The power of the armed forces at the regional and local levels, a consequence of the struggle against the insurgency, has increased significantly. The Fujimori government has given the armed forces what they have been seeking for years: control over all state institutions (including the civilian agencies) in the emergency zones.[30] As the armed forces have lost institutional power at the national level, their strength and operational capability at the regional and local levels has increased.

In summary, over the last two and a half decades, the Peruvian military's power within the state and society has been declining at the national level and increasing at the regional and local levels (see Figure 8.2). During the military government, as one would expect, the armed forces dominated the state and most of civil society. Belaúnde's government produced a reduction of power—not in accord with the new democratic system, but rather in an incoherent fashion. The armed forces lost power where they should have maintained it—in the area of national defense—and garnered power were they should not have—in the protection from prosecution of officers who committed excesses in the counterinsurgency war. Belaúnde thus chose not to intervene in the internal affairs of the armed forces so as not to provoke military instability. At the same time, he failed to support the armed forces in the area of professional effectiveness.

Alan García, on the other hand, chose to intervene in internal military affairs with the intention of controlling the armed forces. But, like Belaúnde, he did not support the maintenance and improvement of their professional capabilities. Today, under the Fujimori government, the policy of intervention in the internal affairs of the armed forces has been deepened. The intention is not only to

Figure 8.2 Variables of Military Power Under Successive Peruvian Governments

	Military 1968–1980	**Belaúnde 1980–1985**	**García 1985–1990**	**Fujimori 1990–**
1. Who decides the organization of the national defense system?	Military	Military	Civilian	Civilian
2. Does the national defense system work?	Yes	No	No	Yes
3. Who appoints the high command and decides promotions and postings?	Military	Military	Military (cooptation by civilian government)	Civilian (cooptation by civilian government)
4. Who decides who the enemy is?	Military	Military	Civilian	Civilian
5. Power and scope of intelligence services	Great power; monitors all society	Almost no power; does not include society	Relative power; monitors subversives & military	Great power; watches all society
6. Pressure capacity for approval of budget and acquisitions program	Yes	Yes	No	No
7. Privileges	Yes	Yes	Yes; status incongruous	Yes; status incongruous
8. Income	High	Medium	Very low	Low
9. Protection from civil prosecution for human rights violations and corruption	Yes	Yes	Yes	Yes
10. Power at local or regional level	Total in the entire country	Partial, and only in Ayacucho	Partial, in one third of country	Total, in one third of country

control the military, but also, as the *autogolpe* and the close watch over civil society demonstrates, to use it as a political base for the government. Fujimori has supported the armed forces by increasing their operational capability and professional effectiveness in the war against the insurgents. He has also, however, used a co-optation policy that has divided the armed forces and generated great unease within the institution that could backfire in the future.

French emperor Napoleon once stated, "You can do anything with bayonets, except sit on them." Fujimori has sat on his bayonet, which could produce a number of outcomes. Fujimori could decide to terminate the co-optation of the high command, he could risk facing uprisings within the army against the high command, or both may occur. Evidence of a possible move toward the first scenario is already beginning to appear. According to some sources within the army, Fujimori was considering removing General Hermoza, given the disrepute into which he has fallen due to the La Cantuta case. Hermoza, however, refused to be removed, and Fujimori was forced to ratify him as army commander general until the end of his government. Such a move does not mean that the army is co-opting the president because, as noted above, the army as an institution has no political power. It does mean, however, that the little *cupola,* or small group of generals who now hold power within the army as a result of Fujimori's co-optation policy, are using that power against even his own wishes. They are not co-opting the civilian government as they have no political project of their own. They will not interfere with the Fujimori government's policies, except as they affect their own power—their removal from their current positions or the weakening of their control over the army.

These events could lead to the second scenario: an uprising in the army against its commander general or a continuation of the leaks by dissident army groups of information implicating General Hermoza in human rights violations, or better yet, in narcotics trafficking. A third possible scenario is for the Supreme Court to decide to grant the civilian court jurisdiction to prosecute those officers involved in the La Cantuta killings. If this were to occur, responsibility for the murders could reach all the way up to the army commander general, compelling him to resign. Such a result could have a negative political impact on Fujimori, as he has supported General Hermoza on many occasions, to the extent that it could jeopardize his chances for reelection in 1995.[31]

However, there are potential positive consequences associated with Fujimori's control over the armed forces. The military is becoming accustomed to being under civilian control, and new presidential powers have been introduced into the new Peruvian constitution. In the future, under less authoritarian presidents, these changes could be useful tools in the hands of an elected leader. While such tools may well tempt future governments to use the military as Fujimori is doing today, they could also help both prevent military coups and definitively bring the armed forces under civilian control.

Notes

1. Comando Conjunto de la Fuerza Armada; *Decreto supremo Nº 001–75/ CCFA lineamientos básicos de la doctrina de defensa nacional,* Lima, June 1975.

2. Decreto Ley 22653, in Presidencia de la República, Secretaría de Defensa Nacional; *Compendio de normas legales de la defensa nacional,* Lima, 1985.

3. This is the doctrine of the Center of Advanced Military Studies (CAEM), *TE-100 Planteamientos doctrinarios y metodológicos de la defensa nacional,* Lima, 1982.

4. This was one of the reasons why the Belaúnde government refused to cooperate with the military on national defense issues. For a discussion of this problem, see Enrique Obando, "Combined threats and how to confront them: Peru, social violence, subversion, drug traffic, and the destruction of the environment," in Louis Goodman, Johanna Mendelson, and Juan Rial, eds., *Civil Military Relations toward the Year 2000* (Washington, DC, The American University, forthcoming).

5. Discussion of the ideological differences among the armed forces during the Velasco regime can be found in Henry Pease, *El ocaso de la oligarquía: Lucha política en la escena oficial, 1968–1975* (Lima, El Cid Editor, 1979); Francisco Moncloa, *Que pasó?: 1968–1976* (Lima, Editorial Horizonte, 1977); Hector Bejar, *La revolución en la trampa* (Lima, Ediciones Socialismo y Participación, 1976); and Guillermo Thorndike, *No, mi general* (Lima, Moscazul, 1976).

6. For details on the acquisitions of the Peruvian armed forces between 1968 and 1980, see *SIPRI Yearbooks, World Armaments and Disarmament* for 1975–1984 (London, Taylor and Francis) and Enrique Obando, *Adquisición de armamentos y dependencia en América del Sur* (Lima, CEPEI, 1990, pp. 60–66).

7. In January 1982, a year and a half after the military left power, a second lieutenant earned the monthly equivalent of $556.63. In July 1993, a second lieutenant earned the equivalent of $212.93 (in constant dollars based on December 1992).

8. Enrique Obando, "Combined threats and how to confront them," op. cit.

9. *Constitución política del Perú,* promulgated 12 July 1979, Article 281, in Edición Especial, Cámara de Diputados, April 1988.

10. A historical account of one of these cases of deportation is provided in Alfonso Baella Tuesta, *El miserable* (Lima, Editorial Andina, 1978).

11. See Rita Tullberg, "Deuda relacionada con lo militar en América Latina," in Augusto Varas, *Paz, desarme y desarrollo en América Latina* (Buenos Aires, Grupo Editor Latinoamericano SRL, 1987, p. 175). For information on the acquisitions of the Belaúnde government, see *SIPRI Yearbooks* for 1981–1987 (London, Taylor and Francis).

12. In 1983, Peru's GNP fell 11.7 percent. Inflation in 1984 was 127 percent.

13. In 1984, the departments of Ayacucho, Apurimac, Huancavelica, Huánuco, and a province of the department of San Martín as well as the capital city of Lima were officially in a state of emergency. In 1989, these areas plus the departments of Junín, Cerro de Pasco, Ucayali, the whole of the department of San Martín, the whole of the Department of Lima, and the Ucayali Province of the Department of Loreto were officially in a state of emergency.

14. Decreto Legislativo 435, "Modifican, sustituyen y adicionan varios artículos al Decreto Ley 22653—Ley del Sistema de Defensa Nacional," in *El Peruano,* Sunday, 27 September 1987, pp. 57862–57863.

15. Hugo Van Hemelrijck (Peruvian army major), *La realidad económica actual en la vida del oficial,* thesis presented to the II Course of Technical Administrative General Staff, Escuela Superior de Guerra, Lima, 1990. This study analyzes the income reduction of the members of the armed forces between 1987 and 1990. The following chart clearly demonstrates this phenomenon.

Reduction of the Real Income of Officers and NCOs of the Peruvian Army Between January 1988 and September 1990

	Jan. 1988	Sept. 1990
General of Division	100	21.29
Lieutenant Colonel	100	21.67
Second Lieutenant	100	26.30
Chief Superior Technician	100	20.71
Technician Third Class	100	22.35
NCO Third Class	100	24.73

Source: Van Hemelrijck, p. 45

Some of the descriptions contained in the thesis are symptomatic of the state of the armed forces, such as: "Unfortunately, our institution does not have as one of its policies the assurance of the well-being of its personnel. This is only something that is talked about but never executed" (p. 27). Or: "In an interview with the general inspectorate of the army it was discovered that as a consequence of the present economic situation the following problems and offenses were commited by military personnel:

- Assault and theft of vehicles
- Requests for retirement from military personnel who head the honor charts for promotions
- Offenses due to lack of disposition to work
- Misappropriation of funds
- Smuggling
- Drug trafficking
- Lower ranks' loss of respect for senior officers
- Theft from military institutions" (p. 26)

Even more interesting are the recommendations made in the thesis: "To provide a partial solution to the existing problems, my recommendations are the following:

- That the command appraise the true value of its military personnel
- That the command demand that the government respect the levels that it determines are appropriate for its personnel" (p. 57).

To appreciate the fall in military income since 1981, one can consider the change in income of a second lieutenant:

	Gross Income	Constant Dollars (Dec. 1992)	Month's US CPI*	Month's Exchange Rate
January 1981	95,504	435.40	80.74	351.00
July 1981	164,146	518.90	85.02	428.00
January 1982	199,888	556.63	84.54	530.00
July 1982	229,005	467.61	90.52	699.00
January 1983	318,340	432.91	90.83	1,046.00
July 1983	598,674	491.19	92.74	1,698.00
January 1988	10,850	145.11	107.34	90.00
January 1989	126,806	75.87	112.29	1,923.00
January 1990	2,722,625	232.06	115.80	13,090.00
July 1993	442.59	212.93	131.00	2.05

Source: Author's computations.
*Consumer Price Index

16. Between January and December 1989, the task force of the National Human Rights Coordination Group, working to prevent political assassination and disappearances in Peru, registered some 441 cases of missing persons, of which only 135 were settled. Amnesty International reported that in 1987, almost half of the missing persons were turned over to the police by the armed forces following interrogation. This high proportion of "reappearances" did not continue in 1988, when only about one-fourth of the reported cases of missing persons was resolved by the armed forces freeing the detainees or turning them over to the police. See Instituto de Defensa Legal, *Perú 1989, en la espiral de la violencia* (Lima, IDL, 1990, p. 119).

17. The general of a division receives 150 gallons; a brigadier general, 100 gallons; a full colonel, 80 gallons; a lieutenant colonel, 60 gallons; and a major, 40 gallons. Ranks below major do not receive gasoline.

18. I came across direct evidence of the coup plans in 1989 as a staff member of the National Secretariat of Defense. Since then, the coup plans have been leaked to the press, appearing in the magazine *Oiga*, no. V 647, 12 July 1993, and 648, 19 July 1993.

19. By 1989, the following departments were declared states of emergency, meaning that they all were led by political-military chiefs: Ayacucho, Apurimac, Huancavelica, Junín, Cerro de Pasco, Huánuco, Lima, San Martín, Ucayali, and the Ucayali Province of the Department of Loreto.

20. Law No. 24150 gave the armed forces in emergency zones command of the police only, not the civilian agencies of the state.

21. In 1987, General Howard Rodríguez, the political-military chief of Ayacucho, sent a letter to his superiors stating that if he did not receive more economic support from the government he would be compelled to halt counterinsurgency operations due to lack of resources. On 21 June 1988, General Enrique López Albujar, then minister of defense, sent a letter

to Cesar López Freyre, the minister of economy, asking for a defense budget increase of 18,056,517,000 intis to meet "the minimal and indispensable needs. . . . [This] makes clear that if these requirements are not met in a timely fashion, the operations of the armed forces will be seriously affected, hindering the fulfillment of its mission as a component of national defense." See Ministerio de Defensa, Oficio no. 1142 MD/OGA-2b.

22. This was what a large number of officers thought about García's last minister of defense, minister of interior, three of the five chiefs of the National Secretariat of Defense, and the last commander-in-chief of the air force.

23. This strategy is detailed in Enrique Obando, "La seguridad interna en la actual coyuntura," in Eduardo Ferrero, ed., *Proceso de retorno a la institucionalidad democrática en el Perú* (Lima, CEPEI, 1992).

24. A good summary of the legislative decrees of November 1991 is in Ana María Vidal, *Los decretos de la guerra* (Lima, IDS, 1993).

25. See *El Peruano,* 12 November 1991, no. 4130, pp. 101700–101708.

26. This was exactly what happened on 21–22 April 1993, when the commander general of the army, General Nicolás Hermoza, sent tanks into the streets of Lima in a successful attempt to press Congress not to investigate alleged human rights violations at La Cantuta University, where several students and a professor had disappeared.

27. On 21 February 1994, responding to growing domestic and international pressure for a resolution of the case, a military court sentenced nine army officers and enlisted men to military prison for the murders at La Cantuta University. A secret military court tried the case after legislation was pushed through the Congress, in a move that produced substantial criticism of the government and eroded Fujimori's popularity, to ensure that the case would be removed from civilian jurisdiction by a decision of the Supreme Court. To many political observers, Fujimori's handling of the case confirmed his dependence on the military.

28. The monthly income of the military as of July 1993 was as follows:

	Gross Income (Nuevos Soles)	Benefits (Nuevos Soles)	Total	Equivalent in US$(2.08 Nuevos Soles/US$)
General of Division	285.53	304.00	589.53	283.42
Brigadier General	285.00	292.00	577.00	227.40
Colonel	274.75	274.00	548.75	263.82
Lieutenant Colonel	263.03	262.00	525.03	252.41
Major	235.03	262.00	497.03	238.95
Captain	232.08	250.00	482.08	231.76
Lieutenant	220.51	244.00	464.51	223.32
Second Lieutenant	212.59	230.00	442.59	212.78

Source: Author's computations.

29. See note 27 above.

30. See *El Peruano,* 12 November 1991, no. 4130, pp. 101699–101700; Legislative Decree no. 749.

31. See note 27 above.

9

Commentary

Gustavo Gorriti

Carlos Iván Degregori's chapter is an important work. I would like to make just two brief observations about it. The first involves Degregori's use of the concept of "fleeing forward" (*fuga hacia adelante*)—whereby fear of defeat and weak morale induce insurgents to intensify their operations in an effort to deliver a mortal blow, rather than to retreat—which he does with exacting care in examining Shining Path. This image, this metaphor used to explain the various strategic and even tactical decisions of Shining Path, has appeared at various times in the development of his analysis of the insurgency.

This is a point with which I disagree. I do not see a presumption of a high level of risk and daring by Shining Path leadership in some of their bold decisions, such as, for example, in 1983 and 1984, when instead of fleeing from the emergency zone of Ayacucho, the group turned as aggressive as possible to produce openings in other zones and regions within which they were organizing. I do not view such a move as a *fuga hacia adelante.* I do not view it as the equivalent of the charge of the light brigade. Rather, it was simply a bold move that entailed a high level of risk and that ultimately ended favorably for Shining Path and allowed it to achieve important advances in a relatively short time.

I believe the approach Shining Path began to use, which is part of what Degregori describes as the *fuga hacia adelante,* was frequently an attempt to create a reality preemptively by merely announcing that such a reality existed. Shining Path became, paradoxically, a nominalist movement. Thus, it declared a strategic equilibrium when it had not achieved it with the hope that this would, first, create pressure

Gustavo Gorriti is a senior research associate at the North-South Center.

within the organization to advance toward that goal, and second, create a pervasive sense of impending success among those who were the main object of the war—the Peruvian population.

In many cases, Shining Path reached the desired equilibria, but in other cases its goals were only partly accomplished, and, assuming they had been achieved, the insurgents advanced to the next step. The guerrilla organization was establishing bases of some precariousness. Thus, by the time it had to confront the great trauma—the capture of Guzmán—many of these partial disequilibria collapsed and multiplied the traumatic effect of the fall of its leader, already quite large. The capture of Guzmán is the nightmare scenario for Shining Path; to use a metaphor I prefer, the intelligence police plucked the queen bee from the center of the honeycomb.

My second point, or cautious observation, concerns the forecasts of "futurology"—predictions about what is going to happen in the future to Shining Path. Prior to 1990, but especially since then, I promised myself that I would no longer become involved in making predictions as analysis of the present was difficult enough. The consistent magical realism that characterizes politics in Peru may prove the point: a president elected by the left and evangelists is now applauded, after a little more than two years, to the point of ecstasy by the ultraviolent right and Opus Dei.

Nevertheless, partially breaking my vow, I would say that we can consider possible future scenarios. One that is within the realm of possibilty is that, given the consistent demolition of institutions from top to bottom, from the roots to the branches, that has occurred during this regime, Shining Path should remain a significant concern. Given that it has maintained a measure of organizational integrity, if the political polarization that exists in the legal realm continues, if at some point one of the regime's solutions is to increase intimidation and repression, and if Shining Path can resolve the dilemma of what to do about the capture of Guzmán, the insurgency cannot be underestimated as a central danger for Peru in the future.

I believe Shining Path should be a central element in the consideration of dangerous potential scenarios for Peru, especially given the difficult foreseeable circumstances the country will have to confront when Fujimori leaves or is forced to leave. When the transition—or a return to democratic legality—comes, when the desire to reestablish normality emerges, there will be periods of great disequilibrium during which it will be difficult to find the common features among diverse parts, between the macrodecisions and the execution of the microaspects. Peruvians therefore have to consider the danger of Shining Path in these scenarios of the future. As long as the situation remains as it is at present, the danger will remain substantial.

Enrique Obando's chapter is a valuable and interesting approach as well, because he attempts systematically to determine the permanent factors to be considered in an analysis of the evolution of Peruvian civil-military relations over the course of a specific period—a decisive period in the history of Peru. Nevertheless, I will make some methodological and factual observations concerning his work.

First, I believe it is important to draw a distinction between the first and second phases of the military government (1968–1980) in determining relative power and the application of that power by the army in power. I believe there is a difference to be considered between the advance of the Velasco period's tone of clearly defined objectives and the retreat evident during the Morales Bermúdez period. In the latter, the retreat became such that there was no objective other than a successful withdrawal at relatively low cost, during which there was a gradual abandonment of political and even doctrinal objectives. These changes began to create what later became an increasingly important characteristic of the army—the internecine disputes. The disputes gave rise to a revolt that, among other things, provoked the departure of army Commander General Maldonado. Additionally, they led to the formation of various groups within the army that later would play a fairly important role in the establishment of counterinsurgency methodologies, which eventually became contradictory or highly distinct.

One should also note that during the Morales Bermúdez era the national intelligence service began to be deactivated. With the expectation of returning to the barracks, the national intelligence service, which is at the disposal of the president of Peru, was an empty shell when it was relinquished by the military. Deactivation lasted two or three years, and the nature of the process became evident with the management of information and intelligence by the Morales Bermúdez government on the preparation of the Shining Path insurrection: it was a total failure—absolutely deficient. As such, the transition occurred with the delivery of a Greek gift to Belaúnde.

A second observation regarding Obando's work is that corruption also emerged to a considerable degree during the government of Morales Bermúdez. Perhaps the most notorious case involved the influence Carlos Langberg developed over Minister of the Interior General Fernando Velit and Vice-Minister General Jorge Lassús during the last part of the government—to some degree foreshadowing what is occurring today.

10

Commentary

Marcial Rubio

Enrique Obando makes an effort to develop variables to be used in measuring the Peruvian military's political power, and he cleverly demonstrates how this power has diminished over the 1980s and 1990s. As measured by these important variables, Obando's analysis is correct.

However, three additional questions should be asked. First, are all of the ten variables equivalent in determining the power of the military, or should some of them be weighted more than others? For example, the procedure for appointing high commanders of the armed forces appears highly political, and, indeed, it is. But most of the military probably sees the procedure in relation to their career paths and to their chances of being promoted to the general command, as opposed to their ability to influence political power. I believe poor management by the current commanders, not the way they are appointed, does more to create dissension within the armed forces. If this is true, then the weight that the politicization of appointments is given among the other variables, such as, for example, the scope of action of the intelligence services, should be reduced.

Second, are all of the variables truly related to *political* power, or are some more bureaucratic than political? For example, I would argue that this is the case with the first and second variables, which relate to the organization and function of the defense system, and to a certain extent, the sixth and seventh variables, which pertain to military budgets and privileges. In view of the country's economic difficulties, these variables are mainly, although not exclusively, bureaucratic.

Marcial Rubio is president of the Center for Development Studies and Promotion (DESCO).

Third, is the Peruvian political process one in which the military's share of power has shifted into the hands of the president? Or, alternatively, is there a complex national and international process in which we can find different forms of acquisition, loss, and transference of power? For example, how much power has evaporated out of the hands of the military of Peru (and Latin American militaries generally) since the United States made it plainly clear that it would oppose any coup? Today, a Latin American president can be relatively secure that a coup is among the least likely of the potential weapons to be used by the military in political conflicts. A president can also be assured of strong support for the government from democratically elected presidents. It is almost certain that a de facto regime will not receive international recognition and will be isolated. This new situation is thus a variable that must be taken into account in exclusively political terms to assess the military's political power.

In this regard, one must also ask how much power devolved to the government and civil society because the Peruvian armed forces could neither develop their prospective institutional design nor their own economic and technological predominance within the country. In the modern era, institutional presence in the fields of technology, communications, and production is a source of power. The Peruvian armed forces recognized this during the 1970s. However, over the years they lost their momentum in these areas, and their commanders were unable to develop a forward-looking conception of their institution. In a way, the armed forces continued to be as they always were during the last two decades. Changes inside and outside the country were not evaluated as evidence of the need for institutional change.

Finally, I think the military still exercises considerable political power, but it is exercised in a more sophisticated way. This is not a result of military decisionmaking, but rather as a consequence of important social changes. First, power is more diffuse. The traditional oligarchy that once controlled the power of the state has been replaced by a more modern and, especially, a more complex social structure, which implies a dissemination of power within society. This change has affected not only the military, but other major institutions, such as the Catholic church and political parties, as well. Second, the evolution of the social classes has changed the focus of many problems and the political impact they produce. For example, acquiring physical security from Shining Path has been a major preoccupation of all Peruvians in recent years. Some paid for walls around their homes, other for alarms or private security services. What was the choice of the poor? In many cases, they reluctantly accepted the protection of the armed forces and the police. This was, of course, accompanied by a variety of abuses, but ultimately it was apparently decided that it is better to sacrifice some human rights rather than life itself. (It should be remembered that neither the military nor Shining Path guarantees the human rights of the average Peruvian.) It may be that military power has benefited from this "unjust" choice.

Aside from the general variables that can be used to measure the military's political power, today's armed forces exert political influence in other ways. The military holds a monopoly on ideas for dealing with insurgency. Fujimori has borrowed those ideas and used them for his global counterinsurgency strategy. For the first time in seven years, the government has accepted the dominant political role of the politico-military commands of the emergency zones. Civilians must develop their knowledge of military theory so as to be in a better position to discuss military matters and therefore influence the thinking of the armed forces.

Moreover, the armed forces are the only institution capable of ensuring public order in Peru, especially when the president does not have a political party that is organized to support the governance of the country. I believe Fujimori's lack of a political party has been and still is one of the greatest sources of military strength since 1990.

11

Commentary

David Scott Palmer

There are any number of questions and concerns we can raise on the basis of the provocative work of Carlos Iván Degregori and Enrique Obando, and I can only begin to scratch the surface. Two specific questions arise from each of the two analyses, which may lead us to additional perspectives, insights, or alternative formulations and patterns.

The first two points concern the subject of Obando's paper, which addresses the power of the military over Peruvian society and the balance of civil-military relations. My first question relates to the literature on military professionalization of the 1960s and 1970s, when many, myself included, wrote extensively on the dramatic increase in the professionalization of Latin America military establishments. Peru was said to have experienced one of the foremost processes of professionalization. Yet, Obando suggests that a quite different dynamic has occurred within the Peruvian military in its relationship with other sectors of society over the past fifteen years.

Given this literature, given our analysis of the increased professionalization of the Peruvian military from the 1950s onward, and given the well-founded research on which it was based, how can we conclude that the military, as an institution, allows itself to be subject to Vladimiro Montesinos, a cashiered military officer operating out of the presidency? Is this not a sign of weakness rather than strength? Does this not demonstrate the sharp divisions and demoralization that have developed within the military institution? Can this not explain at least part of the extraordinary level of human rights violations

---

David Scott Palmer is professor of international relations and political science at Boston University.

that have been occurring in recent years? Can these violations be a function of the eroding sense of mission, of the historic responsibility of the institution, or of professional pride that characterized the Peruvian military in the 1960s and 1970s?

The second question that arises from Obando's work is a key issue: what keeps the Peruvian military from becoming more involved in the counterinsurgency strategy, from providing both economic support and military protection? The military's involvement in dealing with the Shining Path insurgency has tended to be characterized as short-term oriented, as personalistic, and as occasional successes mixed with fairly dramatic failures. Does the failure to become more involved relate to factors beyond the scope of Enrique Obando's ten-variable framework? Does it relate to the long-term Soviet training and provision of equipment? Does it relate to the Ecuadoran incursion of 1981 and the need of the Peruvian military to respond to that event? Or is it a part of civilian resistance to the institutionalization of twelve years of military rule? To what degree does it relate to policies of the military's internal rotation, assignment, and promotion procedures?

Do not the human rights violations emanating from the military partly reflect not only the declining sense of mission and institutional pride, but also these internal rotation procedures? The traditional policy of not allowing a person to serve in the locality of his or her origin, the historic ethnic cleavage of the wider society, and the dramatic difference between the military's historic mission and the goals of ethnic minorities in the country also appear to have a part in explaining human rights abuses. In short, one might at least consider adding some additional factors or variables to explain military political power, such as foreign military training, internal organization, and procedures for promotion and displacement.

It has been occasionally noted that human rights abuses have declined sharply in recent years precisely when the Peruvian government was seeking military assistance from the United States to pursue the counterinsurgency program under the rubric of the drug war. The decline in abuse led to some modest appropriations, which were used over a period of several months. Those several months coincided with a 60 to 80 percent reduction in the level of human rights violations, an unprecedented achievement that has yet to be equaled. So there is apparently a correlation between external military assistance and human rights violations, depending on who is providing the military assistance. This is another issue that deserves consideration when assessing the power of the military.

Two questions arise from Degregori's intriguing work as well. The first is of general interest: can Shining Path overcome the capture of Abimael Guzmán and continue its long-term strategy for taking power? My view has been that because of Guzmán's association with Shining Path since its founding, he and his organization would follow the course of most personalist-directed organizations in Latin America history. That is, it would fade as the response to the individual faded.

As Degregori explores in his work, preliminary indications suggest that Shining Path has been able, perhaps because it has been working to take advantage of the miserable economic and political situation for such a long time, to generate sufficient new forces. Shining Path has been able to place those new individuals into the key positions that have been vacated by the cadres captured during the period of September to November 1992. The organization seems to be regenerating itself. It is regenerating itself, at least in the short term, at a sharply reduced level of activity and violence. There was about a 30 percent decline in the number of deaths in the six months since Guzmán's capture, as compared to the six months prior to Guzmán's capture, and about a 10 percent decline in incidents. But similar patterns have been witnessed in the past; we have seen ebbs and flows before.

I believe the operative question is the qualitative question. How Shining Path regenerates itself is a quantitative question; the qualitative one is how it changes in the process. In other words, will it maintain the same orthodox, hard-line approach in developing a long-term strategy for taking power? Over the course of Shining Path's renovation, can we speak of the possibility of a new cadre, the so-called dissident line within the party, moving into a position of greater prominence? This new cadre would entail the rise of the moderate elements of the party and abandonment of the old strategy of imposing an ideologically orthodox model on local populations in favor of a more responsive approach to dealing with the problems of the communities. This is an open question; I do not know that we have the answer yet, but examining the individuals who replace the captured leaders may provide some insight into any potential qualitative changes in Shining Path as a revolutionary, terrorist organization.

As a final question, how do the continuing political and economic crises affect Shining Path's long-term capacity for eventual success? There is no question that the *autogolpe* of 5 April 1992 delayed a return to economic growth by at least a year. The process of reinsertion into the international community was almost in place when the *autogolpe* occurred. So it appears there was a dramatic short-term economic cost associated with the *autogolpe.* That growth process is going forward, but it appears that a year and a half has been lost.

The double political failure of the Belaúnde and especially the García governments led to an alternative approach, a so-called nonparty, nonpolitical approach that is receiving greater popular support, although experiencing less political institutionalization. So far, this alternative approach seems to have reversed the negative cycle of cumulative causation, as Max Weber would say, to a positive cycle of cumulative causation.

Finally, we have the perverse, but perhaps ultimately positive effect of local political and economic organization, the so-called informalization of economics and politics, as a response to the failure of the system at the center to respond to the needs of the larger population. This informalization at the grassroots level seems simply to be local citizens making efforts to solve their own problems in their own ways. Could this be the beginning of a long-term reversal of the process of top-down solutions, or the beginning of the resolution of problems from the bottom-up? If it is, then the dynamic that led to Shining Path and the organization itself may well be coming to an end.

PART 3

Economic Growth and —or Versus?— Redistribution

12

Macroeconomic Stability and the Prospects for Growth, 1990–1993

Julio Velarde

In 1990, Peruvians elected a new president, Alberto Fujimori. The new leader, an outsider to the Peruvian establishment, would apply one of the harshest economic stabilization programs ever and launch an ambitious set of structural reforms.

The severity of the measures was a response to the enormous disequilibria produced by the previous government, which was perhaps the most extreme example of populism in Latin America. The reforms, almost unthinkable in the past, were also a response to the overextended controls and government intervention that had characterized the García regime (1985–1990). Moreover, the election campaign of the runner-up candidate, who focused on the need for economic shock therapy, contributed to the change in the general popular perception in favor of a more market-oriented economy and against the failed state-as-benefactor policies of the past.

At present, the results of the stabilization efforts have not been as spectacular as expected, but there is a sense that the economy is on the right track. Mistakes have been made during the implementation of the program. If these errors are corrected promptly, the prospects for initiating sustained growth are good. Political instability, however, may delay this process.

Background to the Fujimori Economic Program: Hyperinflation

In July 1985, thirty-five-year-old Alan García became president of Peru. The occasion marked the first time the sixty-year-old center-left

Julio Velarde is professor of economics at the University of the Pacific.

APRA (American Popular Revolutionary Alliance) party attained power. García began his presidency with the highest level of presidential popularity witnessed in recent years. Unfortunately, the optimistic expectations of the Peruvian population were soon reversed. During the APRA government, the country not only experienced the longest and most intense inflation in Peruvian history, but also the largest drop ever in the level of economic activity.

In contrast to most hyperinflationary periods historically, the Peruvian megainflation was induced by an expansionary policy within a framework of generalized price controls. With the ostensible purpose of controlling inflation, fuel, utility, and foodstuff prices were either frozen or allowed to increase at rates substantially lower than the inflation rate. Since taxes were included in the price of fuel and since public utilities were state owned, a growing fiscal deficit emerged.

With the same anti-inflation purpose in mind, the exchange rate was overvalued. Furthermore, a multiple exchange rate system was established, as a result of which the average rate of imports grew at a much slower pace than the average rate of exports. This growing gap between the buying and selling rates was financed by the Central Bank. At the same time, the Central Bank allocated heavily subsidized loans to the development banks, to meet the proclaimed objective of reducing financing costs.

The fiscal and quasi-fiscal deficit financed by the Central Bank gave rise to a continuously increasing expansion of the monetary base, fueling inflationary pressures. The increase in the money supply led to severe distortions in relative prices. Bottlenecks emerged, and pressure for price adjustments, which usually were too little and too late, were implemented in a disorderly fashion. The price controls that were supposed to stop inflation were precisely the key factors behind its emergence. The economic situation became unsustainable, exploding in September 1988, when the monthly inflation rate reached 114 percent. From that point on, the rate of inflation remained above 30 percent per month.

During the first seven months of 1990, just before Fujimori took power, two distinct periods of economic policy can be distinguished. The first period was characterized by the typical expansionary policy that precedes a Peruvian presidential election, when virtually all international reserves are depleted. The second period, although partially forced by the previous overexpansion, had the main objective of avoiding an acceleration of inflation. A policy of crowding out was adopted, so as to impede a significant increase in the exchange rate and prices. As such, the costs of adjustment were transferred to the new government.

As a consequence, during this time the domestic currency was significantly appreciated, the correction of public sector prices was postponed, and arrears in fiscal payments mounted. By July 1990, due to marginal reserve requirements of 80 percent, real interest rates rose to extremely high levels, weakening the financial standing of private firms and of the banking system. Meanwhile, the official exchange rate and public sector prices were so low in real terms that the situation was almost impossible to maintain; prompt action was needed. Change implied a severe correction of inflation.

The García government, which had awakened enormous optimism among the Peruvian people, ended completely discredited. Its failure not only tarnished the popular perception of APRA, but of the whole political establishment. This was the context within which Fujimori, a new figure in political life, one who had no political party behind him and who would ultimately be supported in the campaign by García's political machinery, won the presidential election.

The Stabilization Program: The Economic Shock of 1990

Fujimori was elected on a platform that stressed gradualism in fighting inflation, as opposed to the shock treatment proposed by the opposing candidate, Mario Vargas Llosa. But reality proved stronger than election promises. The economic situation was such that not one economist put forward a policy of consistent gradualism.

At the end of July 1990, the economic picture was dismal (see Table 12.1). The Central Bank was devoid of foreign exchange. Importers were paid dollars only as export proceeds came in. Public sector wages were not being paid; there was simply no money left in the treasury. Utility and other state firms were about to collapse. Therefore, there was no alternative to the economic policies that were ultimately adopted. Even more important, the Peruvian population was expecting decisive measures to combat inflation.

Given the reality of the situation, the main objective of the Fujimori program of August 1990 was to stop hyperinflation. To achieve this end, fundamental disequilibria in the economy had to be addressed. The measures to be taken had to include balancing the budget, unifying exchange rates, and realigning public sector prices. And all of this was to be accomplished by shock treatment, so as to change radically inflationary expectations and to restore the credibility of economic policy.

The effort to achieve fiscal balance involved instituting emergency taxes, particularly a 10 percent surcharge on exports and a

Table 12.1 Peru: Main Macroeconomic Indicators in July 1990

Fiscal Deficit[a]	6.1%
Fiscal Revenues[a]	4.3%
Net International Reserves[b]	-105
Trade Balance[c]	112
Real Exchange Rate[d]	
Market	59.4
Exporter	46.1
Importer	48.5
Lending Nominal Interest Rate[e]	51.0%
Monthly Inflation Rate	63.2%
Real Wages[d]	
Minimum wage	51.0
Private sector average	34.9
Public sector average	42.7
Public Prices[d]	
Fuel	7.7
Electricity up to 100 Kw/h	7.4

Source: Central Reserve Bank of Peru.
Notes:
a. As a percent of GDP
b. Net International Central Bank Reserves (millions of US dollars)
c. Millions of US dollars
d. Index (July 1985 = 100)
e. In percent per month and on loans up to 360 days; includes tax on interest income

once-and-for-all tax of 1 percent on net worth. Tax and tariff exemptions were abolished, and public sector prices were increased significantly. With respect to exchange rate policy, an administered floating system was implemented. After numerous discussions, the alternative of a fixed exchange rate was also discarded. A significant exchange rate overshooting to assure credibility was also discarded due to the magnitude of the increase in public sector prices such a policy implied. Overshooting would have generated not only a bigger initial recession, but also an enormous expansion of the monetary base, which in turn did not guarantee effective control of inflation. The order of magnitude involved in the correction of public sector prices is exemplified by the thirty-fivefold increase in fuel prices. Similar adjustments were made for public utility prices.

The Fujimori government committed itself to refusing to finance the public sector through money creation. This policy has been maintained to date. Only through Central Bank purchases of foreign exchange would the economy remonetize. Simultaneously, interest rates on domestic accounts were liberalized. To help control inflation and promote competition, the government lifted most of the quantitative restrictions on trade. It also established a new tariff structure, lowering the thirty-two existing rates, which ranged from between 0 to 108 percent, to only three rates: 15, 25, and 50 percent.

A one-time bonus equivalent to the full July salary was provided to wage earners. Future wage adjustments for civil servants were frozen. The minimum wage was increased fourfold at the start, and again by an additional 56 percent in September.

When the shock ended, a process of deflation began. The price index fell by more than 30 percent between the second week of August and the third week of September, despite an exchange rate increase of 50 percent during the period. The turbulence created following the price liberalization made it difficult for economic agents to set equilibrium prices. At first, they established very high prices or refused to make all transactions, then they lowered their prices to sell off inventories.

At the same time, rapid remonetization was achieved. The monetary base increased by 396 percent over the two months following the initiation of the program, and the Central Bank accumulated reserves. Interest rates on loans fell from a monthly average of 60 percent in July to 10 percent in October.

The economic program was rather successful until November. The 25 percent decline in economic activity following the shock recovered completely, inflation fell rapidly, and the fiscal situation substantially improved. Fiscal revenues in real terms were 30 percent higher in November than they were the month before. However, some uncertainties emerged. Pressures from interest groups created instability in the new tariff structure, and, as a consequence, the flow of imports was lower than expected, which somewhat hampered the effort to control inflation. Moreover, after the initial remonetization, monetary and exchange rate policy was left unclearly defined.

In addition, the resumption of foreign debt payments to the World Bank and IDB created additional pressures on fiscal expenditures. In December, to preserve a balanced budget, the government decreed further increases in public sector prices. As a result, inflation jumped from 5.9 percent in November to 23.7 percent in December and was at 17.8 percent in January (see Table 12.2).

The rebirth of inflationary expectations forced the Central Bank to adopt a more restrictive monetary policy, so as to avoid a further jump in inflation. This move on the part of the monetary authorities

Table 12.2 Peru: The Hurtado Miller Period: August 1990–February 1991

	1990					1991	
Indicators	Aug	Sept	Oct	Nov	Dec	Jan	Feb
GDP[a]	100.0	90.9	93.9	101.0	108.7	103.5	99.0
Monthly Inflation Rate (in %)	397.0	13.8	9.6	5.9	23.7	17.8	9.4
Central Government Revenues[b]	44.4	86.05	86.32	112.5	97.68	108.1	75.1
Fuel[a]	100	88	80	76	100	85	77
Broad Money in Domestic Currency[c]	120.5	75.1	28.8	11.9	10.6	–8.1	14.8
Base Money[c]	179.9	81.6	33.6	6.3	2.3	1.2	6.9
Foreign Currency Deposits[d]	663	697	838	934	1,031	1,168	1,226
Net International Central Bank Reserves[e]	142	427	565	572	531	451	419
Real Exchange Rate[f]	100.0	121.2	115.9	105.6	105.7	92.0	86.6
Nominal Exchange Rate (S/US$)[g]	0.32	0.43	0.44	0.44	0.52	0.53	0.55

Source: Central Reserve Bank of Peru.
Notes:
a. Real Index (August 1990 = 100)
b. August 1990 millions of soles
c. End of period nominal figure (monthly percentage change)
d. In commercial banks (end of period; millions of US dollars)
e. End of period (millions of US dollars)
f. Index based on the period average banking rate (August 1990 = 100)
g. Period average banking rate

was successful in controlling inflation. However, the squeeze in liquidity produced an increase in interest rates and a fall in the level of economic activity. Interest rates on loans jumped from a monthly rate of 8.4 percent in November to 15.9 percent in January and to 18.7 percent in February. In December 1990, Gross National Product (GNP) was 3.6 percent higher than it was during the last month of the García regime. In January 1991, GNP fell 1.7 percent and an additional 1.8 percent in February.

The period from December 1990 to February 1991 was characterized by uncertainty among the agents of the economy. Leadership in economic policy was lacking due to the conflictive personality of the chair of the Board of Governors of the Central Bank, which obstructed the necessary coordination between the Central Bank and the Ministry of Economy. In addition, in January, the minister of industry presented an alternative economic program that questioned the implementation of the previous policies. These sorts of clashes, coupled with the economic situation described above, damaged the credibility of the Fujimori economic plan, and ultimately ended with the resignation of both the minister of economy and the minister of industry.

The Period of Structural Reforms

On 15 February 1991, Carlos Boloña became the new minister of economy. He launched a new economic package centered on strengthening structural reforms, particularly in the financial and trade sectors. A new tariff structure was put in place, which set only two rates: 15 percent, which covered 80 percent of imports, and 25 percent. The effective rate of protection fell from 44 percent to 24 percent for manufacturing and from 17.2 percent to 12.7 percent for the economy as a whole.

At the same time, the foreign exchange market was completely liberalized. Interest rate controls on foreign accounts were removed and capital was permitted to flow freely. Later, the labor market was partially liberalized by a decree providing flexibility in work contracts. Also, the market for agricultural land was deregulated. Customs was reformed and some port services were privatized. The government instituted new incentives for private investment, including allowing profit remittances for foreign investment. Finally, Fujimori's economic team began slowly to privatize public enterprises.

Although this set of structural changes improved expectations for the Peruvian economy, and was in accord with the original economic program, oversight of the earlier stabilization policies was set aside. The structural reforms were a necessary complement to stabilization efforts, but did not guarantee the success of the fight against inflation. Thus, by July, fiscal balance was not completely consolidated. The inflation rate was at a rather high level of more than 9 percent in June and July 1991. In addition, the overvaluation of the domestic currency increased, and monetary and fiscal policies exhibited a continued lack of coordination.

Since the Central Bank tended to overreact to exchange rate fluctuations, it was unable to meet monetary targets. In the end, it was controlling neither the exchange rate nor the monetary base. For example, in April and May, when the exchange rate was tending to increase, the Central Bank applied a restrictive monetary policy; in June, this approach was reversed. Also during this period, public sector pricing policy was erratic. Fuel prices increased 5 percent in April, were adjusted by 3 percent in May, by 24 percent in June, and then frozen in July.

In July, the Central Bank began to follow monetary targets more strictly. The monetary base began to grow at decreasing rates in the effort to control inflation. Moreover, the Fujimori government adopted a more orderly public sector pricing policy. Prices were adjusted at decreasing rates from August to November 1991. As a result, inflation declined gradually from 9.1 percent in July to 3.7 percent in December, the lowest rate since the program was initiated (see Table 12.3).

Interest rates, however, fell from a monthly rate of 19 percent in July to 9.9 percent in December. In general, economic expectations improved, not only due to the reassertion of economic leadership, but also because in September the government successfully completed an agreement with the International Monetary Fund (IMF).

Also during September, Peru signed a so-called shadow program for 1991–1992, cleared its arrears with the Inter-American Development Bank (IDB), and reached agreements with the World Bank and the Paris Club. The shadow program allowed Peru to accumulate drawing rights to be used to clear arrears with the IMF. In exchange, Peru had to reach a set of quarterly macroeconomic targets. A similar program was approved by the World Bank, under the condition that Peru implement structural reforms that were to a great extent already in place. Clearing arrears with the IDB was achieved through an immediate disbursement of $325 million (with an additional financing of $100 million from Japan to be disbursed afterward). Meanwhile, the government completed negotiations, in which it received generous terms, with the Paris Club.

The exchange rate, however, continued to be overvalued, to a great extent as a result of persistent capital inflows. Dollar deposits in Peruvian banks increased by more than $100 million per month. The inflow of capital financed a growing current account deficit that emerged in the third quarter of 1991 and allowed the Central Bank to accumulate $550 million in reserves during the second semester. In addition, fiscal reform was delayed.

The more sound economic policy applied until November; problems appeared the following month. One was that in Peru there is a seasonal increase in money demand during this month that is difficult to estimate. Another was that public sector prices were frozen, creating uncertainty about their future evolution. All of this made it more difficult for the Central Bank to define a path for monetary growth.

In general, the period between December 1991 and Fujimori's coup the following April was one of fiscal disorder. Not only were public sector prices frozen between November and April, but a set of tax measures implemented in March was partially rescinded after a few days. In clear conflict with Congress, the Fujimori government unilaterally decreed an increase in the value-added tax from 16 percent to 18 percent, eliminated exemptions from the tax on foodstuffs, and imposed a 20 percent tax on the interest rate on foreign exchange deposits.

Congress and the general population fiercely opposed these measures, forcing the government to withdraw some of them. The exemption from value-added tax on foodstuffs was restored and the tax on interest rates was eliminated. But these steps were too late. Inflationary expectations reemerged, forcing the Central Bank to adopt a more restrictive monetary policy. As a consequence of the jump in expectations, inflation in March reached 7.4 percent.

Meanwhile, the political situation deteriorated. The conflict between Congress and the executive branch grew in intensity. Instead of seeking compromise with the Congress, the Fujimori government adopted a confrontational approach. As a result, opinion polls showed decreasing popularity for Fujimori and his economic policies. It is within this context that the president, on 5 April 1992, dissolved the parliament and courts, accusing the political parties and Congress of obstructing his policies. Unexpectedly, the *autogolpe,* or self-coup, was supported by a majority of Peruvians, presumably because they thought that it was the only way to deal with the severe problems the country was facing.

The Consequences of the Self-Coup of 5 April

The Fujimori coup produced negative consequences domestically and damaged Peru's relations with the international financial community. Apparently, the government did not consider the potential extent of the international reaction. Fujimori believed that keeping Carlos Boloña as minister of economy would assure the international community that the economic program would be preserved, and that this would be enough to continue receiving support.

This proved not to be the case. Credits from the IDB were delayed. The financial sector reform loan that was to be subscribed by the IDB a day after the coup was also postponed. Also, disbursement of the last two tranches of the trade reform loan was deferred. Similar steps were taken with some foreign financial flows from most of the members of the Paris Club of nations.

The uncertainty generated by the coup had negative repercussions in Peru's financial sector. Hence, $232 million were withdrawn from deposit accounts during the month following Fujimori's move, restricting credit available to the private sector. During the months

Table 12.3 Peru: The Boloña Period, February 1991–December 1992

	1991										
Indicators	Feb	Mar	Apr	May	Jun	July	Aug	Sept	Oct	Nov	Dec
GDP[a]	99.0	104.1	120.7	123.5	117.5	120.3	115.0	111.1	112.1	112.0	111.5
Monthly Inflation Rate (%)	9.4	7.7	5.8	7.6	9.3	9.1	7.2	5.6	4.0	4.0	3.7
Current Central Govt. Revenues[b]	7.7	6.7	8.6	6.8	6.1	7.6	6.7	8.1	8.0	7.7	8.0
Fuel[a]	77	72	71	68	69	72	74	77	78	78	76
Broad Money in Domestic Currency[c]	14.8	21.2	12.5	6.1	8.8	7.8	6.1	10.1	6.6	5.3	12.6
Base Money[c]	6.9	13.4	3.9	1.5	9.3	7.3	8.1	4.0	3.7	3.5	7.3
Foreign Currency Deposits[d]	1226	1300	1396	1641	1783	1968	2098	2153	2245	2399	2539
Net Intl. Central Bank Reserves[e]	419	499	599	623	754	802	900	944	1014	1155	1304
Real Exchange Rate[f]	86.6	80.8	84.4	97.9	93.9	84.5	76.7	73.7	82.2	89.3	84.5
Nominal Exchange Rate (S/US$)[g]	0.55	0.56	0.63	0.79	0.85	0.82	0.80	0.80	0.92	1.02	1.00

Source: Central Reserve Bank of Peru.

a. Real index (August 1990 = 100)

b. August 1990 millions of soles

c. End of period nominal figure (monthly percentage change)

d. In commercial banks (end of period; millions of dollars)

e. End of period (millions of US dollars)

f. Index based on the period average banking rate (August 1990 = 100)

g. Period average banking rate

Table 12.3 (Continued)

Indicators	1992 Jan	Feb	Mar	Apr	May	Jun	July	Aug	Sept	Oct	Nov	Dec
GDP[a]	104.9	100.7	107.0	111.5	116.5	114.1	111.6	108.3	106.9	108.1	108.3	115.8
Monthly Inflation Rate (%)	3.5	4.7	7.4	3.2	3.4	3.6	3.5	2.8	2.6	3.6	3.5	3.8
Current Central Govt. Revenues[b]	8.5	8.5	8.6	9.1	7.9	8.0	8.3	8.7	8.7	8.9	9.0	8.3
Fuel[a]	73	70	65	66	66	67	66	65	64	65	63	63
Broad Money in Domestic Currency[c]	0.0	6.6	3.1	5.1	2.1	1.5	11.3	–0.4	1.9	1.7	2.4	14.0
Base Money[c]	2.5	2.4	3.0	3.4	4.2	4.6	5.5	3.6	3.5	2.0	4.4	0.0
Foreign Currency Deposits[d]	2685	2740	2725	2489	2538	2603	2651	2642	2807	2885	2959	3045
Net Intl. Central Bank Reserves[e]	1355	1398	1415	1326	1418	1578	1670	1679	1846	1842	1857	2001
Real Exchange Rate[f]	82.1	77.1	69.6	72.8	78.8	80.6	82.8	84.5	88.5	95.3	93.3	91.0
Nominal Exchange Rate (S/US$)[g]	0.99	0.98	0.96	1.02	1.13	1.18	1.24	1.29	1.37	1.55	1.62	1.63

a. Real index (August 1990 = 100)
b. August 1990 millions of soles
c. End of period nominal figure (monthly percentage change)
d. In commercial banks (end of period; millions of dollars)
e. End of period (millions of US dollars)
f. Index based on the period average banking rate (August 1990 = 100)
g. Period average banking rate

of May and June, monetary policy became restrictive. Although high-powered money increased by 4.2 percent and 4.6 percent, respectively, money supply grew by only 2.1 percent and 1.5 percent. This outcome reflected the government's running of an unnecessary surplus. The decrease in the money supply, along with reduced credit in foreign exchange, further squeezed the availability of credit to the private sector. Interest rates on domestic currency loans increased from 7.3 percent in April to 7.9 percent in May, and to 8.9 percent in August. Rates for loans in foreign currency increased from an annual 17.2 percent in April to 19.1 percent in May, and to 19.9 percent in August (see Table 12.4).

This restrictive monetary policy, which was unintended, combined with still high inflationary expectations and a supply shock, led to a drop in the level of economic activity. Adverse weather conditions negatively affected the agriculture sector and caused power rationing, forcing manufacturing firms to rely on their own supply of more costly electricity. As a result, manufacturing production fell by 15.7 percent in July, as compared to the same month a year earlier. High interest rates and recession contributed to the growing share of nonperforming loans in the banking system (see Table 12.5).

The recession was partially reversed during the final months of 1992 by fiscal expansion. During the second semester, inflation was slightly lower, reaching about 3 percent per month. This level, which was still high, is attributable to erratic public sector pricing policy and to the Central Bank's attempts to increase the nominal exchange rate.

Despite the remaining short-term problems, structural reforms continued at a rather fast pace. The Fujimori government continued public sector reform, improved tax administration, and accelerated the privatization of state-owned firms.

The combination of poor macroeconomic results and the inflexibility shown by Minister Boloña toward any suggestions of policy change led to increasing criticism from a variety of sectors. Boloña was, consequently, replaced in the first week of January 1993.

Under the leadership of the new minister of economy, Jorge Camet, the situation did not change much, at least for the first four months of his tenure. Inflation remained at the monthly rate of about 4 percent and overvaluation of the exchange rate was still a problem. Inflation did not fall as far as expected by the government, mostly as a result of actions by the government itself. The erratic nature of public sector prices and the exchange rate continued to signal to economic agents that inflation would persist at about the 4 percent monthly level. Inflationary expectations have been validated by the government's monetary policy. Fortunately, since May 1993, the Central Bank's monetary policy has been more defined, which has led to much better results.

Structural reforms, however, have continued at a slower pace, although Peru has reached a new agreement with the IMF, which provides for its participation in the Extended Fund Facility Program for the next three years. Arrears with both the IMF and World Bank have been cleared, and, finally, the Fujimori government has completed renegotiations with the Paris Club for the same three-year period.

Perspectives

There is general agreement that the economic program of the Fujimori government is sound. But the management of economic policy has not been very successful, and several important mistakes have been committed in the process, which has created some disillusion among economic actors. It is expected that Minister Camet, or a subsequent minister, will take more decisive action to correct the existing problems.

Ambitious structural reforms aimed at opening the economy to world markets is providing good prospects for future economic growth. Poor macroeconomic performance, however, has created pessimism among entrepreneurs, which is working to delay investment in Peru. In general, managers tend to be procyclical; when investment begins, it rapidly sets other investors in motion.

If current macroeconomic problems can be addressed promptly, and considering that foreign investment has begun to move into Peru, economic recovery is a real possibility. At present, the investment in sectors like mining, oil, and fisheries allows one to view the future with optimism. Unfortunately, the rather positive economic prospects are blurred to some extent by the present political instability. That instability may delay the resumption of sustainable growth.

Table 12.4 Peru: Nominal Interest Rates: 1990–1993[a]

Year and Month	Domestic Currency[b]				Foreign Currency[c]			
	Lending[d]	TAMN[e]	Deposit[f]	TIPMN[g]	Lending[h]	TAMEX[e]	Deposit[f]	TIPMEX[g]
1990								
August	51.00	n.a.	35.60	n.a.	n.a.	n.a.	n.a.	n.a.
September	40.00	n.a.	20.00	n.a.	n.a.	n.a.	n.a.	n.a.
October	14.08	n.a.	7.15	n.a.	15.91	n.a.	7.21	n.a.
November	12.51	n.a.	6.12	n.a.	16.24	n.a.	7.46	n.a.
December	12.45	n.a.	5.10	n.a.	16.32	n.a.	7.84	n.a.
1991								
January	17.41	n.a.	6.02	n.a.	15.16	n.a.	7.18	n.a.
February	22.17	n.a.	8.49	n.a.	16.59	n.a.	6.43	n.a.
March	23.75	n.a.	9.42	n.a.	17.34	n.a.	6.74	n.a.
April	18.73	19.05	7.49	n.a.	20.80	19.41	8.40	n.a.
May	14.94	15.95	6.67	n.a.	20.47	20.07	9.18	n.a.
June	17.10	17.47	7.28	n.a.	20.21	19.18	9.51	n.a.
July	18.20	18.98	9.28	4.91	21.00	20.14	11.23	8.64
August	17.29	18.38	9.62	4.44	21.55	20.27	11.31	8.89
September	12.10	12.68	5.56	3.23	22.53	19.80	9.41	7.76
October	9.83	10.99	4.42	2.71	22.92	20.69	8.40	7.73
November	9.67	10.54	4.42	2.70	23.07	20.30	8.53	7.64
December	9.86	10.85	4.44	2.73	23.18	21.07	8.54	7.76
1992								
January	9.61	10.60	4.40	2.61	23.43	20.83	8.54	7.80
February	8.56	8.84	3.93	2.29	23.26	19.14	8.43	5.92
March	8.00	8.33	3.40	2.00	22.15	19.86	7.78	6.93
April	7.11	7.29	2.96	1.86	19.54	17.21	6.59	6.50
May	7.29	7.93	3.07	1.71	19.89	19.10	6.65	6.18

June	7.81	7.84	3.17	1.67	20.37	19.03	6.59	6.28
July	7.94	8.11	3.21	1.74	20.61	19.90	6.64	6.32
August	7.95	8.14	3.20	1.66	20.58	19.89	6.61	6.22
September	7.17	7.38	3.10	1.51	18.68	16.91	6.42	5.97
October	6.85	7.49	3.03	1.48	18.17	17.40	6.29	5.88
November	7.00	7.14	3.03	1.39	18.23	16.75	6.32	5.79
December	7.05	7.64	3.02	1.42	18.30	17.53	6.28	5.80
1993								
January	6.93	7.47	3.00	1.41	18.21	17.32	6.26	5.72
February	6.90	6.50	2.98	1.40	18.39	15.32	6.16	5.77
March	6.49	6.72	2.77	1.40	18.40	16.35	5.83	5.72
April	6.25	5.86	2.70	1.39	18.39	16.19	5.76	5.72
May	5.91	5.76	2.67	1.36	18.37	16.53	5.89	5.69
June	5.70	5.47	2.57	1.32	18.34	15.77	5.85	5.63
July	5.67	5.38	2.53	1.31	18.25	15.61	5.91	5.52
August	5.42	5.43	2.48	1.21	18.17	15.99	5.79	5.41
September	5.30	5.19	2.35	1.24	18.07	15.34	5.63	5.30

Source: Central Reserve Bank of Peru.
Notes:
a. Average rates
b. In percent per month
c. In percent per year
d. On loans up to 360 days; includes tax on interest income
e. Weighted average lending rate
f. Savings deposits
g. Weighted average deposit rate
h. Overdraft rate

Table 12.5 Peru: Nonperforming Loans: 1991–1993[a]

Date	% of Total Loans
1991	
Dec. 31	10.8
1992	
Feb. 29	13.1
Jun. 30	13.3
Sep. 15	17.2
Dec. 31	22.9
1993	
Mar. 30	23.8
Jun. 30	22.7
Aug. 15	23.0

Source: Bank and Insurance Supervisory Agency.
Note:
a. In commercial banks.

13

Peru's Difficult Road to Economic Development

Efraín Gonzales de Olarte

The search for economic development is a forward-looking task. What is done today will define the future, but it is based on what was done in the past. Even though history never exactly repeats itself, we must understand the past in order to look to the future. We must relate the economic events of the present with those of the past, which, taken together, constitute the long term. This is especially true in countries such as Peru, where the economic past has not proved useful for building a better future, perhaps because the short-term economic horizon became ever more limited and because economic adjustments were given greater priority than growth.[1]

One can see evidence of this in the considerable influence of economists on short-term economic policies, as opposed to development policies. Macroeconomists became intensive-care physicians, while we development economists limited ourselves to acting as forensic specialists. Shock treatment is of no use in saving a patient dying of anemia. Ideally, the patient should not develop anemia, which is achieved only if we concern ourselves with the conditions and determinants of development. Today, given the political and institutional changes that have led to the so-called structural adjustments in Latin America, we must think about and work on development from a short-term perspective. Consequently, the objective of this paper is to analyze Peru's long-term problems[2] together with closely related short-term problems in order to seek answers to one question: what is needed in Peru to open the way to development? We can hope that the analysis of the past will provide insight into proposals aimed at resolving the problems of today.

Efraín Gonzales de Olarte is a senior researcher at the Institute for Peruvian Studies (IEP).

In the current context, development means economic growth with equity, with democracy, and without environmental degradation. That is, more complex and challenging objectives are demanded. However poor or critical a country's situation, we must seriously consider the three to be long-term objectives in the civilized construction of a country. Even in Peru, a country beset by almost all possible plagues and problems, we should adopt these same objectives for the future. This should be the case even though we are starting from the point of a lengthy recession (almost thirteen years of economic decline), with growing poverty and unequal distribution of income and wealth, with violence, with a fragile democracy to strengthen, and with increasing signs of environmental degradation.

This paper will not address the problems of violence, democracy, and the environment. Nevertheless, I am convinced that if we achieve economic growth with redistribution it will be much easier to build a peaceful, democratic Peru and to ensure that growth will not come at the cost of leaving even scarcer resources and increased environmental destruction for the next generation (Gonzales 1993).

Long-term problems require that one's analysis consider macroeconomics, microeconomics, politics, history, and the institutional economy, so as to be able to offer a plausible view of economic phenomena. There is a risk of developing a very general interpretation, which is almost useless for normative purposes, or an encyclopedic perspective. To avoid these extremes, I will focus on the determinants of the economic dynamic in Peru (growth and decline) and their relationship with short-term economic phenomena. I will try to show that the crisis of development, or the long-term crisis, has resulted from a perverse combination of investment crises and economic and political instability, as reflected in the chronic short-term perspective of economic policymaking and in the behavior of economic agents and political actors. All of this has been coupled with external constraints that are subject to exogenous changes and with Peru's propensity for suffering external shocks.

The first part of this chapter will analyze the variables that best explain Peru's growth or decline at the macroeconomic level. The second part will address the economic and political instability, or the "Peruvian pendulum" that serves as a brake on growth. I will then examine briefly the economic mechanisms of the pattern of Peruvian growth to determine which of them have been the principal constraints. On this basis, I will subsequently analyze microeconomic behavior and the role of the entrepreneur in the processes of economic growth and decline. In the fifth part, I will try to relate the short term to the long term with respect to stabilization policies. The final section will analyze the effects of the hysteresis left by the crises as well as short-term adjustment policies and policies that affect future economic growth.

Finally, this chapter should be viewed as an initial effort to synthesize a series of research efforts by me and others on issues that are highly complex and with statistical information limited in both quality and quantity (de la Torre 1990). This chapter is for the most part an essay that seeks to demonstrate that the long-term issues are more pressing than is generally thought to be the case.

The Determinants of Peru's Economic Growth and Decline

An Aggregate Perspective

The Peruvian economy grew until the middle of the 1970s. Thereafter it ceased growing, and in the last ten years has experienced a recessive tendency. In the 1980s per capita GDP dropped to the levels of the late 1950s (see Figure 13.1).

The long-term cycle hit its inflection point during the 1973–1975 period. From 1950 to 1975, per capita GDP grew at an annual rate of 2.4 percent, whereas from 1976 to 1982 it declined at a rate of 2.2 percent per year. Growth during the expansive phase of the cycle was steadier, while there was pronounced economic instability during the decline (see Figure 13.2 and Table 13.1).

Over the last forty-two years per capita GDP grew at only 0.5 percent on average per year, and showed great variability.[3] Obviously, something that was done or something that happened during the expansive phase led to a long-term crisis from which the country has yet to emerge.

One factor of considerable significance to Peru's economic growth has been its demographic evolution. From 1940 to the 1970s, the population growth rate reached 2.8 percent per year. It began to decline in the middle of the 1970s, and in 1992 it was estimated that the rate would be at about 2.3 percent. Obviously, such high rates slowed the country's ability to achieve higher rates of investment. However, a causal relationship between demographic trends and economic growth is still not clear. Nor has it been demonstrated that the slowdown in population growth rate was due to the economic crisis and falling real incomes, or to other factors, such as increased participation of women in the labor force, greater urbanization, and the increase in the rate of school enrollment. In both cases, the changing population would appear to be an endogenous variable, but with

Figure 13.1 Peru: Per Capita Gross Product and Investment, 1950–1990

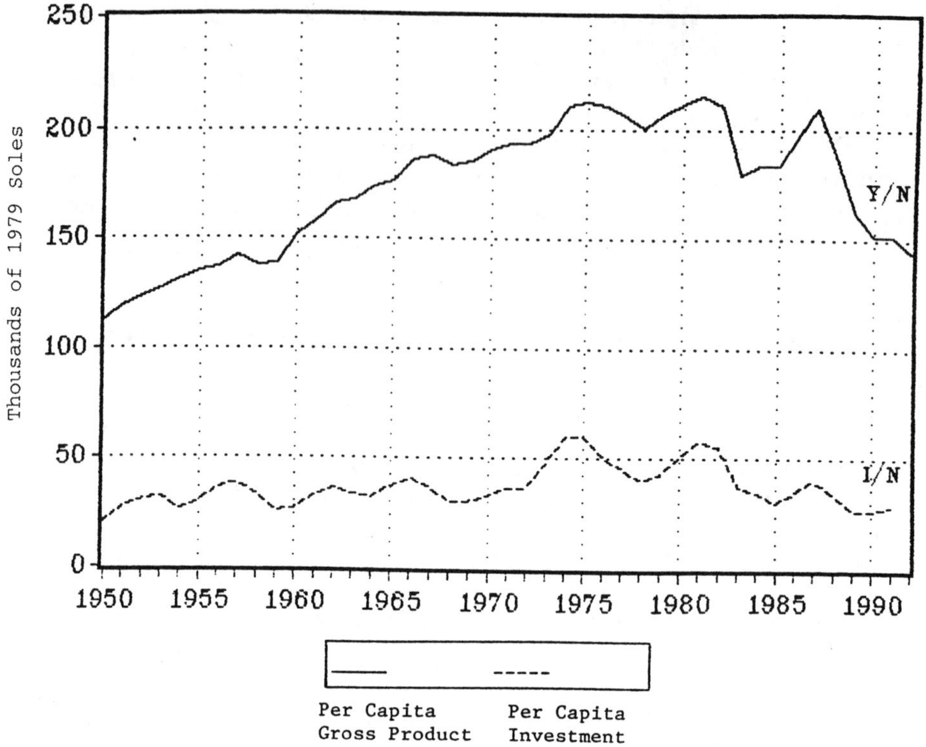

the opposite sign, and it is not known if its decline was due to economic growth or to the crisis. Certainly, the lower the rate, the greater the possibilities of development.

What explains this economic and demographic dynamic, which is similar to that of other Latin American countries?[4] To answer this question, almost all theories of growth attribute economic dynamism to three factors: investment, improvement of the work force, and technical progress[5] as a residual element. Actually growth is due to long-term quantitative and qualitative improvements in the factors of production, which allow the productivity growth of a country. From this perspective, we can estimate a growth function[6] that gives us an idea of the factors that have influenced the long-term evolution of the Peruvian economy.

First, investment alone explained only 45 percent of growth (or decline) in per capita GDP.[7] Including labor, both factors explained 72 percent of the change in per capita GDP.[8] The increase in workers'

Figure 13.2 Peru: Rates of Growth of Per Capita Gross Product and Investment, 1950–1990

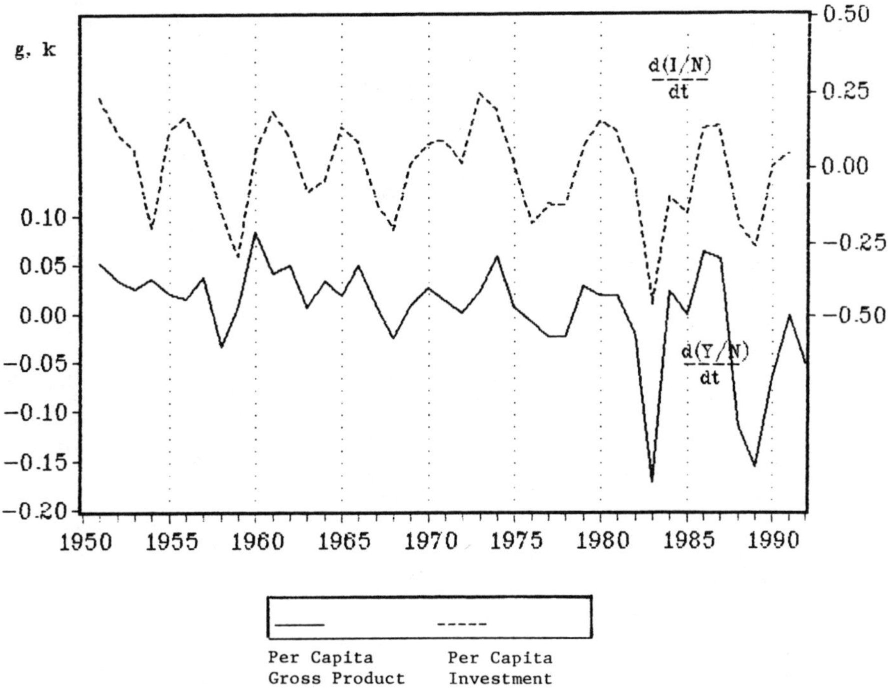

incomes has been a important source of growth of per capita GDP in the long term, with a more or less clear causality.[9]

The remaining 28 percent could not be attributed to technical progress alone;[10] rather, other factors must also be considered, such as education, external constraints, domestic and external economic stability, and political-institutional stability. These factors are usually considered residual in theories of growth. Yet we find that growth is due not only to factors that add up arithmetically, but also to a successful combination of these factors. The empirical results suggest some analytical leads and force us to pose new questions.[11]

Internal and external economic stability, measured by the variation in annual rate of inflation[12] and the annual rate of variation in the exchange rate, have been important factors for growth and investment. That is, there was investment when inflation varied between 2 and 5 percent and when the nominal and real exchange rates were stable. In addition, in the long term, inflation appears to

Table 13.1 Percentage Rates of Growth, 1950–1992

	GDP	Per Capita GDP	Investment (K)	Remuneration (L)	Inflation (p)
1950–1992					
Means	3.14	0.45	1.97	1.38	269.8
Variances	5.3	5.27	15.9	11.9	1080.2
Rates of Variability	0.592	0.085	0.124	0.116	0.249
1950–1975					
Means	5.08	2.44	5.82	5.77	9.7
Variances	2.47	2.55	14.1	3.05	4.9
Rates of Variability	2.057	0.957	0.413	1.892	1.98
1976–1992					
Means	0.23	–2.16	–4.89	–3.89	293.5
Variances	7.31	7.41	17.81	15.6	662.9
Rates of Variability	0.031	–0.292	–0.275	–0.249	0.443
Governments					
M. Odría 1950–1956	5.53	3.46	10.21	7.05	6.82
M. Prado 1956–1961	5.19	3.02	2.73	5.79	8.12
F. Belaúnde 1963–1968	4.37	1.7	–0.98	4.82	30.83
J. Velasco 1969–1975	4.69	2.07	11.5	5.8	11.76
F. Morales 1976–1980	2.48	–0.08	–1.62	–2.05	52.2
F. Belaúnde 1981–1985	–0.63	–2.46	–10.1	–0.21	105.26
A. Garciá 1986–1990	–2.11	–3.52	–1.53	–13.67	1952.7
A. Fujimori 1991–1992	–0.35	–3.4			97.95

Based on data from the INEI (National Institute of Statistics and Information Science), Perú Compendio Estadístico 1991–1992, Dirección Técnica de Indicadores Económicos, Lima, 1992.

be the result of the lack of growth of aggregate supply, or to a lack of investment, as is noted by Tello (1990).

Incorporating qualitative variables, such as the type of government (civilian or military) and the economic policy regime (orthodox or heterodox), as indicators of political stability or instability, we find that alternating periods of civilian and military government, and the swings in economic policy regimes had a negative impact on growth in Peru. Nevertheless, the changes in economic policy regime were the endogenous outcome of the short- and medium-term evolution of the economic cycle. That is, in each expansive cycle since the 1960s, more or less heterodox policies were adopted, and when they produced crises the country ended up with an orthodox adjustment.

Second, when including education, which is considered one of the most important factors for long-term growth, in Peru its impact would have been minor. The correlation between per capita public spending on education and growth of GDP has been very low (r^2=0.224), as have the regression coefficients. A significant aspect here is that education expenditures have been highly cyclical; the state spent more during the phases of economic expansion and drastically reduced spending with each economic adjustment. But the most important element has been the incompatibility between quantitative and qualitative improvements in education and the limited expansion of demand for labor, basically a result of the decline of investment, which has created a structural disequilibrium in the labor market. The results of this process have been: (1) considerable international migration of the highly skilled work force; according to Altamirano (1992), the population of Peruvians abroad has increased to 1.1 million, which is equivalent to 5 percent of the total; and (2) Peru's underemployment with respect to income and occupation. In 1970, underemployment affected 46.9 percent of the economically active population, increasing in 1980 to 51.2 percent, and in 1990 to 70 percent.[13] In short, public investment in education did not translate into greater development, but into international migration and lower real incomes that did not reflect the higher levels of education that the Peruvian population had obtained.[14] In other words, the economic and educational system of Peru has generated a mass of educated poor.

Third, there was limited availability of foreign exchange for investment, which can be viewed in two distinct phases. During the first, which continued until the end of the 1960s, foreign exchange receipts depended on the trade balance, or basically on the expansion of exports. The subsequent phase centered on the balance of payments, or foreign loans, as a source of exchange. Thus, the foreign exchange constraint became acute during the period of decline given the burden of the external debt.

One important element often forgotten in analyses was the trend in the quality of aggregate investment. The composition of gross fixed capital formation as a ratio of equipment to construction grew from 35 percent in the 1950s to 55 percent in 1975, reflecting a steady increase in investment in machinery. Later, investment in construction began to account for a larger proportion; by 1989–1990, 78 percent of gross fixed capital formation went to construction and only 22 percent to machinery. We do not know whether this trend was a response to the long-term crisis or the factor that set off the crisis.

A Less Aggregated Perspective

Trends in investment. Aggregate investment per capita has shown a slightly downward trend over the last forty years, which has yet to be sufficiently explained. Nevertheless, the most notable phenomena during this period were the persistent decline in the investment/profit ratio (I/π), especially in the private sector (Gonzales and Samamé 1991), and the strong fluctuation in the level of investment. Figure 13.3 illustrates just how sharp these changes have been.

The decline in the (I/π) ratio is one way to present the drop in the level of savings converted into investment (I/S), a trend that has been accentuated in Peru since the 1970s. The investment of savings has been falling over time for four reasons, which have not been the subject of much research. First, since the 1960s there has been a progressive reduction in private sector expectations of the profitability of investments with a long period of maturation (Thorp and Bertram 1978). Second, there has been a hysteresis effect of adjustment policies since the middle of the 1960s; that is, the growing need to use savings to cover the losses of entrepreneurs and workers during and after the adjustment stages. I will return to this issue below. Third, since the 1970s there has been progressive use of a portion of savings to pay for the mounting external debt (Dancourt 1986). Finally, capital flight due to political and institutional instability has been a factor since the 1970s (Devlin 1985; Dornbusch 1991).

These factors appear to have deeper roots in the pattern of economic growth, which neither created a domestic market (greater demand) nor transformed part of the industrial sector into exporting industries. Thus, the pattern of growth did not create the stable

Figure 13.3 Peru: Profits Invested (I/n), 1950–1990

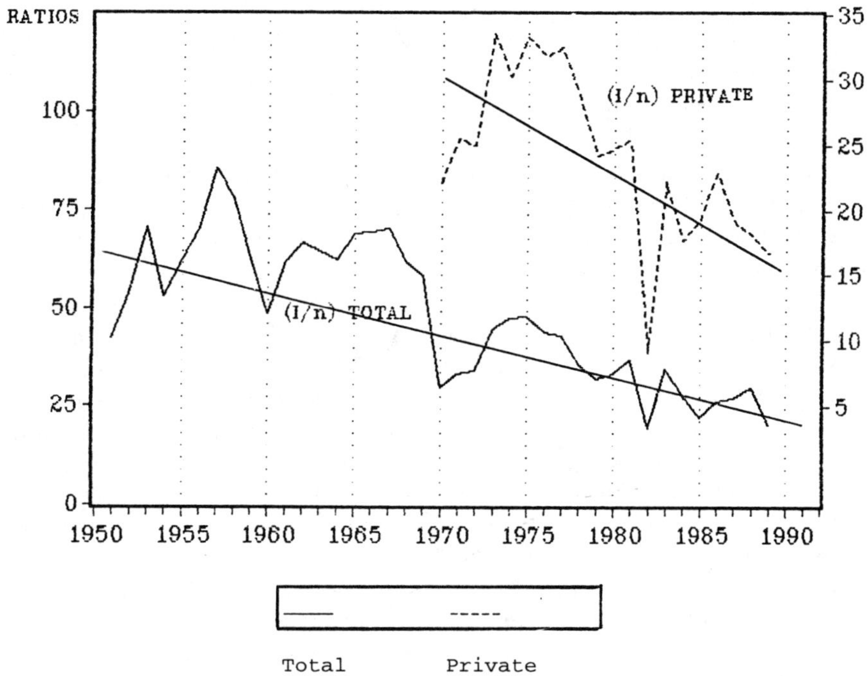

conditions for profit making either inside or outside the Peruvian economy. But, the macroeconomic equality that says the investment-savings differential (I-S) equals the exports-imports differential (X-M) defined the limits of investment as a function of the increase in exports or of the substitution of imports. Exports grew by leaps and bounds, generally as a result of foreign or state investments, and import substitution did not actually develop (Schydlowsky and Witch 1979; Iguiñiz and Távara 1985; Gonzales 1991). As a result, expectations of profitability were influenced by the performance of the external sector.

Fluctuations in aggregate investment have followed the economic cycle, which is driven by the behavior of the external sector. When exports were expanding, investment followed, among other reasons because investment depends on the availability of foreign exchange and the exchange rate, and when the crisis in the balance of payments crisis occurred, investment declined as much a result of shrinking savings as of the drop in domestic demand. A small open economy that exports primary commodities, such as Peru, dramatically illustrates how the evolution of the international economy, in trade and finance, affected the behavior of total investment. Obviously, the governments failed to reduce that vulnerability.

Private and public investment: Was there a "crowding-in" effect? The trends in private and public investment have differed. Private investment, both foreign and national, led the investment process in the dynamic (export and industrial) sectors until the middle of the 1960s, while public investment was complementary. Subsequently, beginning with the first government of Belaúnde and continuing with the military government of General Velasco, public investment became the driving force of the process of accumulation, replacing private investment, which diminished out of fear of the military regime's nationalizing reforms (Thorp 1978; Fitzgerald 1981; Alarco and del Hierro 1989). Private investment became complementary.

In this phase, public investment was based on external indebtedness (savings). In the long run, this deepened the problem of the external constraint reflected in the (I-S=X-M) equation, as investment was earmarked in part to boost exports (mining and petroleum) and as the rate of return on investments was insufficient to service the external debt, especially in the early 1980s, when world interest rates were so high. Finally, in the 1980s public investment fell and private investment once again accounted for the principal share, albeit investment of short maturation (construction), high profitability (agribusiness, coca, and gold), and limited-scale.

Given these particular trends, one must determine whether there has been complementarity (crowding-in) or displacement (crowding-out) between public and private investment in Peru, and what effect this would have had on growth. The limited research that has been done in this area (Jiménez 1987; Ascarza 1990) reaches contradictory conclusions. For Jiménez, there was crowding-in from 1956 to 1983; the state appears to have stimulated private investment through its own investments. In contrast, Ascarza, covering a shorter but more recent period (1968–1987), finds that there was a crowding-out effect due to the structure of public investment, which in part has competed with private investment, such that the negative effects have more than offset the positive effects of the complementary, crowding-in investments.

In a study still underway, my associates and I found that whether there is a crowding-in effect between public and private investment or not also depends on the stability of the institutional framework. The effect of complementarity has been less a result of the changing normative association between public and private investment with respect to sectors, incentives, and financing. From 1968 to date there has been greater institutional instability than in the preceding periods, although we did not find a clear crowding-out effect, but rather a slight complementarity for the 1970–1991 period.[15] In other words, the possibilities of cooperation between the private and public sectors appear to depend more on the existence of lasting rules of the game than on changing "good" rules of the game.

The real income of workers and concentration of the functional distribution: Redistribution without growth. Workers' real incomes grew in the period from 1950 to 1975 and have declined steadily as the crisis has unfolded since 1976. This led to a reduction in their relative share of national income from an average of 48 percent of the total in the 1960s to 38 percent in the 1980s. During the same period, the relative share of profits grew from 26 percent to 42 percent. This meant there was a concentration of income on the profit side, which, as profits were not invested proportionally, reduced effective demand and left worker income as the principal source of economic dynamism on the demand side.

This is why economic activity has been so sensitive to the evolution of workers' incomes, which has been the factor underlying the recovery of the urban-industrial economy. Hence the importance of income policies. In addition, the incomes of workers have been, at least since 1990, the factor to be adjusted in the process of addressing the short-term as well as long-term crises, as reflected in current levels of underemployment and unemployment, which together affect 82 percent of the population (Verdera 1993).

Until the beginning of the 1970s, the link between investment and an increase in workers' real incomes came about through improvements in productivity; this connection has been lost since the 1976–1978 period. It will therefore be difficult to emerge from the current crisis, as the only way to resolve the long-term distribution problem is to return to the path of private investment and to increased productivity. The reduction of real incomes, impoverishment of workers, and concentration of profits without greater investment have been the principal effects of the crises and of successive adjustment policies, which together have reduced the size of the market for goods and labor.

Instability as a Factor Limiting Growth: The Peruvian Pendulum

A few years ago, in our book *The Peruvian Pendulum*, my co-author and I argued that one of the principal problems of development in Peru was the oscillation of economic policy regimes and the dramatic shifts brought about by successive civilian and military governments (Gonzales and Samamé 1991). The essential idea is that the instability of relative prices and of the institutional framework has been the worst enemy of investment. Instability has been the rule since the middle of the 1960s, which is why Peru did not find the road to sustained growth and cannot find its way out of the crisis.

Table 13.1 provides an empirical illustration of Peru's economic instability over the last forty-two years. This long cycle is comprised of a growth phase up to the mid-1970s, during which time the 2.06 rate of variability (mean/variance) of annual growth of GDP indicates stability. This contrasts with the 1976–1992 period, when this rate fell to 0.03, reflecting considerable instability. But if we take into account the variations in per capita GDP, that is, if we include demographic pressure as a source of economic instability, stability during the growth phase was less (0.96) and instability during the downturn has been dramatic (-0.29). This cyclical trend is also reflected in the rate of variability of inflation, which yields an interesting fact: the Peruvian economy experienced stable growth (1950–1975), while the annual rate of inflation was on average less than 10 percent, with a small variance. We can therefore infer that as long as the adjustment programs are not able to bring inflation down to a similar level, it will be difficult to return to the path of growth with investment.

The original source of this instability is, as indicated above, the great variability of investment, which is greater than the variability in GDP in both phases of the long cycle (see Table 13.1). Investment has occurred in leaps and bounds (see Figure 13.2). Meanwhile, worker income (remuneration) was stable during the growth phase of the cycle (t=1.89), but during the economic downturn it obviously became highly unstable.

If we break down this long cycle into periods corresponding to the respective governments, we find that the governments of Generals Manuel Odría and Juan Velasco promoted investment. During both administrations investment increased at rates of more than 10 percent annually (see Table 13.1). In the first case, foreign direct investment was the impetus behind overall investment. In the second, state investment, financed primarily by external loans, drove the accumulation process. External savings have always been the driving force of investment, and Peruvian capitalists have not led or even sought to lead the investment process. I will return to this issue below.

The determinants of the long-run cycle first appeared from 1956 to 1968, during the Manuel Prado and Fernando Belaúnde governments, when the rates of growth of investment were low and negative, respectively (see Table 13.1). During this period the pattern of Peruvian growth was redefined (from exporter of primary commodities to dependent, semi-industrial exporter) based on limited investment.

Economic instability has been a result of two factors. The first is the pattern of growth, which tends to be subject to exogenous crises due to abrupt changes in export prices or quantities, or to excessive increases in imports. The second factor is economic policies that failed to avoid these crises, to address them in a timely manner and effectively correct them by reestablishing macroeconomic equilibria and aligning relative prices. The political cycle has been at the root of the instability of economic policy (Gonzales and Samamé 1991).

There has been a political will that has defined, both through development policies and in the short term, the basic orientations of the Peruvian economy. Specifically, the basic orientation has reflected the political interests of both civilian and military governments, and the result has been oscillations in economic policy because those policies reflect particularistic interests, which are rarely in the national interest. In my view this has been the case for two reasons. First, to date Peru has not been able to develop an integrated market economy in which "the capitalists earn what the workers spend," or, in the absence of that, to create an economy with few external constraints. Second, to date Peru has not been able to develop a political system capable of institutionally channeling and resolving particular conflicts, such that the taxes that capitalists and workers pay could yield socially equitable benefits for all. The result of an institutional framework of this nature was the persistence of an unequal distribution of income and, above all, the inability of the economic and political system to alleviate class differences (Webb and Figueroa 1975; Webb 1989; Figueroa 1991; Gonzales and Samamé 1991).

In other words, the investment process described above did not lead to the establishment of a market economy that later created a state to serve the needs of such an economy. Rather, the governments, representing distinct interests, used the market and the state itself for their own specific purposes. The oscillating economic policies—or the Peruvian pendulum—have been the result of this fragmentation and socioeconomic inequality (Gonzales and Samamé 1991).

The Pattern of "Dependent, Primary Exporter Semi-Industrial" Growth

One of the reasons for economic instability has been found in the disequilibria in the trade balance brought about by falling exports or rising imports. The level of economic activity and investment has always depended on the availability of foreign exchange, which should have increased as a function of legal exports or would have no longer been necessary had import substitution occurred. Exports increased during the first phase of the long cycle at a rate of 4.7 percent per year. But during the recessive phase they grew at a rate of only 1.8 percent. Imports expanded at 6.8 percent per year from 1950 to 1976 and have declined at 5.6 percent annually since 1976 as a consequence of the successive adjustments. Legal exports per capita have been stagnant for the last ten years.

The essential problem of the pattern of Peruvian growth was the relative absence of links between the export sectors that generated foreign exchange (mining and fisheries, with a high degree of participation of foreign companies) and the sectors that used foreign exchange (industry, modern agriculture, and services). Exporters sell little in the domestic market, while the industrialists import most of their inputs and capital goods. As a result, the operation and expansion of the industrial sector have been dependent on the exchange rate, which measures the relative scarcity of foreign exchange and which simultaneously affects real wages. It was obviously a pattern of growth that functioned on the basis of a latent conflict between exporters and industrialists. An overvalued exchange rate favored the industrial sector, as it made its inputs cheaper and increased real wages, while sacrificing the profits of exporters. Under these circumstances, economic policy swung back and forth, and over the long term amounted to a zero-sum game; that is, it did not foster growth.

Population pressure and urbanization "imposed" the overvalued exchange rate over the long term. Voters and political interest groups pressured for high real wages and low inflation, which were only possible as long as foreign exchange was available from the export boom, from external loans, or by fixing exchange rates on the basis of political considerations independent of their market value.

The death knell for this pattern of economic growth came with the 1966–1967 crisis in the balance of trade, which emerged as a crisis of incompatibility between exports and imports and between exporters and industrialists. It was resolved without increasing the supply of exports, by resorting to easy external indebtedness. Structural adjustment was needed at that time, but it did not occur basically because of the APRA-UNO (National Odriist Union) coalition's opposition to the reforms proposed by the minister of economy in 1966.

The military government of Juan Velasco, which replaced the Belaúnde administration with the 1968 coup, strengthened the pattern of primary export, semi-industrial growth and made the country much more subject to external constraint. It prolonged a model of growth that had demonstrated its principal weakness thanks to easily obtainable foreign loans.

Obviously, the epilogue has been harsh, for since 1976 the structural imbalances have become greater and more complex. The external gap (X-M) affected the process of accumulation (S-I) to the extent that part of savings had to be earmarked to pay the debt, thereby reducing the amount remaining for potential investment and compromising the fiscal future of the economy, given that more than 90 percent of the external debt is public. As a consequence, gradually a trade-off between paying the debt and growing had to be made. This problem persists today without any definitive solution. Moreover, it has left latent macroeconomic imbalances between revenues and fiscal expenditure (committed in part to debt payment), between exports and imports (foreign exchange is required to pay the external debt), and between savings and investment (part of savings must be used to pay the debt).

Some Microeconomic Characteristics of Investment and the Entrepreneurial Factor

An aggregate perspective of investment provides an idea of the major trends and overall oscillations that obviously result from an infinite number of investment decisions on the part of private entrepreneurs and/or capitalists and of public enterprises and officials. These need to be analyzed, despite the limitations of the existing literature on the topic.

The microeconomic functions of private and public sector investment differ because they are determined by distinct parameters and variables. In Table 13.2 I have tried to synthesize the various determinants of investment in Peru according to type of enterprise.[16] I have included state institutions such as ministries and municipal governments.

In my view, there are five distinct types of investors in Peru: formal-sector foreign entrepreneurs, formal-sector national entrepreneurs, informal-sector entrepreneurs, state enterprises, and

Table 13.2 Determinants of Investment of Various Types of Enterprises

Variables/ Enterprises	Limiting Variables	Attitude toward Risk	Technical Change	Institutional Framework Affecting Investment	Economic Objective of Investment
Formal Sector Foreign	National Resources Stability of Legal System	Takes Risk	Incorporated	Type of Government Economic Policy	Maximize Profit
Formal Sector National	Relative Prices	Risk Averse	Incorporated Learning by Doing	Economic Policy	Maximize Income
Informal Sector National	Credit	Takes Risks	Learning by Doing	Formal Legalization	Maximize Employment and/or Profit
State Owned	External Credit	Implicitly State Guaranteed	Incorporated	Economic Policy	Social Welfare
State Institution	Fiscal Resources External Credit	Implicitly State Guaranteed	Incorporated	Economic Policy	Social Welfare and Redistribution

government institutions. The general question is: have entrepreneurs been a factor in the economic growth of Peru? Obviously, the response will be exploratory given that this issue has been studied so little.

Private companies, national or foreign, invest to obtain profit. Nevertheless, there are some differences among them that influence the levels and continuity of investment. The first difference is that foreign entrepreneurs invest where there are profitable and exportable natural resources and a stable legal framework; national entrepreneurs invest as a function of present and future relative prices, largely in the production of goods and services for which there is domestic demand. The second difference is that the former are willing to take some risks in exchange for greater expected profits; the latter have an aversion to risk, which is why they search for maximum rent differentials when they take any risk. Hence they are characterized as rentiers. Informal-sector entrepreneurs, in contrast, are limited in their ability to invest by their lack of access to formal-sector credit but are accustomed to taking risks. The problem of risk stems from incomplete information about future prices and from changes in the economic policy regime and in institutions.

In contrast, investment in public enterprises has more altruistic objectives—social profitability—even though the feasibility studies of these enterprises anticipate the use of profits to cover financing costs. The factor limiting investment in this area has been the lack of sufficient financial resources. As a result, most of Peru's state-owned enterprises were created or expanded during the 1970–1989 period, with foreign loans accounting for one-third of total investment (BCRP, Sub-Gerencia del Sector Público). Such investments entail little risk to the extent that they are implicitly guaranteed by the state. The state institutions, which invest in projects such as highways, irrigation systems, schools, and health centers, seek to improve social welfare and provide for redistribution and depend on the state's capacity for fiscal expenditure, based on the level of domestic or external resources.

Since most investment in Peru is made by the private sector and since the structural adjustment program underway today assumes that private investment should be the key to future development, we must consider how Peruvian entrepreneurs have acted with respect to investment. It appears that national investors have gone through two distinct stages, although both have been based on the same behavior of accepting low risks only in exchange for high profitability.

The first period was from 1950 to the middle of the 1960s, when Peruvians invested in the sectors or activities in which foreign capital invested (Thorp and Bertram 1978); they were followers of the economic and political assessments made by foreign investors, who also provided the information on risk levels. At the time, one Peruvian investor stated that, "This fish meal business always had a bad smell, but if Ralston Purina is interested, it smells like roses to me."

The second stage began in 1968. The Velasco government clearly influenced Peruvian investors, not only because it nationalized several foreign enterprises, but also because it created state enterprises as an alternative. Subsequently, the government of General Morales and the three succeeding democratic governments could not stabilize the economy. These events influenced entrepreneurial behavior, making it ever more averse to risk, which, as Alcorta notes (1992), led the largest Peruvian entrepreneurial groups (which Alcorta calls the new financial capital) to operate according to the principle of portfolio diversification. They adopted as their standard the maximization of portfolio profits, or of the complete set of firms and assets that each group controls; they did not focus on one single investment, activity, or firm in particular, so as to diversify the risk to the maximum extent possible.

This would explain why entrepreneurs have supported any government and any economic policy over the last fifteen years, for their interests are so diversified that their portfolios earn a profit under any circumstances. If this is the case, it suggests two facts that are extremely important for development. First, economic policy has been unstable because the profits of the economic pressure groups (business associations) have not depended on economic stability; they have tailored their portfolios to deal with unstable conditions. And there has been instability for almost twenty-five years. Second, national private investment in fixed capital goods, and especially in equipment and machinery, will only be forthcoming if it maximizes portfolio profits, which are comprised of productive, financial, and commercial activities as well as services. As a consequence, if inflation continues at a level of more than 50 percent each year, it is likely that investment will be more speculative or in real estate, and not in productive sectors. These hypotheses merit special study, since the empirical evidence has only begun to be gathered in studies by Alcorta (1992) and Iguiñiz (unpublished paper).

Have Peruvian entrepreneurs been important factors in the country's development? Based on the evidence reviewed, in Peru we have not seen Schumpeter's innovative entrepreneur, but rather a passive entrepreneur who is consistently averse to risk. That is, the entrepreneur has responded rationally to the institutional framework and to the rules of the game set by governments. In this sense, the

Peruvian entrepreneur has not been a determinant of the economic cycle but has been dragged along in its wake.

The Connection Between the Short Term and the Long Term in Economic Policy

For empirical analysis, inflation and the exchange rate were introduced as control variables[17] to determine how internal and external economic instability affected growth. The estimates improved considerably and demonstrated that in the long term the overvalued exchange rate has had a negative impact on economic growth. Inflation has also had a negative impact, but in another sense, as it has permanently altered relative prices, hindering investment decisions in productive sectors and facilitating investment in tertiary sectors in which there is a high capital turnover. The exchange rate appears to be either a variable or instrument of economic policy, depending the theoretical orientation of each government, the long-term impact of which needs to be discussed.

Several works (Larios 1989; Escobal and Saavedra 1990; Ferrari 1990) point to the persistence of an overvalued exchange rate from 1950 to 1980, with the exception of some years, and then from 1986 on. The causes of this persistent overvaluation appear to be, first, the existence of differential rents[18] in the mining and fishery sectors that allowed for profits even with overvalued exchange rates. After 1980 the "coca sector" also contributed to this overvalued exchange rate. Second, since the middle of the 1960s and especially since the military government, most primary-sector exports came under state control. As a result, setting the exchange rate became a political issue, allowing for exchange rate overvaluations at the cost of profits of state-owned enterprises and, later on, producing losses that led to disaster. In all of these cases, the essential problem was that there was no correlation between the productivity of exporters and importers and the exchange rate, which obviously had long-term effects on the allocation of investment resources and expenditures and on the determinants of real wages and salaries. In this context, import substitution as an export strategy was impossible, or, from another point of view, the exchange rate policy, which kept the Peruvian sol overvalued for long periods of time, was counterproductive relative to the model of import substitution.

Obviously, given this exchange rate tradition, the devaluations provoked economic commotion, which was translated into the reduction of exporters' profits, although not necessarily of exports. At the same time, they provoked a reduction of the real incomes of workers, given that almost one-third of the consumer basket of goods is imported. So the governments tended to avoid and postpone devaluations because of the political costs involved. But the effects of delayed adjustments were fatal for the stabilization of relative prices and, obviously, for growth. Due to these considerations, the exchange rate policy, if there is one, must not be seen merely as a short-term instrument. It must also be viewed as a tool that sets one of the most important relative prices in the economy, on which the stability and relative scarcity of long-term investment, savings, and employment decisions so greatly depend.

The current overvalued exchange rate, the determinants of which are even more complex given the use of the dollar as a financial asset, is the Gordian knot that must be untied so as to ensure that the exchange rate can begin to be determined by variables other than those used in the past. True structural adjustment will come when the exchange rate is a function of the productivity of marketable goods, and not of the income differential, be it natural or artificial.

The lack of a consistent connection between short- and long-term policies has been one of the key elements retarding economic growth in Peru. One of its principal results has been the appearance of various hysteresis effects, which make it more difficult to return to the generation of income through investment and to growth. I will now examine why this is so.

Some Hysteresis Effects on the Peruvian Economy and Their Impact on Growth

The concept of hysteresis is taken from nineteenth-century physics, not unlike several other concepts that have been adopted in economics, to explain the persistence in the present of prior circumstances even when the causes of such phenomena have been removed.[19] In the field of economics, the development of this theory and its empirical application began only in the 1980s. The theory has been applied mainly to employment problems. Increases in unemployment, for example, have a direct impact on the "natural" rate of unemployment (Blanchard and Summers 1988). It has also been applied to international trade theory (Dixit 1989). In Peru, this concept has been used by Martinelli and Chiney (1991) to analyze the long-term effects of structural adjustment policies.

In the analysis of this long period abrupt swings provoked by the export cycle or by adjustment policies are observed. These have been phenomena of short duration, but once the economy has returned to "normal" the effects have persisted. We see the hysteresis effects in three areas: employment, the stock of capital and natural resources, and macroeconomic disequilibria.

Regarding employment of the labor force, the fundamental problem, according to Verdera (1983), has been underemployment, and in the last ten years open unemployment has grown considerably. Since 1970, the period for which statistical information is available, these levels have increased after each crisis and adjustment. The problem is that being underemployed or unemployed has become a normal situation. This effect influences growth and the possibilities of overcoming the crisis in two ways. First, any future growth must absorb those who are underemployed and unemployed today and also try to absorb the youths who are entering the labor markets. Considerable investment is certainly required to carry out this task. Of course, if the adjustment policies had been adopted on time, they would be less drastic, and this problem would be less serious. Second, underemployment and unemployment reduce workers' capacity to save and increase pressure on the state to make social expenditures, and thus also reduce the capacity for future investment. From this perspective, the structural adjustment underway today should assign priority to public investment in order, above all, to absorb underemployment.

In a country such as Peru, where underemployment and unemployment are due to the lack of capital and resources to employ the labor force adequately, a measure of capital stock has been lost with each crisis and economic adjustment. This loss is due to the bankruptcy and closing of businesses, the need to depreciate capital more rapidly, the opportunity cost of keeping a factory closed, or the need not to produce on a given piece of land. Once the short-term crisis is resolved, one is left with less capital and resources, which obviously has repercussions not only for the gross product, but also for employment and investment. As Martinelli and Chiney (1991:33) point out,

> A profound depression during the economic cycle reduces the potential growth of GDP, creating a feedback effect through the sensitivity of investment with the logical repercussions on the level of adequate employment, as indicated by the analysis on employment series. The series demonstrates that beginning in 1977 the structural lack of sufficient employment has increased each year, as witnessed by the growth of the absence of adequate actual employment from 38 percent for 1976–1980 to 49 percent for 1986–1987,

coupled with the certainty that this gap is expanding further in the current recession.

A more complex hysteresis effect, on macroeconomic disequilibria, is provoked by adjustment policies. None of the adjustment processes since 1966 led to stable macroeconomic equilibrium; that is, they could not simultaneously meet the criteria that exports equal imports, investment equal savings, and taxes equal government spending (X=M, I=S, and T=G). Almost all the adjustments narrowed the external gap and in some cases the fiscal gap, but never the accumulation, or savings-investment, gap. As a result, there was always a latent disequilibrium that would set off the next crisis, which is why the subsequent adjustment has been harsher each time. As indicated above, this has been due to the pressure of the external debt on fiscal expenditure, foreign exchange, and savings, making the macroeconomic equilibria ever more unstable and leading the economy to tend increasingly toward chronic disequilibrium. Consequently, to the instability "inherent" in the Peruvian economy since the middle of the 1970s one must add the hysteresis effect of the adjustments, which makes it difficult to move to a phase of recovery and growth.

Obviously, these issues require greater theoretical and empirical refinement, but they are realities that must be taken into account to integrate the long-term effects of the crises and the adjustment programs. In a country with a shortage of productive resources and an excess supply of labor, the cumulative effects of successive short-term crises have created an ever increasing need for larger amounts of resources that are not available. They have also caused the processes of recovery and return to growth to require a long period of time, from five to ten years. The lesson is that there is no long-term development policy more important than timely and appropriate short-term policies.

Final Thoughts

The information we have analyzed above suggests that the path to development in Peru will be difficult. The past holds some lessons for the future, but a repetition of some of these experiences is unlikely, or would be undesirable. But even if there were the will and favorable international conditions, the development process will take time, especially because nothing guarantees that the crisis is being overcome or that the Peruvian pendulum is not going to swing again. Perhaps contrary to the past, today the conditions for economic recovery and growth are occurring in a context marked by a great deal of uncertainty, albeit within a context favorable to free enterprise and the market economy, which in theory can facilitate a return to the model of export-led growth.

Let us now turn to the initial question: What does Peru need to return to the path of development? Based on my analysis I find that the requirements for development are part of a process of economic and institutional reconstruction that requires that:

- Annual inflation is brought below 10 percent
- The exchange rate is set as a function of marketable and non-marketable goods
- Private investment, both national and foreign, drives the process of accumulation, and stable investment rates are maintained
- The complementarity between public and private investment is improved
- Income distribution is a function of productivity and not the control of power
- The educational system serves to support economic growth
- The political system is capable of producing stable institutions

The problem is what to do to ensure that all of this can come to pass, and then how to do it. Again, this analysis of the past can be useful in searching for clues as to how to bring about this process of change.

The first lesson from Peru's experience is that growth depends on stable investment and on the quality of such investment. Technological change that promotes growth is change that is incorporated in new machinery and technical processes. At the same time, and confirming general theories of growth, investment should create jobs and improve workers' incomes, for this represents the additional demand that any expansion of supply requires. Nevertheless, the specific nature of the Peruvian case requires that new investment should also create new, dynamic export sectors (or expand the supply of exports), which creates employment[20] directly, as opposed to indirectly as in the past. Yet there is a latent problem of underemployment and unemployment that requires a certain type of investment in labor-intensive technology. Perhaps state investment can play an important role in this regard. It is under these terms that a new pattern of growth can be redefined.

The second lesson is that education as investment has only in part served to promote development in Peru, in large measure because the quantity and quality of the supply was greater than the demand. As a result, there is simultaneously a need for change in the educational system through mechanisms that would bring supply into line with demand with respect to educational quality and for massive investment to increase the demand for labor. But beyond the economic sphere, education is an established right of the citizenry that the population expects to receive; consequently, the state's role must be redefined and improved.

The third lesson is that private investment is highly sensitive to economic and political instability. Peru therefore needs a process of reconstruction of the frameworks for economic, institutional, and political stability, so as to set its sights on a cumulative and permanent process of investment. Under these circumstances, the role of public investment can be crucial, to the extent that there has been a complementarity or crowding-in effect attracting private investment and diminishing the national entrepreneurs' aversion to risk. Nevertheless, for this to work it requires an institutional framework that defines in a lasting way which investments should be made by the private sector and which by the state. This would ensure that the jurisdictions of the respective sectors are not invaded.

The fourth lesson is that instability in Peru has two origins, one in the economic cycle, when the external constraint becomes acute, and another in the political cycle, when meeting the demands of political clienteles moves beyond the available economic resources (foreign exchange and fiscal revenue). When the two factors have converged, they have produced changes in political regime and economic policy, thus giving rise to the Peruvian pendulum. There will be no solution to this situation without changes in the anticyclical policies aimed at correcting or cushioning the external shocks through mechanisms that make timely external adjustments possible. Such steps would serve to shorten the political cycle. On the political level, a system of checks and balances clearly is required to ensure that governments earn votes and support not on credit, but with cash.

The fifth lesson is that the crises and adjustment policies have had an undesired hysteresis effect on production, employment, savings, and macroeconomic equilibria. The crises in countries such as Peru tend to worsen because the adjustment policies leave remnants that accumulate, such that they end up becoming perverse long-term policies. This has become even more acute in Peru as external indebtedness has a major impact on short-term fiscal management, the availability of foreign exchange, and domestic savings, which are essential ingredients for economic recovery and growth.

The final lesson is that growth depends on the stability of an open economy, which to date has depended on short-term policies. Thus the exchange rate, which has been overvalued for the larger part of the last forty years, has inhibited export growth, which only occurred in sectors with a high income differential, and import substitution. In general, countries that use the exchange rate as an instrument of development set it at levels above its parity. However, adjustment policies could not consistently bridge the three gaps (external, savings-investment, and fiscal); only two of the three were closed, and so macroeconomic stability was quite precarious.

There is a lesson from the past that must not be repeated. The highest rates of investment and growth were attained by military regimes with external financing, suggesting that military regimes induce greater confidence and are more credible than civilian governments. This period concluded or is concluding not only because of the crisis in the functioning of military institutions, but also because the modern version of development must be forged in a democracy. Democracy should guarantee the permanence of institutions and therefore stability—the secret for returning to the path of renewed investment. Today democracy is a condition for development, not only for reasons of principle, but because if democratic government works it should provide stability for investment and economic activity. Stability will be the future test of development with democracy.

Notes

1. This chapter was written primarily while I was a senior research associate at the North-South Center in Miami. I completed the final version in Lima in August 1993. I am grateful to Carol Wise and John Sheahan for their comments during and after the Woodrow Wilson Center's conference. They have been most useful not only for improving this chapter, but also for providing direction for future research. Likewise, I thank Richard Webb, Gustavo Gorriti, Roxana Barrantes, and Steve Stein for their comments and suggestions. Obviously, this chapter as written is solely my responsibility.

2. There is no consensus on the concept of the long term in economics. For A. Marshall, the long term is characterized by the time it takes the prices of all factors to change. For others, the short term is one year or less, and the long term ten years or more. For a more detailed discussion, see Granger (1993) or Pamico and Petri (1987). I define the long term as a period greater than the length of one generation of the population, that is, approximately fifteen years.

3. The standard deviation (s.d.) was 5.3 percent, and there was one year when per capita GDP grew 8.3 percent, while in another year it declined 17.1 percent.

4. See Sheahan (1987), Thorp and Whitehead (1987), Hirschman (1986), and Cardoso and Helwege (1992).

5. In general, technological changes are incorporated in new investments, thus technical progress is a type of additional technical change.

6. I use what is called the computable growth model, $y_t = \alpha_L l_t + \alpha_K k_t + \mu$, which allows simple estimation of the determinants of growth of per capita GDP for the 1950–1992 period. The variable (y) is the rate of growth of per capita GDP, while (l) and (k) represent the rate of growth of labor and capital, respectively.

7. Corbo and Rojas (1992) estimate for Latin America that "the rate of investment has a positive and statistically significant effect on growth, but explains only about 37 percent of the variation in growth of per capita GDP" (p. 274).

8. The empirical results for a forty-year period were as follows:

$$y_t = \underset{(0.006)}{0.007} + \underset{(0.042)}{0.237}\, I_t - \underset{(0.042)}{0.017}\, I_{t-1}$$

$$r^2 = 0.453 \quad F = 16.29 \quad DW = 1.17$$

$$y_t = \underset{(.005)}{0.096} + \underset{(.0339)}{0.138}\, I_t = \underset{(.044)}{0.253}\, L_t$$

$$r^2 = 0.735 \quad F = 47.36 \quad DW = 1.82$$

Where: y_t is the annual rate of growth of per capita GDP
I_t is annual growth of total investment per capita
L_t is the annual rate of growth of labor income per capita.

9. There is a problem of causality between growth of GDP and growth of workers' incomes. The Granger causality test was performed to be certain that changes in workers' incomes are a source of changes in GDP. The test yielded a null hypothesis, and so long-term growth in GDP would depend on the growth of the incomes of workers, which in turn reflects increases in productivity or real income policies.

10. Vega-Centeno (1983), in a pioneer work, points out that most technical changes in the industrial sector were incorporated in investments, and that there was a lesser technical change as a result of ingenious adaptations and modifications of machinery in use.

11. Two functions were chosen to explain the determinants of growth of per capita GDP, one linear and the other a double logarithm, so as to capture the elasticity of these factors.

$$y_t = \underset{(.009)}{0.03} + \underset{(.035)}{0.13}\, I_t + \underset{(.082)}{0.21}\, L_t - \underset{(.0003)}{0.0003}\, dp_t + \underset{(.0000003)}{0.000004}\, (e/p)_t$$
$$- \underset{(.009)}{0.005}\,\mathrm{RP}_t - \underset{(.0009)}{0.005}\,\mathrm{TG}_t$$

$$r^2 = 0.77 \quad F = 18.2 \quad DW = 1.94$$

$$\log y_t = \underset{(.304)}{4.835} + \underset{(.065)}{0.054}\,\log I_t + \underset{(.063)}{0.792}\,\log L_t + \underset{(.016)}{0.038}\,\log Dp_t$$
$$+ \underset{(.008)}{0.026}\,\log (e/p)_t + \underset{(.022)}{0.036}\,\log \mathrm{PR}_t - \underset{(.019)}{0.247}\,\log \mathrm{TG}_t$$

$r^2 = 0.987$ F = 479.49 DW = 1.89

Where: Dp is the variation in annual inflation ($p_t - p_{(t-1)}$), an indicator of domestic economic stability.
e/p is the annual rate of change in the real exchange rate, an indicator of stability in the external sector.
PR is the economic policy regime, orthodox or heterodox, a dummy variable.
TG is the type of government, civilian or military, a dummy variable.

12. That is, the amount the rate of inflation changes in year (t) in relation to year (t-1), or $dp = p_t - p_{(t-1)}$.

13. Underemployment with respect to income is defined as people who work more than thirty-five hours a week who receive income below the legal minimum wage. In metropolitan Lima, this problem has become critical, for whereas in 1980 underemployment was 26 percent, in 1985 it rose to 42.5 percent and in 1991 to 78.5 percent (General Directorate of Employment and Cuánto 1992).

14. Illiteracy declined from 57.6 percent to 13 percent from 1940 to 1988. From 1986 to 1989, the enrollment rate for secondary school was 65 percent, while it stood at 36 percent in Brazil and 37 percent in Bolivia. (UNICEF, 1992).

15. We found the private investment function (Ipr_t) to be a function of present and lagged public investment (Ipu_t), of growth of the gross national product (DGNP), of private investment itself with a lag, and of the changes in the real exchange rate $(e/p)_t$. The period covered is 1970-1991. The result was as follows:

$$\underset{(87964)}{Ipr_t = 230364} + \underset{(.361)}{0.706(Ipu_t)} + \underset{(.407)}{0.007(Ipu_{t-1})} + \underset{(.217)}{0.277(Ipr_{t-1})}$$

$$+ \underset{(.009)}{0.182\text{DGNP}_t} + \underset{(.55)}{0.71(e/p)_t}$$

$r^2 = 0.456$ F = 6.94

16. The main characteristics of entrepreneurial behavior were drawn from various authors (Vega-Centeno 1983; Carbonetto and Carazo 1986; de Soto 1986; Chávez 1988; and Alcorta 1992). Entrepreneurial behavior is examined relative to investment, technical change, and economic policies. There is without doubt no systematic comparative study of Peruvian firms and entrepreneurs.

17. Actually these variables were introduced not only as controls, but also as instrumental variables, especially the exchange rate, which has been an exogenous variable over the long run.

18. It appears that Peru has had a "Dutch disease" problem since the middle of the 1950s, which inhibited investment in other export sectors with lower income differentials. This topic has not been studied for that period.

19. For a conceptual discussion of this phenomenon, which only recently has been applied in economics, see Cross (1993).

20. Actually, sectoral growth with these characteristics has occurred in Peru since 1980, with the emergence of the "coca economy," which exhibits

all the paradigmatic characteristics of economic development: it is an export sector; there are no barriers to the entry of new producers, as the scale of investment and production is divisible; it creates considerable employment since the technology is labor intensive; it allows for the integration of the agriculture, industry, and service sector; the income elasticity of international demand for the product is high; and it is highly profitable. It is a shame that coca and its by-products are harmful. But in reality other legal, beneficial products with the foregoing characteristics must be sought, for they hold the key to economic growth.

References

Alarco, Germán and Patricia del Hierro
1989 *La inversión en el Perú: Determinantes, financiamiento y requerimientos futuros.* Lima: Friedrich Ebert Foundation.

Alcorta, Ludovico
1992 *El nuevo capital financiero: Grupos financieros y ganancias sistemáticas en el Perú.* Lima: Friedrich Ebert Foundation.

Altamirano, Teófilo
1992 *Exodo: Peruanos en el exterior.* Lima: Fondo Editorial de la Pontificia Universidad Católica del Perú.

Ascarza, Illich
1990 "La inversión pública como determinante de la inversión privada en el Perú. Master's Thesis. Lima: Catholic University of Peru.

Blanchard, O. J., and L. H. Summers
1988 "Hysteresis and the European Unemployment Problem," reprinted in Rod Cross, ed., *Unemployment, Hysteresis and the Natural Rate Hypothesis.* Oxford: Basil Blackwell, pp. 306–364.

Carbonetto, Daniel, and M. Ines Carazo
1986 *Heterogeneidad tecnológico y desarollo económico: El sector informal.* Lima: Friedrich Ebert Foundation.

Cardoso, Eliana, and Ann Helwege
1992 *Latin America's Economy, Diversity and Conflicts.* Cambridge: MIT Press.

Chávez, Eliana
1988 "El sector informal urbano: De la reproducción de la fuerza de posibilidades de producción." *Diagnosis and Debate Series* no. 32, Lima: Friedrich Ebert Foundation.

Corbo, Vittorio, and Patricio Rojas
1992 "Crecimiento económico de América Latina." *Cuadernos de Economía,* vol. 29, no. 87 (August), pp. 265–294.

Cross, Rod
1993 "On the Foundations of Hysteresis in Economic Systems." *Economics and Philosophy,* no. 9, pp. 53–74.

Cuánto S.A. (Richard Webb and Graciela Fernández Baca)
1992 *Perú en 1992 números.* Lima: Cuánto S.A.

Dancourt, Oscar
1986 "Sobre las políticas macroeconómicas en el Perú, 1970–1984." *Working Paper no. 4.* Lima, Institute for Peruvian Studies (IEP).

de la Torre Postigo, Carlos
1990 "En el laberinto de las cuentas nacionales: Defectos metodológicos y implicancias sobre nuestra visión del desarrollo." *Revista Economía,* vol. XIII, no. 26.

de Soto, Hernando
1986 *El otro sendero.* Lima: Instituto Libertad y Democracía.

Devlin, Robert
1985 "La deuda externa en América Latina." Lima: Peruvian International Studies Center (CEPEI).

Dixit, Avinash
1989 "Hysteresis, Import Penetration and Exchange Rate Pass-Through," *Quarterly Journal of Economics,* CIV 2 (May), pp. 205–228.

Dornbusch, Rudiger
1991 "Policies to Move from Stabilization to Growth," Proceedings of the World Bank Annual Conference on Development Economics 1990. Washington DC: The World Bank.

Escobal, Javier, and Jaime Saavedra
1990 "Las variaciones del tipo de cambio real y el ingreso agrícola." *Revista Debate Agrario,* no. 9 (July–September), pp. 11–42.

Ferrari, César
1990 *Comercio exterior y desarrollo.* Lima: Friedrich Ebert Foundation.

Figueroa, Adolfo
1991 "Perú: Distribución de la crisis y crisis de la distribución," in Efraín Gonzales de Olarte, ed., *Nuevos rumbos para el desarrollo.* Lima: IEP, Problems of America Series.

Fitzgerald, E. V. K.
1981 *La economía política del Perú: 1956–1978.* Lima: IEP Economic Studies Series.

Gonzales de Olarte, Efraín, ed.
1989 *Economía para la democracia: Siete conferencias.* Lima: IEP, Economic Analysis Series.

Gonzales de Olarte, Efraín
1991 *Nuevos rumbos para el desarrollo del Perú y América Latina.* Problems of America Series. Lima: IEP.

Gonzales de Olarte, Efraín
1993 "La dimensión ambiental de las políticas económicas." *Permanent Seminar on Agrarian Research.* Working paper no. 2.

Gonzales de Olarte, Efraín, and Lilian Samamé
1991 *El péndulo peruano: Políticas económicas, gobernabilidad y subdesarrollo, 1963–1990.* Economic Analysis Series no. 13. Lima: IEP.

Granger, Clive W. J.
1993 "What are we learning about the long-run." *The Economic Journal,* vol. 103 (March), pp. 307–317.

Hirschman, Albert O.
1986 *The Political Economy of Latin American Development: Seven Exercises in Retrospection.* San Diego: Center for US-Mexican Studies, University of California at San Diego.

Iguiñiz, Javier, and José Tavara
1985 "Crecimiento económico y restricción externa." Diagnosis and Debate Series no. 12, Lima: Friedrich Ebert Foundation.

Jiménez, Félix
1987 "El comportamiento de la inversión privada y el papel del Estado: Notas sobre la acumulación de capital en una economía no integrada." *Socialismo y Participación,* no. 38.

Larios, Fernando
1989 "Impacto de la política cambiaria sobre el sector agrario del Perú." Diagnosis and Debate Series, no. 43. Lima: Friedrich Ebert Foundation.

Martinelli, César, and Jorge Chiney
1991 "Efectos de largo plazo de las crisis de ajuste en el Perú." Working paper no. 29. Lima: IEP.

Pamico, C., and F. Petri
1987 "Long-run and short-run," in M. Milgate and P. Newman, eds., *The New Palgrave Dictionary of Economics,* vol. 3. London: Macmillan Publishing.

Portocarrero, Felipe, Arlette Beltran, and J. Zimmerman
1988 "Inversión pública en el Perú (1900–1968): Una aproximación cuantitativa." Lima: Research Papers of the University of the Pacific (CIUP).

Schydlowsky, Daniel, and Juan Julio Witch
1979 *Anatomía de un fracaso económico. Perú 1968–1978.* Lima: Research Center of the University of the Pacific.

Seminario de Marzi, Bruno, and César Buillon Buendía
1992 "Ciclos y tendencias en la economía Peruana." Research paper no. 15. Lima: Research Center of the University of the Pacific and the Economic Research Consortium.

Sheahan, John
1987 *Patterns of development in Latin America: Poverty, Repression, and Economic Strategy.* Princeton: Princeton University Press.

Tello, Mario D.
1990 "Sobre el concepto de causalidad en economía: El caso de la relación entre inflación y el tipo de cambio en el Perú, 1950–1990." *Revista Economía,* vol. XIII, no. 26.

Thorne, Alfredo
1984 "The determinants of savings in a developing country: The case of Peru." Ph.D. dissertation, Oxford University.

Thorp, Rosemary, and Geoffrey Bertram
1978 *Peru, 1890–1977: Growth and Policy in an Open Economy.* New York: Columbia University Press.

Thorp, Rosemary, and Lawrence Whitehead
1987 *Latin American Debt and the Adjustment Crisis.* Pittsburgh: University of Pittsburgh Press.

United Nations Children's Fund (UNICEF)
1992 *State of the World's Children.* New York: Oxford University Press.

Vega-Centeno, Máximo
1983 *Crecimiento, industrialización y cambio técnico: Perú 1955–1980.* Lima: Fondo Editorial de la Pontificia Universidad Católica del Perú.

Verdera, Francisco
1983 *El problema del empleo en el Perú.* Economic Analysis Series, no. 7. Lima: IEP.

Verdera, Francisco
1993 "La situación actual del empleo." *Revista Actualidad Económica,* no. 141.

Webb, Richard
1989 "Los problemas de redistribución en contextos democráticos." Efraín Gonzales de Olarte, ed. *Economía para la democracia: Siete conferencias.* Economic Analysis Series. Lima: IEP.

Webb, Richard, and Adolfo Figuerora
1975 "La distribución del ingreso en el Perú." Economic Analysis Series. Lima: IEP.

Wise, Carol
1986 "Economía política del Perú: Rechazo a la receta ortodoxa." Working paper, Political Economy Series, no. 1. Lima: IEP.

14

Commentary

John Sheahan

In the early 1980s, many of us involved in economic analysis spent a significant amount of time explaining why things went so wrong during the Velasco period. We attempted to explain why, at that time, after the election of a new government promising a more classically liberal style of economics, import liberalization, better relations with the private sector, and an end to state-centered tendencies of the period—a program that appeared would really help the situation because it was reversing many past policy errors—the economy continued to deteriorate. It was inconceivable then that events would turn out as badly as they have. Efraín's Gonzales's chapter is marvelous at highlighting the main interacting factors responsible for the continued economic decline after the policy had turned in what appeared to be such a positive direction. It is an excellent explanation of how a variety of explanatory economic factors are linked in a systematic fashion.

Julio Velarde's work can be interpreted as a rather positive assessment of Peru's present economic stabilization and liberalization program. And, in fact, one can say something positive about it. The program is definitely not the wild program of Alan García; it is clearly trying to reverse everything that appeared to be wrong with the García approach. But, at the same time, such an assessment is also a bit like saying that a government that has a bad habit of shooting itself in the stomach is an improvement over the previous government that had a bad habit of shooting itself in the head; it is not quite the improvement that one would want. It does not seem to me that Fujimori's economic adjustment program is at all well designed,

John Sheahan is professor of economics at Williams College.

well implemented, or moving in the right direction. It is a terrible, strain-aggravating program that has no future as it stands now. The program has to be changed if Peru hopes to progress.

I want to choose two points from Velarde's work and then explain what I feel is wrong about them. The points are, first, that "there is a sense that the economy is on the right track." The second is that "there was no alternative to the economic policies that were ultimately adopted." Let me start with the second phrase first.

I have done some studying of the stabilization and liberalization programs of other Latin American countries. Of those I have studied, those of Chile and Mexico and the very mild liberalization in Colombia, which actually took the form of export promotion, Peru's program is by far the most extreme, the most drastic, the most unlimited, and the least careful about the damage it is doing to society. Whereas the Chileans decided to be careful with their economic reforms, the Peruvians decided to throw dynamite at the problems they were facing. The Peruvian program was certainly not implemented within the framework of a society that was basically stable, within which it might have been all right to take a radical approach. Peruvians need to be more careful because Peru is a society that faces the greatest danger of never recuperating.

What are the specifics of the problem? The chapters of Gonzales and Velarde, I believe, agree on this point. One of the greatest difficulties over the last twenty years has been a consistent overvaluation of the currency that has made it practically impossible for the industrial sector to export unless it receives direct aid for that purpose, and even then it is very difficult. An overvalued currency makes it very difficult for Peruvian producers to compete against lower-priced imports, unless those imports are restricted. Overvaluation is one of the major crimes that we accuse all of the governments from Velasco to García of committing.

What has the present program produced? It has increased the overvaluation. It has pushed the exchange rate in the wrong direction for more than two years. How did that happen? Let us consider how much room there was to do something different. When the Chileans faced their 1981–1983 crisis, when they fired the economic advisers who were running the liberalization program and brought in a new group, the first move they made was to devalue drastically in real terms, in an attempt to get the industrial sector to compete in the international market. What did the Mexicans do when they were hit with a debt crisis in 1982? They, too, devalued drastically in real terms. What did the Colombians do when they wanted to move away from high levels of protection, reduce barriers to trade, and compete in the world market? Adopting a crawling peg, they, first, devalued in real terms and, second, prevented the real exchange rate from appreciating for more than a decade.

In all three cases, economies that were severely depressed began to demonstrate export growth, and Mexico and Chile experienced incredibly successful export growth. Increased foreign exchange earnings provided the impetus for economic expansion, coupled with quick growth in industrial exports and change in the entire character of their trading systems.

What did the Peruvians do? The Peruvian government decided that devaluing and subsequently pegging the exchange rate violate the purity of a free-market approach. So, they let the exchange rate float. The Central Bank never fully agreed with that policy and attempted from time to time to intervene. As Velarde writes, such attempts were awkward because the policymakers were trying to control the domestic money supply and simultaneously intervene in the foreign exchange market. But in the end the exchange rate was allowed to float. How did the exchange rate react? It moved in the wrong direction; that is, the direction opposite to the rate movement of every successful stabilization and liberalization program that I know of.

What caused it move to that way? The mechanics have been very similar in every country. If the authorities clamp down hard on the monetary side and remove all controls on interest rates in a society that is scared to death that inflation is going to continue, the result is fantastically high real interest rates. In Peru, real interest rates were on the order of 9 to 10 percent per month, and at the end of 1992, Peru's rates remained very close to 50 percent per year.

What happens when a country experiences real interest rates at that level? First, long-term investment is an impossibility. Second, domestic borrowers seek foreign financing at interest rates of, say, 15 percent. The result is capital inflow. The currency appreciates in a constant and perfectly natural, predictable, and understandable fashion. If a country removes all controls and tightens the money supply, its currency will increase in value.

Does the country want its currency to appreciate? In some instances, possibly, because cheap imports help reduce inflation. Making imports cheap and discouraging exports, removing the incentive to export by lowering the value of foreign exchange, does counter inflation. But what does this begin to sound like? It begins to sound like every populist government we have ever seen in Latin America: fight inflation by appreciating the currency. Then, when somebody asks what has happened to Peruvian exports under such conditions, the answer is that they have not fallen much—yet they have not increased at all, despite the enormous excess capacity of production, the tremendously depressed wages, and the like.

Imagine an economy with output that has been declining for most of a decade, and very quickly for the past five years. Relatively speaking, the country is in a depression deeper than the United States experienced in the middle of the 1930s. Now assume the policy response for recovery is to remove import restrictions, greatly reduce tariffs, and then make foreign currency cheap, that is, appreciate the domestic currency. What happens? Imports flow in and replace domestic production, and exports fail to respond. The policy also produces a current account deficit, but that is not worrisome because there is plenty of money to finance the deficit. This is not a financial crisis; it is a crisis of production and survival. I am not fully up-to-date on the data for Peru, but I believe the employment level has fallen in each year, beginning in 1990. One might argue that this is natural with an economic shock program. Yet employment fell again in 1991. I believe employment in the industrial sector fell 9 percent in 1992. Output per capita declined about 5 percent.

The economy did start to recover. It really snapped back at the end of 1990 and at the beginning of 1991. Then somebody objected. So, policymakers tightened the rope and strangled the economy with an extremely tight monetary policy, with the goal of fiscal balance, which was then turned into a fiscal surplus. As a result, Peru's output has fallen in the second year of the Fujimori program. Employment is continuing to fall. Finally, goods are being imported at lower and lower prices and replacing domestic output.

The Peruvian economy is not only facing a depression. There is also a strong sense among young people that there is no future in the society and that the only alternative is to leave. We see people leaving the society both physically and by joining the violent organizations that are attempting to tear the society apart. It is safe to presume that an economy that is perpetually in decline and that fails to offer any evident future to its youth is going to face a lot of violence. And capturing leaders is only going to stem the violence, because the driving force behind it continues.

In Colombia during the 1960s, a trip to Peru was like a trip to heaven. Colombia was experiencing a great deal of violence, and the government could not seem to control it. The economy was stagnant—really stuck—in the middle of the 1960s. Inflation was higher than Peru's, income was lower, and growth rates were much lower. The status of the two countries today, of course, is quite different. How have the Colombians been able to turn their situation around? Keep in mind that Colombia has had as much or more of a drug problem than Peru. Colombia has at least as many revolutionary movements, and they are very tenacious; there has been substantial blackmailing of oil suppliers, and so forth. Colombian society is not, however, experiencing disintegration like Peru, rather, it is moving right along. Income per capita is rising; employment continues to rise. Moreover, people leave the agricultural sector quickly enough so that agricultural incomes increase as well.

Peru has not accomplished any of this. Why? I believe Gonzales's work is correct on almost every point. Increased employment is required to restart the economy; the present program is causing employment to decline. In addition, exports need to increase, so that the economy can pay for imports with its production and earnings, as opposed to borrowing, a point that Gonzales emphasizes. The present system is paralyzing exports and not providing output. And poverty—the inequalities are even greater than they are in Colombia—is underlying the social conflict. The Cuánto index of Peruvians in critical poverty, which rose under the García government, has increased by more than 45 percent in the two years of the current program.

How can one argue that this economic program is on the right track? What is it accomplishing? I am not arguing that Peru was wrong to stop shooting itself in the head; it was right in that sense. It was right to move away from quantitative restrictions on imports; it was right to unify relative tariffs. However, it was wrong to remove incentives to export. And it was wrong in a deep recession to reduce tariff revenues so sharply and to cut public services on the grounds that the country cannot afford a social welfare program while also reducing tariffs and government revenue from trade. These latter policies are all perverse.

Assume Peru decided to correct the exchange rate, production incentives, or the degree of competition, for example. What would have to be done? The government would have to act under an assumption of responsibility for ensuring that the economic situation improves. This requires action and the assumption of responsibility, as distinct from the approach of former Minister of Economics Carlos Boloña, which was based on the belief that an end to government intervention would allow everything to be fine. The Peruvian situation has not been fine, however, and there is no reason to expect it to be. Wages are falling because employment is falling. So, consumption is declining; investment is paralyzed. The government cannot increase spending because it must avoid increasing the budget deficit, and it cannot raise taxes while reducing its tariff revenue. This is the essence of the story: the economy is in a straitjacket.

I can think of about ten steps that could be taken to reactivate the Peruvian economy without aggravating inflation and without diverging from liberalization. As Velarde writes, moving away from an inward-looking industrial sector, from the protected system of production, is movement in the right direction. Clearly, it was no coincidence that the inflection point of the Peruvian economy, the shift from growth to decline, came when Peru stopped trying to compete in international markets and retreated behind protected barriers in an effort to develop. That was fatal. Reversing those policies is a good step, but a country does not have to shoot itself in the stomach in the process.

Many steps can be taken—the reaction to all of which, when I have advocated them in Peru, is: "Ah, García and populism again." For example, instead of cutting tariffs from an 85 percent average to a 15 percent level in the midst of a depression, do what the Chileans did during the 1981–1983 period when they were in this situation. They raised tariffs from 15 to 35 percent. Nobody claimed that Pinochet had quit liberalizing. I believe that under the prevailing conditions, such a policy is the correct one, provided strong export incentives are also included so that producers do not turn inward again.

Peru today could raise its average tariff level from 15 to 35 percent and rapidly devalue in real terms. The devaluation would produce a fall in real wages, which is unfavorable. But in Peru today, with all of the reforms that should have increased real wages and with currency appreciation, wages have still fallen. The situation in Peru could not have been worse: simultaneously, the currency appreciated, exports dropped, and real wages fell. Consumption, production, and employment all declined as well.

What did the Chileans do? The Chilean authorities intervened in the interest rate market. They lowered real interest rates, as they had climbed to over 30 percent ten years after the initiation of the adjustment program. The 30 percent interest rate level meant that the Chilean economy had no way to recover. Hence, the Chileans brought them down to 11 percent; they did not make them negative in real terms, which would have produced a terrible result. There is a big difference between interest rates at an impossible level of 50 percent and interest rates at a difficult but reasonable level of 10 percent.

Peru's Central Bank could announce, with government backing, that it was going to target the interest rate level instead of the money supply, much like the Federal Reserve does in the United States. The Central Bank could further set a goal of an interest rate level of, for example, 10 percent—not a rate that is negative in real terms. Then the exchange rate would begin moving in the correct direction. Such a step would not be tantamount to a rejection of capitalism, free markets, or anything else associated with them. It just involves *managing* an economy so that it can float instead of sink.

The Chileans, like the Koreans when they faced the same situation in the early 1980s, set lower real interest rates, provided very strong export incentives, ensured the exchange rate was at the right level, and then kept the economy open and allowed it to work. There was a driving force behind the restoration of growth. In Peru, there is nothing behind it; it is a terrible situation. I would like to think that very soon someone in Peru will argue that the current approach is unnecessary; that Peru can remain on the liberalization track and also allow the economy to begin growing; that such a policy may improve the employment situation, but if it does not, something specific can be done; and that such a policy may produce an expansion of exports, but again, if it does not, a specific policy can be implemented there as well.

As Gonzales writes, the incentive to increase supply can be raised. I suspect that if formal sector employment rose on a fairly steady basis, perhaps 3 to 5 percent per year, the violence in Peru would begin to diminish. The number of people choosing to join the armed opposition would decrease. The real danger is not in Peru's rejecting liberalization again, but rather that the country could blow itself apart. The economy cannot solve everything, but it can provide the opportunity for society to reconstruct itself in a much better way.

15

Commentary

Carol Wise

Julio Velarde's work is a very good macroeconomic update on Peru that will be helpful to individuals who are seeking to catch up with the complicated trends occurring in the country. His essay contains much of what one would want to know about the numerous economic reforms for both the short and medium term that have been implemented since 1990.

Let me offer, however, a suggestion for making this work more understandable to individuals who are not well versed in economic analysis. Velarde notes that the management of economic policy has not been very successful. Then later he argues that some otherwise positive economic prospects are blurred to some extent by the present political instability. I agree that economic management and political instability are intricately linked. But the analysis could be strengthened by elaborating on those economic management problems and on the politics behind the program. Is this a new kind of economic management program? Or is it the same old approach that we have been witnessing, as Efraín Gonzales argues, for the last twenty or thirty years? My hunch is that part of the program is new and part of it is old. Exploring this issue would further produce an interesting analysis.

Gonzales, on the other hand, takes a much longer-term view of Peru's political economy; he does not focus solely on economics. Such long-term analysis is long overdue. Gonzales begins, I believe correctly, in the late 1950s by explaining that during this period

---

Carol Wise is assistant professor of Latin American Studies at the Paul H. Nitze School of Advanced International Studies (SAIS) of the Johns Hopkins University.

relations between the public and the private sector first turned sour, and the country began to lose its political and economic footing. He also explains why the 1965 to 1970 period was crucial and extensively probes the determinants of this deterioration of relations between the public and the private sector. By the late 1980s, the entire relationship was completely out of sync.

What are the underlying factors of the long-term development trends of the Peruvian economy? The issue is how, beginning in the late 1950s, a small, open, very successful, classically liberal, primary-export economy with a balanced budget, low inflation, and fairly peaceful social relations completely deteriorated by the late 1980s into a situation characterized by hyperinflation, among other economic and social ills. Such an outcome is the result of unbelievable fiscal and monetary flagrancy and of a broad set of unpleasant political relationships.

Gonzales's emphasis on the long term is especially important because uncovering the long-run determinants of Peru's development can provide direction for policymaking and allow the formulation of responses to the present situation. He points to the tension among the short term, medium term, and the time horizon of policymakers. He points to the destructive policy flip-flopping, not just between civilian and military governments, but between orthodoxy and heterodoxy as well. In my own study of Peru, I count at least four major periods between the early 1960s and the present during which these major reversals have occurred. I am not referring to the manipulation of a couple of variables, say wages and prices, but rather to great shifts in the direction of policy, movement from one extreme to the other.

Gonzales also discusses complementarity between public and private investment in Peru. It is a complementarity that I believe holds true throughout the region and that has been documented in some interesting recent articles in *World Development.* In Peru, the complementarity of public and private sector investment has not been evident in relations between business and government, which is to say that the two need each other. Business and government have been involved in a love-hate relationship since about the late 1950s.

Another issue Gonzales mentions, which is quite disturbing in policy terms because its resolution remains unclear, is the disjuncture between investment rates and real wages. As investment increases, for example, wages fail to respond. There is also a disjuncture between exporters and importers, both of whom operate according to their own logic, and one does not see the link between import substitution and export promotion that is seen in some more successful cases in the region. Finally, Gonzales addresses the disturbing disjuncture between the formulation of macroeconomic policy and its implementation. What is being formulated by the central bank or the ministry of finance is not necessarily what is implemented.

Overall, what we see in this chapter is a character analysis of a state that by the early 1990s matched what the old dependency school thinkers would call a classically disarticulated economy. Nothing operates as one would think it should. The key question is what to do about it.

Having summarized Gonzales's major points, I want to attempt to reformulate the patterns he highlights. I group the facts, figures, and interesting patterns that Gonzales has identified into four long-term trends. Every country in the region has been dealing with similar development problems; why has Peru been dealing with it to a greater extent, and why has it turned out to be the worst of the seven states major in resolving them?

The first trend is the increasing reliance on external debt and external savings as of the middle-to-late 1960s, which provided the "breathing room" with respect to macroeconomic policy; that is, it allowed adjustment to be postponed. It was a mixed blessing because such breathing room led to what Gonzales correctly points out as destructive, overvalued exchange rates, wild fluctuations of interest rates, and price signals that do not appeal to investors, be they domestic or foreign.

The second trend—and Peru suffered the most here—was the increasing reliance over the same period on the expansion of state enterprise. The significant period in this regard was the early 1970s, when the bulk of the economy was nationalized, mainly for ideological reasons. The problems that emerged have, of course, given rise to today's tremendous rush toward privatization. I have my doubts about the privatization schemes of some of these countries; Chile, for example, is selling off very productive enterprises. Peru, however, is a case in which the private sector actually needs to be privatized before investment can be successfully promoted there.

The third trend, and Gonzales mentions it in a number of ways in his chapter, is the hostility that has developed between the public and the private sector. The relationship in Peru is no longer love-hate. In developing countries generally, the private sector acts selfishly as a rent-seeker, looking out for its short-term interests. Peru is an especially disturbing case because the private sector made out like bandits with a great deal of debt-backed public investment. Profits were very good, particularly during the 1970s, but the private sector complained bitterly all the way to the bank and was often complaining about erratic price signals, among other unfavorable economic signs.

The fourth trend that has emerged is the inability of most states in the region—and again, Peru more so than others—to coordinate social policy or redistributive measures with any of the unorthodox development models that have been attempted. To label some of them development "models" is an exaggeration; "experiments" would be a better term. The inability to formulate true social policy with any of these plans has been a significant failure.

Gonzales's chapter includes a fascinating and disturbing table that illustrates Peru's trends in investment, wages, and growth, among other variables, over the 1950 to 1992 period. The table shows convincingly that the movement has been fairly steadily downward. The consistently negative trend and the fact that Peru has experienced so many erratic government changes and policy shifts leads me to believe other factors are at work. All signs are negative for Peru, yet in other Latin American countries the economic trends are beginning to move in a positive direction.

Two factors appear to be involved. The first is the international setting, which Efraín points to time and again. I will not dwell on it, except to note that the setting has been rather hostile to the developing world over the past twelve to fifteen years. The second factor contributing to this downward trend, independent of regime type and policy, is the domestic setting, that is, the broad array of Peruvian state institutions—financial institutions, the executive branch, and Congress, for example—and the way the state is tied to organized societal interests. If we compare Peru to other countries that are supposedly pulling through a difficult period—the Colombias, the Mexicos—we see a world of difference.

Yet there is also a certain institutional continuity operating in the region today. There are, briefly, four institutional contours of these states that are affecting efforts at sound economic management. I will address them as they relate to Peru. First, there is the nature of the leadership coalition. In Peru, the tendency toward a highly presidentialist management style has been widely discussed. And the new constitution is probably the most presidentialist of any in the region and, certainly, in Peru's history. What has happened is that the somewhat healthy presidentialism established in the 1960s and codified in the 1979 constitution has become extreme. By late 1987, this presidentialist management style meant that highly insulated economic teams of four or five people controlled all decisionmaking. These teams carried a lot of technocratic pretensions, but throughout the 1980s they were mainly political party hacks. Of course, by the late

1980s, as García began to lose his footing, the presidential style was paranoia. No one could get access to any decisionmakers even just to talk.

The second institutional contour is clearly the quality of state financial and planning institutions. Here, in Peru, there has been a gradual deterioration. As Gonzales notes, the decay began in the middle of the 1960s. If I had to choose between the Central Bank of Peru of 1967 and the Central Bank of Peru of 1991, I would take the former. The Central Bank of 1967 was at least trying to function as a financial institution with a measure of autonomy or pretensions to autonomy in the policymaking process. Since the middle of the 1960s, particularly with García's blatant firing of the Central Bank president in 1987, which violated the constitution and the rules of the bank itself, we have witnessed a deterioration in the economic policymaking process. As the Central Bank, the institution with the most integrity, begins to deteriorate, substantial infighting between the finance minister, the chief of the Central Bank, among others, emerges. This is another reflection of the downward trend.

A third contour is the quality of the bureaucracy. My own research shows that there was a period in the late 1960s to early 1970s in which it was actually prestigious to be a bureaucrat or a public policymaker in Peru. There was what political scientists now call a corps d'esprit, a vibrant group of individuals who cared about policy and government. Since the middle of the 1970s, those individuals have been the first to be dismissed from the top echelons. Wages have been squeezed and, of course, they are now completely eroded. Workers are being paid to leave the bureaucracy. The situation has turned into the typical case of a venal, underdeveloped bureaucratic setting.

The final contour that I want to mention is that the state, again broadly defined, is the least-developed feature of the policymaking framework in Peru. It never really sufficiently developed, even though in the early 1980s with the formation of the National Confederation of Private Business (CONFIEP), an umbrella private sector organization, there were efforts to begin organizing the private sector to a greater extent so as to form stronger links with government, to allow *concertación*, or a coming together to agree on policy. Those efforts failed for many complex reasons that I will not address here.

Obviously, all of these four trends are linked, but we really have not witnessed the establishment of a stable relationship between the state and the private sector, on the one hand, and between the state and all of the other societal and organized interests, on the other. As a result, policymaking is affected. When it is time to sell the policy package to society-at-large, each component must be renegotiated and each effort at implementation redesigned. Peru developed the classic model of the politicized state; the wheel is constantly being reinvented.

There is a vague sense of the existence of rules of the game in the relationship between the state and business and labor, and between the state and societal interests. If some kind of negotiating framework on the rules of the game can be firmly established among the state, capital, and labor, the country can begin to move forward with some kind of policy and plan for the future. This has been the case in many studies of the early postwar reconstruction of Europe, in the context of a war-torn economy, and a completely chaotic and ideologically divided set of political parties.

The notion in Peru is that all of the ideological wrangling of the political parties makes it very hard to accomplish anything. I would argue that Peru today—although it is not clear that the early postwar reconstruction literature in Europe can be applied to Peru—is similar to the experience of early postwar European reconstruction in many ways, notably with respect to the war-torn economy and the set of chaotic and ideologically divided political parties. Most of that literature demonstrates that a country can experience a great deal of ideological division, but if that logic of cooperation can be established, if the stable rules of the game can be developed based on the current modes of interaction, if some kind of communication among the state, the business sector, and labor can occur, the country will be on firmer ground at the start. The country can begin to move forward with a policy framework and plan for the future.

It is easy to be pessimistic about Peru today, to assume that the situation is heading only downward. I will attempt to conclude on an optimistic note by asking: how does a country begin to pick up the pieces?—or how does it begin the process of reconstruction? I believe we must consider Peru as a case of early postwar European reconstruction.

Let me point to three hopeful trends. As Richard Webb has documented in the introduction to *Peru's Path to Recovery: A Plan for Economic Stabilization and Growth*, by Jeffrey Sachs and Carlos Paredes, the Peruvian state has been collapsing for some time. It collapsed fiscally. It collapsed institutionally as well. The state is not what it was less than a decade ago; it has disappeared as we knew it. People have even been paid to leave the bureaucracy. If they have not been paid to leave yet, they are still reading comic books or working on crossword puzzles, waiting to depart. Given this destructive long-term trend within the state and between the state and society, maybe this is not so terrible a development. It is a situation that is making it difficult to develop and implement policy. But following its complete collapse in the middle of 1991, the state is beginning to reconstruct itself in some fairly interesting ways.

What is positive about Fujimori is that he does not have a party as a base. So, there are not as many party hacks to deal with, and one can determine what is happening within the government. And what Peru is experiencing, interestingly, is that more of its highly talented people are entering the public sector than at any time since I have been studying the country. Peru still has many talented professionals in small organizations like the Commission for the Promotion of Private Investment (COPRI), which is the privatization commission. Others are in the National Tax Administration Superintendency (SUNAT). There are small pockets of expertise where talented individuals are actually beginning to carry out the tasks necessary for renewal.

The second favorable trend I want to emphasize—and I know if one is living in Peru at present it is difficult to see or feel it—is that the country is finally adjusting. Peru is buckling down and making the adjustment in both macro- and microeconomic terms for the first time since the 1967–1968 program. Since that time, there have been a number of attempts at economic stabilization and adjustment. Those attempts were thwarted either because the external sector expanded to relieve the pressure for adjustment or because it was just too difficult for the government to implement. Alan García made virtually no attempts at adjustment. So, adjustment is finally occurring, and it not easy, but the economy will not turn around until it succeeds.

Index

About the Book

On 5 April 1992, Peru's twelve-year-old system of democratically elected government was plunged into crisis. Alberto Fujimori, a political unknown before winning the presidency two years earlier, carried out a coup against his own government—an *autogolpe*—suspending the constitution, dissolving the congress and the courts, arresting members of the congress and the media, and for a time harshly censoring the press. The events of that day brought one surprise for Fujimori—a strongly negative reaction from the international community—and another for many observers—among Peruvians, Fujimori's actions proved highly popular.

The *autogolpe* is one of at least three major Peruvian events that have occurred since the rise to power of the Fujimori government. Coupled with the *autogolpe* was the "Fujishock," a radical economic adjustment that is aimed at reviving the Peruvian economy after years of economic stagnation and decline. Fujimori then shocked the world in September 1993 with the announcement of the capture of the revolutionary guerrilla leader of Shining Path, Abimael Guzmán, and several other members of the organization's leadership.

In this book, leading Peruvian scholars and analysts address this extraordinary series of events and the response of the international community to them, all within the broader context of Peru's political and economic development over the past four decades.